Narrating Medicine in Middle English Poetry

Narrating Medicine in Middle English Poetry

Poets, Practitioners, and the Plague

Eve Salisbury

BLOOMSBURY ACADEMIC
LONDON • NEW YORK • OXFORD • NEW DELHI • SYDNEY

BLOOMSBURY ACADEMIC
Bloomsbury Publishing Plc
50 Bedford Square, London, WC1B 3DP, UK
1385 Broadway, New York, NY 10018, USA
29 Earlsfort Terrace, Dublin 2, Ireland

BLOOMSBURY, BLOOMSBURY ACADEMIC and the Diana logo are trademarks of Bloomsbury Publishing Plc

First published in Great Britain 2022
Paperback edition published 2024

Copyright © Eve Salisbury, 2022, 2024

Eve Salisbury has asserted her right under the Copyright, Designs and Patents Act, 1988, to be identified as Author of this work.

For legal purposes the Acknowledgments on pp. xi–xii constitute an extension of this copyright page.

Cover design by Rebecca Heselton
Cover image: Sloane 182, f.18, by permission of the British Library.

All rights reserved. No part of this publication may be reproduced or transmitted in any form or by any means, electronic or mechanical, including photocopying, recording, or any information storage or retrieval system, without prior permission in writing from the publishers.

Bloomsbury Publishing Plc does not have any control over, or responsibility for, any third-party websites referred to or in this book. All internet addresses given in this book were correct at the time of going to press. The author and publisher regret any inconvenience caused if addresses have changed or sites have ceased to exist, but can accept no responsibility for any such changes.

A catalogue record for this book is available from the British Library.

A catalog record for this book is available from the Library of Congress.

ISBN:	HB:	978-1-3502-4979-0
	PB:	978-1-3502-4983-7
	ePDF:	978-1-3502-4980-6
	eBook:	978-1-3502-4981-3

Typeset by Integra Software Services Pvt. Ltd.

To find out more about our authors and books visit www.bloomsbury.com and sign up for our newsletters.

For Evan Andrew

Contents

List of Illustrations	x
Acknowledgments	xi
List of Abbreviations	xiii
Introduction	1
The Making of a Medical Discourse	3
Narrative Medicine and Medical Humanities	5
Microcosmic Bodies	9
Chapter Overview	13
1 Honoring Stories of Illness in Chaucer	17
Physician, Heal Thyself	23
Charting "Pestilence"	29
The Wounded Child	32
Diagnosing the Summoner and the Friar	35
Diagnosing the Pardoner: "This" Pestilence	36
Wounded Knight / Wounded Storyteller	39
Medicinal Barnyard	40
Medicinal Gardens and the *Hortus Conclusus*	44
Toward a Healing Philosophy	45
2 Gower and Langland: Therapeutic Dialogue and	
Intersubjective Medicine	49
Pestilence and Penitence	53
Confession and the Seven Deadly Sins	55
Medical Consciousness and the Psychophysiological Body	56
Practitioner and Priest	61
Reading the Cardiocentric Body: Langland	63
Reading the Cardiocentric Body: Gower	67
Gower's Physique and the "Parfit Practisour"	72
Health in an Unhealthy World: Langland	75
Health in an Unhealthy World: Gower	76
Diagnosing the Storyteller's Illness	78

3 Lydgate and Hoccleve: Dietetic Medicine and the Medicalization
   of Madness   81
   A Diet and Doctrine for the Pestilence   85
   How the Plague Was Ceased in Rome   89
   Fabula Duorum Mercatorum (The Story of Two Merchants)   91
   Death and Its Dance   94
   Death and the Physician: A Dialogue   98
   Lydgate Meets Hoccleve Virtually   99
   Knock, Knock, Who's There?   105
   Learning to Die   107
   Fables from the *Gesta Romanorum*   108
   Reading the Fables Allegorically   111
   Go Little Book, Go!   114

4 Inscribing Medicine: Thornton Household Remedies   119
   John of Burgundy's *De Epidemia* and Thornton's "Medcynes
   for the Pestilence"   126
   From Pestilence to Wounds   133
   From the Literal to the Literary: Wounding   135
   Reading for Disease   138
   The Healing Power of Blood   144
   Medical Charms: Fever   147
   Medical Charms: Toothache   148
   Medical Charms: Childbirth   149
   Narrating Medicine in Thornton Household Recipes   153

5 Women Healers, Life Writing, and Therapeutic Reading   155
   Women Healers and Communal Medicine   160
   Pestilence and Household Healing   161
   Chronicling the Pestilence   165
   Passion to Compassion   170
   Heart and Soul   171
   Therapeutic Reading for Women   173
   Medicine for Disease   174
   Therapeutic Reading and the *Vertu* of Women's Healing   178
   Two Virtuous Women of Romance   179
   Bad Medicine: The Vilification of Women Healers   182
   Narrating Medicine for Women   186

6	Afterword: A Prognosis	189
	Illness Narratives versus Plague Narratives	193
	Looking Back	195
	Looking Ahead	197
Bibliography		199
Index		216

Illustrations

1 Microcosmic Man in the center of the Macrocosmic Universe — 10
2 Chaucer's Physician holding up a "jurdon" to inspect a urine sample — 27
3 Cells of the brain as an exemplum of the Doctrine of Cells — 58
4 The connections between the heart and other senses — 59
5 Death and a Dying Man — 97

Acknowledgments

My work in the Medical Humanities began when Western Michigan University decided to launch a School of Medicine and invited humanists across campus to contribute ideas about the building of a medical curriculum. Faculty members in the humanities were asked to suggest readings that would speak to the needs of students and fit into an already-full schedule. Several years later the program now includes courses on ethics and law as well as narrative medicine and physician-storytellers. While I cannot claim credit for the evolution of the Medical Humanities program at WMU, what I can say is that I was there at its inception, strategizing with colleagues involved in thinking about an exciting new enterprise. This is the scenario that led to my participation in the Medical Humanities conference organized by members of our philosophy department, Fritz Allhoff and David Charlton, which provided additional opportunities for me to converse with health-care practitioners about the narratives they wrote, the kinds of stories they heard from their patients, and what they gained from such exchanges.

When I met Rita Charon and learned about her theory and practice of medicine, I was convinced that this would be applicable to my study of Middle English literature. She had, after all, applied literary interpretation to her readings of the body and her teaching of "radical listening" to medical students. Invited to speak at The Sischy Lecture in Humane Medicine at the University of Rochester, Charon recounted her work as the founder and executive director of the program in narrative medicine at Columbia University and the successes it had generated. But when she encouraged audience members to join in a close reading of poetry, what became clear to me was how a poem had the capacity to "speak" in ways in which the body speaks, its rhythms and cadences interpreted as if it were a text. For those who listened attentively and engaged in what amounted to a diagnostic reading of a poem, that evening's activities were both uplifting and informative. For me, Charon's presentation prompted a change in the direction of my work.

As this brief narrative suggests, there are many people to thank in bringing a book project such as this to fruition. First and foremost, of course, is Rita Charon, whose talk inspired the reorientation of my research that evening in Rochester. Also present that evening and equally enthusiastic were Pamela Yee and Jenny Boyar, who later participated, along with Sarah Gillette and M. W. Bychowski, in a conference session on medicine and the poetry of John Gower, organized by Georgiana Donavin, friend and co-director of The Gower Project, for the International Congress on Medieval Studies held at WMU. Another session on the topic, this time for the International John Gower Society Conference held at the University of Rochester, continued what had proven to be a productive line of inquiry.

Writing on this topic during the time of Covid, with its restricted travel, social distancing, and mask-wearing, has been challenging. At the same time, however, such restrictions have urged me to think more substantively about the benefits of modern medicine, especially in relation to the era of bubonic plague in England, the historical context for my study. Such restrictions have also made me more aware of online borrowing systems that made much of the research for this book possible. Not only would I like to thank the Interlibrary Loan team at WMU but also Anna Siebach-Larsen, Director of the Rossell Hope Robbins Library and Koller-Collins Center for English Studies at the University of Rochester, for lending books during lockdown and enabling a space for study afterward. The Robbins Library is a place where I spent many hours during my graduate years and where fond memories were made. Returning to this space was thus less daunting than it could have been during this difficult time. It was there that I met Caleb Prus, a student with an interest in Medical Humanities who reminded me that conversations with students on topics of mutual concern are to be cherished for the clarity they bring to unsettled textual matters. To that end I would like to thank all the students over the years who have engaged in such clarifying conversations with me. I would also like to thank the editors at Bloomsbury, Ben Doyle, Laura Cope, and their production team for setting the book into motion and keeping it on track. So too I would like to thank the anonymous reviewers of an early draft who offered suggestions for improvement and the equally anonymous reviewer of a final draft who noted that such changes had been made.

Thanks also go to friends Sarah Higley, Jill Miller, and Edith Jaffe for their willingness to listen to my musings in the project's early stages, and Muriel Lederman, whose participation in WMU's Medical Humanities conference furthered my immersion in the subject. I would also like to thank my partner of many years, David Bleich, for his support and encouragement, as well as daughter Meghan, son-in-law Andy, and grandchildren, Maddie and Evan, for keeping the spirit alive throughout the writing process. Lastly, I would like to take this opportunity to extend my gratitude to all the primary care physicians and practitioners of narrative medicine for injecting humanity into an oftentimes impersonal health-care system. Having the Medical Humanities and narrative medicine as an integral part of medical education makes a difference.

Abbreviations

METS	Middle English Texts Series
TEAMS	Teaching Association for Medieval Studies
MED	Middle English Dictionary
DMVE	Dictionary of Medical Vocabulary in English, 1375–1500
DPS	Documents of Practice Series
EETS, o.s	Early English Text Society, original series
EETS, e.s.	Early English Text Society, extra series
EETS, s.s.	Early English Text Society, supplementary series

Introduction

Narrating Medicine in Middle English Poetry: Poets, Practitioners, and the Plague is designed to fill a gap in what we know about medical writing and its convergence with other forms of literature in England in the 100+ years after the advent of the "great mortality" (pestilence, Black Death, plague).[1] Predicated upon the assumption of a discernible link between a traumatic disease event and an upsurge in medical consciousness, this study foregrounds a discourse that includes forms of writing not often associated with premodern medicine and its practice. Composed of several genres and written as frequently in poetry as in prose, this body of literature answers questions about how to interpret symptoms of disease, how to devise effective treatments, and how to implement regimens of health thought to be preventative.[2] When read in conjunction with medical treatises, plague tractates, and remedies in poetry and prose, storytelling enriched in this way discloses experiences of illness that medical writing in and of itself falls short of expressing. In so doing the telling of tales exposes a kinship between the art of writing and the art of healing. It also demonstrates a marked interest in self-care and prevention as indicated in the genre of *regimen sanitatis*, motifs of which are incorporated into manuals of governance as well as narrative poetry and medical writings.

Since this study addresses a disease that has reached into our own time with cases erupting sporadically in various parts of the world, it seems appropriate to deploy a modern medical theory of interpretation for the purpose of

---

[1] "Black Death" was a postmedieval coinage based upon the buboes that erupted on the body (usually the armpit, groin, and neck); since then, two other strains of plague have been identified: one pneumonic and the other septicemic, the former a respiratory illness, the latter a blood infection. As is well known to modern medical science, the causative bacillus for the bubonic strain of the disease has been identified as *Yersinia pestis*, named after the French bacteriologist who discovered it, Alexandre Yersin.

[2] Julie Orlemanski, *Symptomatic Subjects: Bodies, Medicine, and Causation in the Literature of Late Medieval England* (Philadelphia: University of Pennsylvania Press, 2019).

understanding stories told about the etiology, transmission, and effects of that disease on individual bodies and communities. One such interpretive methodology proven effective in modern Medical Humanities programs is Rita Charon's practice of narrative medicine, which teaches how to engage a text both by observing its representation of physical symptoms and by listening closely to the stories told by patients in practice and, in this case, by some of the most innovative and perceptive English poets and prose writers of the late Middle Ages.[3] The witness of recurrent plague events offered by the authors and texts included in this study enables us to access another level of experience of the pandemic traditionally identified as "the plague," or the Black Death as it came to be known. This study brings the practices of poets, prose writers, and medical practitioners who found themselves in the middle of a public health crisis to the attention of a twenty-first-century audience aware of the global impact of infectious diseases. One need only think of the ongoing battle with new and antibiotic-resistant strains of bacteria and spontaneous outbreaks of viral illnesses for which there are no vaccines to underscore that point. Our experience with the pandemic sparked by Covid-19 is but the most recent example.

Narrating Medicine in Middle English Poetry asks these key questions: What does the recognition of a medical discourse emerging during the late medieval period contribute to what we know about actual diseases, especially the bubonic plague, or "pestilence" as it was commonly known? How does the medical discourse of the fourteenth and fifteenth centuries intersect with faith practices and scientific knowledge? How do regimens of health and assumptions about a body-soul continuum affect a population in the throes of a traumatic disease event? How do we recuperate stories told by patients through literary works too often considered fiction and therefore meaningless entertainment? How do household codices and verse remedies factor into our understanding of medical procedures carried out by premodern families without consultation with a physician? What roles do women play in medicine and empirical practice, and what do their writings tell us?

---

[3] The study of plague has advanced significantly in recent years, and especially in the present moment as we face the devastating effects of Covid-19. Both geographic spread and chronology, the traditional narratives of the Black Death, have been altered as a result, the appearance of the plague earlier than presumed and its spread far wider. See "The Mother of All Pandemics: The State of Black Death Research in the Era of Covid-19," https://www.medievalacademy.org/page/PandemicWebinar

The Making of a Medical Discourse

During the period under consideration here, that is, the 100+ years following the appearance of the plague in England in 1348, the confluence of literature and medicine begins to crystalize into a discourse that experiments within and beyond the inherited assumptions of Hippocrates and Galen, encouraging new ways of thinking about medical treatment. Expanding on the view of Marion Turner that "there was a particularly noticeable upsurge in the production of medical texts in England and in English,"[4] a claim also taken up by medievalists such as Julie Orlemanski and others,[5] the literature addressed here marks a divergence from premodern medical studies based upon inherited texts to an emphasis on shared knowledge both textual and experiential among vernacular readers, many of whom were caregivers and householders. Medical treatments depicted in what otherwise would be considered "literary" texts convey empirical practices and everyday remedies as effectively as treatises written in Latin or Arabic and relegated to other disciplinary categories and specialized audiences (Guy de Chauliac's *Chirurgia magna*, for example).[6] At the same time, such texts introduced medical terminology and the ailments to which this specialized lexicon referred to a reading audience in need of a language in which to narrate their illnesses.[7] While most studies of plague writing focus on Boccaccio's *Decameron*, Machaut's *Le Jugement dou Roy de Navarre*, and Petrarch's "anguished outcry" in his many letters,[8] the poetry of Chaucer, Gower, Langland, Lydgate, and Hoccleve, the writings of Margaret Paston, Julian of Norwich, and Margery Kempe, and the anonymous authors of Middle English romance and writers of medical treatises, also have something to offer. While demonstrating an awareness of the catastrophic nature of an infectious disease, these writers and their works also point to the efficacy of dialogic therapy,

---

[4] Marion Turner, "Illness Narratives in the Later Middle Ages: Arderne, Chaucer, and Hoccleve," *Journal of Medieval and Early Modern Studies* 46.1 (2016): 61-87. See also Orlemanski, *Symptomatic Subjects*; Bryon Lee Grigsby, *Pestilence in Medieval and Early Modern English Literature* (New York: Routledge, 2004), and Daniel McCann, *Soul-Health: Therapeutic Reading in Later Medieval England* (Cardiff Wales: University of Wales Press, 2018).
[5] Michael Leahy, "'To speke of phisik': Medical Discourse in Medieval English Culture," PhD diss. Birkbeck (London: University of London, 2015).
[6] Peter Murray Jones, "The Surgeon as Story-teller," *Poetica* 72 (2009): 77-91. See also, Jeremy J. Citrome, *The Surgeon in Medieval English Literature* (New York: Palgrave Macmillan, 2006).
[7] Julie Orlemanski, "Jargon and the Matter of Medicine in Middle English," *Journal of Medieval and Early Modern Studies* 42.2 (2012): 395-420.
[8] See Siegfried Wenzel, "Pestilence and Middle English Literature: Friar John Grimestone's Poems on Death," in *The Black Death: The Impact of the Fourteenth-Century Plague*, ed. Daniel Williman (Binghamton, NY: Center for Medieval and Early Renaissance Studies, 1982), 131-59 (at 132).

therapeutic reading, and the stories told by the sick as well as those attempting to care for them. These are some of the authors whose writings enable medical expertise to be disseminated among a popular audience not only in need of information and practical advice but also in need of strategies for assimilating medical knowledge to prevent a gruesome and sudden death among household and community members. When works such as Chaucer's *Canterbury Tales*, Gower's *Confessio Amantis*, Langland's *Piers Plowman*, Lydgate's "A Diet and Doctrine for the Pestilence" (among others), and Hoccleve's *Series* are read in conjunction with plague treatises and remedies found in household codices such as Thornton Lincoln Cathedral MS 91, the merging of categories of writing, reading, and the disciplines they represent becomes increasingly legible. When Middle English medical narratives and the life writings of Margaret, Margery, and Julian are factored into the medical discourse developing during the plague years, the identification of what I believe to represent a significant shift in medical treatment and disease prevention, or what one modern physician sees as the beginning of internal medicine, is all the more apparent.[9] Premodern medical practitioners such as those recounted by Chaucer's Physician as well as medical writers such as John of Burgundy, John of Arderne, Gilbertus Anglicus, John of Gaddesden, Guy de Chauliac, Henry Daniel, John Mirfield, Henri de Mondeville, and even Henry de Grosmont, who as a patient speaks so movingly of "holy medicine,"[10] factor into the dialogic interaction of the works noted above. At the same time, scenes of therapeutic practice appear in disparate writings in Middle English oftentimes cast in religious language. As more than one scholar notes in this regard, the Latin word *salus* means both health and salvation, signifying a linguistic conflation of theology with the care of body and soul. Through narrative poetry, medical knowledge begins to disseminate more widely among a vernacular audience in answer to an increasing demand for pragmatic treatments as well as a deeper understanding of how to live in a world besieged by recurring attacks of a lethal pathogen. Whether written in a sophisticated poetic style or more humbly and plain, narrative poetry and life writing provide ways in which the medical imagination may be expanded, efficacious remedies conveyed to a wider audience, and traumatic experiences of a devastating epidemic communicated to future generations.

---

[9] John Pearn, "Two Medieval Doctors: Gilbertus Anglicus (c1180-c1250) and John of Gaddesden (1280-1363)," *Journal of Medical Biography* 21 (2013): 3-7 (at 6).

[10] See Naoë Kukita Yoshikawa, "Holy Medicine and Diseases of the Soul: Henry of Lancaster and *Le Livre de Seyntz Medicines*," *Medical History* 53 (2009): 397–414. See also, Catherine Batt, *Le Livre de Seyntz Medicines, the Book of Holy Medicine* (Tempe, AZ: ACMRS, 2014).

Narrative Medicine and Medical Humanities

The recognition of narrative medicine as a productive discipline within the more broadly defined Medical Humanities has prompted new directions in the study of literature, especially in relation to diseases still present in the twenty-first-century population, including occasional outbreaks of bubonic plague but also leprosy (Hansen's disease), cancer, influenza, and the common cold. Like modern storytellers, some of whom are doctors who relate their personal grappling with illnesses of various kinds,[11] premodern medical writers not only speak of their own experiences as practitioners but also consider the voice of the patient to be as significant as their own. In many cases, in fact, not only do poets and prose writers engage in subjective narration but physicians aware of the need to disseminate strategies of self-care in the face of a global medical emergency do as well. Since its inception in the late twentieth century, narrative medicine has made significant inroads into health care in the institutions across the United States and the UK as well as in Medical Humanities programs worldwide. Designed to teach medical students how to listen more attentively to stories of illness and carry out treatments with a deeper understanding of the patient as well as a heightened awareness of what it takes to be a conscientious medical professional, this approach to medical care has proven effective. A turn toward a more empathetic clinical practice, one that features dialogic engagement and intersubjectivity, contributes to a holistic assessment of the patient's body while also establishing an atmosphere of mutual trust and respect on an individual level as well as confidence in medicine and its practitioners as a collective enterprise.

Rita Charon, author of *Narrative Medicine: Honoring Stories of Illness* and originator of this approach to medical practice, trains medical students and other health-care workers how to listen to their patients' stories, as well as how to write about them in a way that helps establish interpersonal bonds among health-care providers: "narrative medicine gives doctors, nurses, and social workers the skills, traditions, and texts to provide nuanced, respectful, and singularly fitting clinical care to the sick while also achieving genuine contact with their own and their colleagues' hopes and ideals as health professionals."[12] As Charon has explained, writing about patients, engaging with them vis-à-vis experiences that all humans share, oftentimes reveals as much about the clinician as it does about

---

[11] Oliver Sacks' autobiographical work comes to mind here as does Arthur W. Frank's, *The Wounded Storyteller: Body, Illness, and Ethics* (Chicago: University of Chicago Press, 1995).

[12] Charon, *Narrative Medicine*, 13.

the conditions of the patient. Health-care specialists such as those noted above are required to enter the world of their patients "if only imaginatively, and to see and interpret these worlds from the patients' point of view."[13] Just as those in premodern religious orders (Charon cites medieval Franciscans in this analogy) move from a state of initiation and naiveté to one that is more authoritative and knowing, so too fledgling practitioners become more confident as they learn more about themselves through the stories of their patients and their experiences in treating them. The point of teaching "readerly skills" to medical personnel, in Charon's view, is to foster their ability to

> follow a narrative thread, to adopt multiple and contradictory points of view, to enter into the teller's narrative world and see how that teller makes sense of it, to identify the images and metaphors used to recognize the temporal flow of events, to follow allusions to other stories, to tolerate stories' ambiguity, and to be imaginatively transported to wherever the story might take the one who surrenders to it.[14]

This is an approach that both enriches and humanizes the clinical methods and impersonal technologies typically used to gather data and provide a statistical baseline for treatment. It is the difference between a humanistic approach to medical practice and an approach driven by technologies that tend to dehumanize the human body.

Charon's recognition of the correspondences between medical practice and the body's functions, between clinical observation and literary interpretation, is especially applicable to the recuperation of narratives that disclose something about the realities of illnesses of the past, whether derived from the patient's personal history or the social context in which that history was lived. The theory and practice of narrative medicine is especially appropriate for examining how storytelling constructs events that unfold over time in a patient's life. The five narrative features of medicine identified by Charon—temporality, singularity, causality/contingency, intersubjectivity, and ethicality—correspond to "time, characters, narrator, plot, and the relationships that obtain between teller and listener," all of which can be applied to the reading and interpretation of premodern narrative. Especially significant in this regard is the attention to trauma caused by events—social and political as well as personal—over which

---

[13] Charon, *Narrative Medicine*, 9.
[14] Rita Charon, "The Self-telling Body," *Narrative Inquiry* 16.1 (2006): 191-200 (at 194). See also Charon's "Narrative Medicine as Witness for the Self-Telling Body," *Journal of Applied Communication Research* 37.2 (2009): 118-31.

individuals have little control. As Donna Trembinski has pointed out, trauma is now an accepted category of analysis for reading literatures of the Middle Ages, rendering the past "more visible and more explicable to present eyes. It allows for a reading of texts that has the potential to deepen and nuance our perceptions of historical emotions and actions and historical interactions between [and] with people."[15] She alerts us to "narrative disjuncture, disordered prose, formulaic language or metaphors standing in for description of potentially traumatic events," as signs and symptoms of something gone awry, something painful to remember and impossible to forget.[16] These are the points at which narrative medicine and trauma studies intersect, especially when the story seems fragmented or displaced or when there are discernible strategies of denial or evasion and signs that the storyteller is wounded in some way.

Time past, as constructed in many of the narratives presented here, features the importation of classical works and their authors, the creation of narrators removed from the action yet fully implicated in the plot. So too the frame narratives offer a model of dialogic exchange between the storyteller and the recipient(s) of the tale. As in Charon's model of medical practice, to engage attentively as part of the listening audience enables that audience to experience "loss perhaps more powerfully in the light of another... [and to] recognize in catastrophic and public suffering that which is always present and needful of attention in local and private suffering."[17] This is precisely the level of engagement in reading that exposes the links between the public and the private that distinguish illness narratives from collective accounts of pandemic disease. At the same time twenty-first-century understandings of the private and the public, especially when it comes to health care, are not always as distant from past perceptions as we may imagine. The illness of an individual registers in the disease of the larger sociopolitical environment just as surely as the microcosmic human body resonates with the macrocosmic universe.

How can we recuperate the illness narratives of the Black Death when we have so little direct testimony of individual experiences of the disease, memoirs that speak subjectively of the body and its responses? Other than chroniclers' accounts, which may not be eyewitness narrations and therefore distanced from the illness itself, there are few written documents in the English vernacular of the time that contribute to what we know about individual experiences of

---

[15] Donna Trembinski, "Trauma as a Category of Analysis," in *Trauma in Medieval Society*, ed. Wendy Turner and Christina Lee (Leiden: Brill, 2018), 13-32.
[16] Ibid., 21.
[17] Charon, *Narrative Medicine*, 181.

the plague.[18] Do stories told in narrative form mediated by fictional narrators, personas created by their writers, substitute for the stories of "real" patients? Indeed, what constitutes "illness" in the minds of authors who approach the topic from nonmedical perspectives? By emphasizing narrative medicine's focus on the efficacy of storytelling and the need for interpretive methods that emphasize close reading and listening to the speakers in the text, this study reveals something that may be of value to a twenty-first-century audience of practitioners and patients as well as to medievalists and readers interested in learning how literature and medicine can be mutually illuminating for more obscure eras. So too a more broadly conceived interdisciplinary approach to the study of past medical practices and stories about them, as the Medical Humanities provides, can contribute valuable insights into patient care as well as telling us more about the role of the practitioner in the middle of a pandemic. Moreover, by explaining how premodern medicine was practiced as effectively by empiricists (mostly women) as by academically trained physicians (mostly men), we gain a better understanding of what appears to be a turn toward a more experiential and pragmatic approach to healing that benefits those who rely on their own resources. "Innovation" and "experimentation," two terms rarely associated with premodern medicine or early literature for that matter, speak to the urgent need felt by practitioners, poets, and prose writers alike to respond to the crisis of care prompted by the "great mortality." As one historian notes, and as ironic as it may seem, observable changes in the status of physicians and surgeons as well as an attitude toward life among the devout were discernible during this time of crisis.

As Robert S. Gottfried puts it, "the Black Death brought not so much a stoic acceptance of pain and suffering as it did a desire for an active, temporal life."[19] Such a statement is not wholly in accordance with the writings of mystics such as Julian of Norwich, whose anchoritic circumstances restricted active engagement in the world, especially when her experience is compared with that of Margery Kempe. Nor is it adequate to talk about hermits or recluses, like Richard Rolle, whose activities revolve around meditative devotion and physical isolation. Nonetheless, there are ways in which such individuals participate in an

---

[18] The few testimonies from physicians who experienced the illness are written in Latin and other non-English languages such as the *consilium* of Jacme d' Agramont, written in Catalan.

[19] Robert S. Gottfried, *The Black Death: Natural and Human Disaster in Medieval Europe* (New York: Free Press, 1983), 79-80. For a more recent understanding of the pandemic see Monica H. Green, ed. *Pandemic Disease in the Medieval World: Rethinking the Black Death* (Kalamazoo and Bradford: Arc Medieval Press, 2015). See also Green's essay, "Taking 'Pandemic' Seriously: Making the Black Death Global," 27-61.

"active, temporal life" when reading and writing are taken to be actions capable of eliciting change. By offering a religious mode of healing in their writings, as Laura Kalas has made clear in her work on Margery Kempe, mystics whose approaches to devotion are unique in style and form can play an active role in delivering "spiritual medicine."[20]

The need to address the medical challenges facing the English populace after the first appearance of the plague in England (c. 1348) had its effect on many writers, in other words, yet what began to emerge during its many subsequent outbreaks were new ways of thinking about health and an increased attentiveness to innovation born not of an idealized desire for theoretical medical knowledge but rather a pragmatic need to combat a real-life health threat. The focus on the humoral body and how to treat it effectively became, as one modern physician-writer asserts, the advent of internal medicine whose practitioners—Gilbertus Anglicus and John of Gaddesden—in this case, were "pioneers" of the "emergent discipline."[21] To that claim I would add, as others have, that there is something of a silver lining in the experience of the Black Death in the form of innovation and experimentation.[22] The increased knowledge and use of medicinal compounds, the discernible consumption of vernacular treatises on pestilence by nonprofessionals, the creation of networks for sharing medical information, and an emphasis on preventative strategies indicate a heightened medical consciousness both for individuals and communities of vernacular readers. One of the notable functions of a medical discourse that includes literary texts is that it expands the medical imagination, making possible what otherwise would seem too daunting even to contemplate.[23]

Microcosmic Bodies

The Hippocratic-Galenic medical tradition and its focus on the elemental composition and form of the humoral body, its relation to the macrocosmic structure of the universe, its four temperaments and qualities, the significance

---

[20] Laura Kalas, *Margery Kempe's Spiritual Medicine: Suffering, Transformation and the Life-Course* (Cambridge, UK: D. S. Brewer, 2020).
[21] Pearn, "Two Medieval Doctors," 6.
[22] John Aberth, *The Black Death: The Great Mortality of 1348–1350* (New York: Bedford/St. Martin's Press, 2005), 3. See also Faye Marie Getz, "Black Death and the Silver Lining: Meaning, Continuity, and Revolutionary Change in Histories of Medieval Plague," *Journal of the History of Biology* 24.2 (1991): 265–89.
[23] Aberth, *The Black Death*, 4.

of cosmology to bodily procedures such as uroscopy, bloodletting, and other methods of treatment were integral to the academic training of physicians. Many of the presumptions about the body were inherited by medieval practitioners from a pre-Christian understanding of the kinship between the body and the world. Integrated into the model of the Ptolemaic universe *that* body becomes a microcosm or "little world" at the center of the cosmos encompassing it (Figure 1). As this illustration from a medical miscellany of the fifteenth century suggests, the placement of the human body in the center of the scheme of things visually alludes to the abstract notions undergirding the study of medicine. That the human at the center of the known universe is shown within a series of concentric rings consisting of planets, constellations,

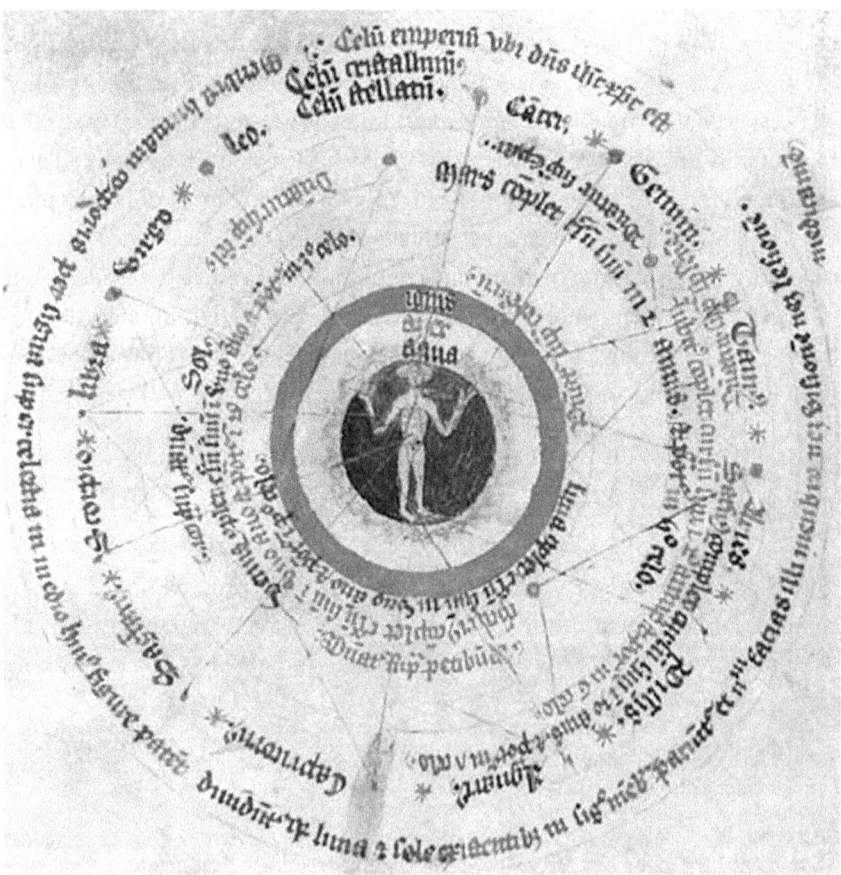

Figure 1 Microcosmic Man in the center of the Macrocosmic Universe. MS Sloane 282, f. 18, British Library. By permission of the British Library.

and astrological signs enables visualization of the interconnectedness between the human and the celestial. In this depiction the body is bounded by the four elements—fire, water, air, and earth—which recall the four humors—blood, yellow bile, black bile, and phlegm—the four qualities of the humors—hot, cold, wet, dry—the four temperaments associated with those humors—melancholic, sanguine, choleric, and phlegmatic—in a symbolic numerical system resonant with the four seasons, the four directions, the twelve winds (four primary, eight secondary), the four Ages of Man, as well as classical and biblical narratives featuring the number four.[24] As Esther Cohen so aptly observes, the assumption of this scheme is "that the basic building blocks of the human physique—the humors—were inherent within the human frame, not borrowed from preexistent matter,"[25] which means that individuals were presumed to have been born with a certain psychophysiological makeup subject to the influences of external forces, factors of everyday human life that came to be known as the "nonnaturals." Over time premodern physicians consolidated such forces in their identification of six of the most influential: "air, motion and rest, sleeping and waking, diet, evacuation and retention, and finally the 'accidents of the soul' or passions."[26]

It is important to note in view of the above that a study to gain an understanding of the body and its relation to the cosmos was required for medieval medical students. Astronomy/astrology and Man as microcosm, sometimes depicted as having the signs of the zodiac superimposed on his body, were considered essential to comprehensive medical education. As Nancy Siraisi observes, "the good physician was supposed always to take astral influences—on the patient at conception and at crises of life and of health or illness, on medication, and on parts of the body—into account."[27] Yet such a highly educated purview did not necessarily translate into practical applications at the level of patient care, especially in the face of the plague. As many have commented upon, the reputations of professional physicians suffered as a result of their not being able to "cure" the scourge ravaging the populace, though some died trying.[28] Perhaps

---

[24] The four gospels, the four living creatures that represent the gospels, the four rivers of Paradise, and the four generations of people from Adam to Christ. Latin writers such as Horace and Ovid also took up the symbolism of the number four, the former in his Ages of Man theory (in the *Ars Poetica*), the latter in *Metamorphoses*.

[25] Esther Cohen, *The Modulated Scream: Pain in Late Medieval Culture* (Chicago: University of Chicago Press, 2010), 23-4.

[26] Ibid., 24.

[27] Nancy G. Siraisi, *Medieval & Early Renaissance Medicine: An Introduction to Knowledge and Practice* (Chicago: University of Chicago Press, 1990), 67.

[28] Gentile da Foligno and Jacme d'Agramont, while Guy de Chauliac recovered briefly before succumbing.

the disillusionment with professional medicine as well as the recognition that patients needed to take responsibility for their own health is one reason that there emerges a discernible movement toward self-care and household medicine necessitating popular access to medical treatises and remedies of all kinds. The world of theoretical medicine gave way to a more pragmatic mode of medical care among the nonprofessional population; at the same time the language used in medicine as a discipline retained its links to the celestial realm and the assumptions such connections implied. There is, in fact, a conflation of terminology that brings the material world into conversation with the world of theological abstraction wherein a *Christus medicus* was presumed to reside and healing was a sacred process; certain medicinal substances are given names that render them metaphorical in some way. *Gratia Dei*, the Rose of Mary (rosemary), Virtue given of God, the drink of Antioch, Armenian bole, and *terra sigillata* (sealed earth) as well as a variety of charms and prayers were thought to aid in treating medical needs, not the least of which was childbirth.[29] As cited by three prominent professional practitioners, stones and herbs, amulets and parchments, as well as other objects and the rituals that accompanied them could have as much medicinal effect as the use of language, especially if the patient believed in the efficacy of the treatment.

Refocusing our reading in terms of narrative medicine not only exposes the workings of such treatments but also enables the recognition of a notable level of anxiety as well as a palpable desire to deploy whatever means necessary to treat the plague: to engage in prevention by avoiding "bad air," taking a bath, or having sex, and concentrating instead on eating a modest diet, getting enough sleep, and keeping the vital spirits alive and well through reading, writing, and attentive listening. As George Keiser noted years ago, "books originally copied for clerical practitioners were soon copied for, and even by the laity, a fact that is recognized in vernacular treatises whose translators explain their work as means to permit every person, learned or lewd, to be his own physician."[30] This study seeks to illustrate how twenty-first-century readers living in a pandemic of our own might get closer to the experience of the Black Death as empathetic

---

[29] Many of these are found in the *Dictionary of Medical Vocabulary in English, 1375–1500*, ed. Juhani Norri (Abingdon, UK: Ashgate, 2016). "Virtue given of God," for instance, is described as "ointment for ocular lacerations made of germinal vesicles of egg yolks" (1195).

[30] George R. Keiser, *A Manual of the Writings in Middle English 1050–1500*, vol. 10, gen. ed. A. E. Hartung (New Haven: Yale University Press, 1998), 3653. See also George R. Keiser, "Verse Introductions to Middle English Medical Treatises," *English Studies* 84.4 (2003): 301–17; also, Linda Ehrsam Voigts and Patricia Deery Kurtz, eds. *Scientific and Medical Writings in Old and Middle English: An Electronic Reference* (Ann Arbor: University of Michigan Press, 2001). https://cctr1.umkc.edu/search

witnesses to the awakening of a newly literate audience and its need for medical knowledge. By reading a range of writings that intersect by discipline and perspective in their focus on solving what amounts to a public health crisis, we gain a better understanding of how the "great mortality" registered among the individuals it affected.

Chapter Overview

The chapters that follow address these matters in medically inflected stories with characters who experienced illness or were themselves writers and readers of medical texts, as well as householders, empirics, midwives, and "witches" whose skills were acquired by practice rather than academic study. Listening to the tales told by poets, practitioners, and empirical healers during the plague years reveals connections between the personal and the social in ways that privilege the material body over the abstract notions of astrological medicine. When illness is not only individual but a feature of the social milieu, answering the call for immediate medical treatment becomes a priority.

When Chaucer makes the observation, "the lyf so short, the craft so long to lerne" at the beginning of the *Parliament of Fowls*, the craft he is citing is not of poetry, as one might expect, but rather one of the most famous aphorisms in the Hippocratic corpus. Chapter 1 sets the stage for linking Chaucer's poetic art to the art of healing. Unlike Boccaccio in his *Decameron*, a story collection presumably based upon the author's experience of the plague in Florence, Chaucer refers to the epidemic obliquely and for the most part lets it lurk under the surface only to emerge every now and then in allusions, gestures, characterizations, and figures of speech. Chaucer's own physician notwithstanding, many of the pilgrims of the *Canterbury Tales* produce narratives that foreground a method of healing of both body and soul that begins with dialogue and storytelling. On a journey predicated upon a belief in the imminence of death, Chaucer's pilgrims become patients seeking remedies for their illness, telling tales that reveal something about the human condition and the need for medical treatment.

Since confession is a mode of spiritual purgation and Galenic medicine assumes the purging of harmful bodily fluids, Chapter 2 begins by addressing Gower's stories in the *Confessio Amantis* and their vocalization of an illness of the soul as well as of the body. Dialogues between patient and doctor are replicated in the exchanges between Genius and the youthful Amans, whose lovesickness appears to be the cause of his malaise. Yet there is more than meets the eye in this frame narrative, and the tales subsequently told to alleviate the youth's suffering offer glimpses of another contemporary illness (leprosy) that exemplifies the purgative exchange. Just as surely as bloodletting, cupping, and other procedures were thought to restore the balance of humors in the body, so too, in the act of speaking and listening, Amans begins to return to a sense of equilibrium. Much the same may be said about Will and his dialogues with several interlocutors in *Piers Plowman*, especially the eponymous character from whom he begins to recognize his own illness and the ways in which it affects his well-being. Not simply a form of talk therapy or the congenial data-gathering consultation between a physician and her patient, the dialogic exchanges between these two figures (Amans and Will) and the allegorical characters who guide them enable us to see how the treatment of illness transpires through intersubjective modes of communication. Lurking in the background, alluded to both directly and indirectly and affecting the tone and content of both works, is the plague.

Because the Black Death proved to be a disease resistant to treatment or cure, there was much skepticism about the ability of academically trained physicians to return patients to a state of health. Chapter 3 addresses select works of John Lydgate and Thomas Hoccleve and another aspect of the experience of disease, including ways in which any individual might respond to the anxiety engendered by the threat of imminent death. For Lydgate and Hoccleve, immersion in reading and writing poetry in addition to carrying out the duties of their respective occupations appear to function as personal therapy for dealing with the traumatic emotions provoked by recurrent outbreaks. Both poets were conversant in medical discourse and enfolded their knowledge of medicine into their respective works; both created personas who spoke to the life and death interests of their audiences. For Lydgate, such writings include "A Diet and Doctrine for the Pestilence," "How the Plague Ceased in Rome," the *Fabula Duorum Mercatorum* (The Story of Two Merchants), and the "Danse of Death"; for Hoccleve, such topics appear most prominently in the *Series*, a collection of texts including a complaint, a dialogue, a meditation on death, and two fables from the *Gesta Romanorum*. While there are clear variations among these narratives, and between these two poets, taken together, they underscore the attention being paid to medicine, its practice in the fifteenth century, and its effects on these writers.

Chapter 4 addresses the inscribing of medicine and household remedies into one of Robert Thornton's manuscripts, Lincoln Cathedral MS 91. Middle English poetry and prose as featured in this collection runs the gamut from the treatment of pestilence to the applications of charms and prayers for everyday illnesses. Stories such as the *Alliterative Morte Arthure* and the *Prose Life of Alexander*, romances such as *Sir Degrevant*, *Sir Eglamour of Arois*, and *Sir Perceval of Galles*, hagiography, comical satires, and miscellaneous materials copied into this compendious household miscellany conflate the art of healing with the art of written expression.[31] But what is most intriguing about this manuscript, especially in relation to the focus of this study, is that it includes the *Liber de diversis medicinis*, a collection containing medical advice and recipes for households such as Thornton's. Read in conjunction with scenes from literary texts depicting the treatments of a range of illnesses offers possibilities for alleviating suffering without the intervention of a medical professional. Listening as well as reading provides a household audience with the interpretive skills needed to escape the realities of actual disease, at least temporarily. By lifting the spirits and stimulating the imagination of both young and old, as recommended by physicians of the time, these narratives had a healing effect all their own.

When explicated within the context of late medieval household miscellanies, as Chapter 5 suggests, medical poetry points to the need for immediate and accessible health care. And since women were central to the management of the household and the care of family members, health care became their responsibility (Margaret Paston and Margery Kempe are pertinent examples). As exemplified in the Thornton collection, miscellanies offer the kind of entertaining and instructive works appealing to household members of all ages. The presence of midwives, hospital sisters, wet nurses, and herbalists and Trotula's works on obstetrics and gynecology[32] provide an additional context for readings of literary women of medicine such as Geoffrey of Monmouth's pre-plague Morgan le Fay and the women of the so-called fairy world, whose healing arts expand the medical imagination. So too their less glamorous counterparts, the women more likely to provoke accusations of witchcraft than the divinely ordained healing of the Virgin Mary or the Pearl maiden or virtuous women of romance like Josian of *Bevis of Hampton* and *Le Bone Florence of Rome*, offer comfort in response to despair. Women alleged to be witches and sorceresses are the female characters located in the literary shadows as well as the margins of society from which they occasionally emerge as powerful figures.

---

[31] One scholar even goes so far as to suggest that at least one writer of medical verses may "himself be an author of romance." See Keiser, "Verse Introductions," 309.

[32] Monica H. Green, *The Trotula: An English Translation of the Medieval Compendium of Women's Medicine* (Philadelphia: University of Pennsylvania Press, 2001; repr. 2002). See also Monica Green, "Women's Medical Practice and Health Care in Medieval Europe," *Signs* 14.2 (1989): 434-73.

While literatures and writers of the past may not seem to have anything to contribute to fresh approaches to the Medical Humanities, we might recall that the humanities can be traced back to Francesco Petrarch and the *studia humanitatis* he envisioned.[33] Modeled on the works of Cicero, the Roman orator whose writings provided so much solace in the face of the Italian writer's loss of close friends and family members during the pandemic, this was an idea eventually enfolded into university curricula across Europe. Since this is precisely the time frame during which the English authors highlighted in this study did their work, it makes sense to look more closely at their texts to add another dimension of meaning to what we already know about the devastation caused by the Black Death. That there could be a way to keep the body strong and resistant to disease not only through modifications to diet and daily habits but in the reading of books and the telling of tales surely contributes to the *studia humanitatis* of the time. This, it seems to me, marks the "real" beginning of the Medical Humanities, a moment in the history of medicine that the principles of narrative medicine help to illuminate.[34]

Such is the forward-looking prognosis offered in the Afterword, in which subjective narratives of illness are distinguished from plague narratives that situate the Black Death within a broad historical context. While the former enables personal experience to enter the epidemiological record, the latter constitutes a purview often distanced from such documentation. There is something to be said about listening to the voices of poets, practitioners, and others who saw and felt the devastation taking place around them. Narrative medicine's attention to the stories told by patients to those in positions of care offers a model of interpretation that enables modern audiences to access the disease episodes of the past. These are the tales of illness that lend the official recounting of the Black Death another level of meaning.[35]

---

[33] Howard Brody, "Defining the Medical Humanities: Three Conceptions and Three Narratives," *Journal of Medical Humanities* 32 (2011): 1-7.

[34] See Richard Schiffman, "Learning to Listen to Patients' Stories," *The New York Times*, February 25, 2021. "Narrative medicine is now taught in some form at roughly 80 percent of medical schools in the United States. Students are trained in 'sensitive interviewing skills,' and the art of 'radical listening' as ways to enhance the interactions between doctors and patients."

[35] A note on texts cited in Middle English: I have replaced those words containing thorns and yoghs with slightly modernized spelling to facilitate easier reading. For difficult or unfamiliar medical terms, I have inserted translations in brackets.

1

Honoring Stories of Illness in Chaucer

The lyf so short, the craft so long to lerne,
Th' assay [attempt] so hard, so sharp the conquerynge,
The dredful joye alwey that slit [slides away] so yerne:
Al this mene I by Love, that my felynge
Astonyeth with his wonderful wekynge
So sore, iwis, that whan I on hym thynke
Nat wot I wel wher that I flete or synke.[1]

(ll. 1-7)

When Chaucer wrote "The lyf so short, the craft so long to lerne" at the beginning of the *Parliament of Fowls*, it was to introduce a dream vision of Nature and courtship among birds. In this early work, a female eagle is the object of admiration for three male eagles who argue their worthiness to be her consort in a mating ritual as old as time. The craft referred to in this context, as clarified by the lines that follow, indicate that "love" is what it takes "so long to lerne." This is, after all, a narrative poem about a bird's desire to find a mate. What is curious about the citation of this particular aphorism within the context of what amounts to a thinly disguised allegory about *human* mating rituals, however, is that its source is neither Andreas Capellanus' *Art of Courtly Love* nor Ovid's *Art of Love* nor even the *Roman de la Rose*, as one might expect, but rather a quotation attributed to Hippocrates, arguably the most authoritative figure (along with Galen) in the history of medicine known to the Middle Ages. Translated into Latin, "Vita brevis, ars vero longo," from its original Greek, this is an iteration of the first of the Hippocratic *Aphorisms* in which the "craft" refers neither to human nor avian love but rather to the skills required to be a medical practitioner. That the saying also appears in a fourteenth-century surgeon's work, Guy de Chauliac's

---

[1] All quotations are from *The Riverside Chaucer*, gen. ed. Larry D. Benson (Boston: Houghton-Mifflin, 1987).

Chirurgia magna, translated into Middle English in much the same way as Chaucer deploys it here—"the lyf so schort, the craft forsothe is long"—suggests not only that Chaucer may have known the writings of physician/surgeons such as de Chauliac but that he sees a genuine correspondence between love and medicine. Moreover, because "the phrase's first context of meaning was medicine,"[2] according to Julie Orlemanski, the statement accrues additional validity. What Chaucer does with his poetic declamation here, however, allows healing and love to be read as equivalent endeavors.

Nonetheless, such a statement begs the question of why a poet as savvy as Chaucer would refer to the practice of medicine rather than to the writing of poetry, the kind of work for which he is best known? And why would he, if poetry is also at stake in this opening gambit, consider it to be a craft rather than an art? What is defined as a "craft" suggests that both poetry and medicine require skills that might be acquired by reading a manual or apprenticing with an experienced mentor. To make this craft into a full-fledged art would require mastery that combines "knowledge with skill, reason with experience, and method with intuition," a combining of areas of expertise that "lies beyond the careers of many medical practitioners," according to Luke Demaitre.[3] Perhaps the same may be said for Chaucer's writing of poetry, especially in a dream vision like the *Parliament of Fowls* recounted as it is by a narrator who suffers the disorienting effects of insomnia. When Chaucer's sleep-deprived speaker deploys the Hippocratic aphorism to talk of love and courtship, he borrows language embedded in a medical tradition that recommends getting enough sleep to maintain humoral balance and overall health. Love and medicine merge in these poetic lines, in other words, to suggest the therapeutic dimension of a line of work able to change a person's mood, awaken the senses, and assuage physical and emotional restlessness, if only temporarily. When love and medicine converge in the beginning of this Chaucerian dream vision, there is something to be said about how poetry transforms its practitioner into a physician whose craft becomes an expression of artful healing.[4]

---

[2] Julie Orlemanski, *Symptomatic Subjects: Bodies, Medicine, and Causation in the Literature of Late Medieval England* (Philadelphia: University of Pennsylvania Press, 2019), 46.

[3] Luke Demaitre, *Medieval Medicine: The Art of Healing, from Head to Toe* (Santa Barbara, CA: Praeger, 2013), 2–3.

[4] Pearl Kibre and Nancy G. Siraisi, "Matheolus of Perugia's Commentary on the Preface to the Aphorisms of Hippocrates," *Bulletin of the History of Medicine* 49.3 (1975): 405–28. In a fifteenth-century lecture by Matheolus of Perugia, for instance, the aphorism is defined as both "a short discourse replete with deep meaning" and "a short saying encompassing the essential meaning of a given proposition." On the utility of the work: "This is sufficiently apparent from the explanation of intent in the text…. 'Since man's life is short and the art of medicine long, it was necessary and

There have been many claims that poetry can heal the ills of humankind—that, like music, it has therapeutic value when deployed at moments of despair and loss. Yet many questions of a medical nature remain to be asked in relation to this poem and Chaucer's oeuvre in general. How does poetry in the time of pestilence lift the spirits or enhance the well-being of the soul? Certainly, life is short when there is an epidemic lurking in the background, when human reproduction, like that of the birds depicted in mating rituals, is deferred or postponed. It is probably no coincidence that the *Parliament of Fowls* was written around the time of the marriage of Anne of Bohemia and Richard II (1382), when at least two outbreaks of the plague had already occurred, one in the late 1340s, another in the early 1360s. When the queen died in 1394 at the priory at Sheen, the king reportedly had the property burned to the ground out of grief. Like the Man in Black, the central figure of Chaucer's *Book of the Duchess* written shortly after one of the plague outbreaks and prior to Anne's death, the king is said to have suffered the loss of his beloved consort from an ailment over which neither king nor court physician had any control. Like the bereaved Richard II or John of Gaunt, the historical personage frequently cited as the model for Chaucer's Man in Black, the character captures a sense of the frustration experienced by many of those who lost friends and family members to this sudden and unexpected illness. The relationship between poetry and medicine, suffering and Love, Nature and a traumatic disease event affects the birds of the *Parliament* no less profoundly than the readers who share the sorrow of the Black Knight in the *Book of the Duchess*.

The intermixing of physical pain with emotional trauma and spiritual unease is embedded in poems of unrequited love and loss. As divergent as these dream visions are from Boethius' influential *Consolation of Philosophy*, wherein Lady Philosophy as medical empiric offers anxiety-reducing medicine to the prisoner, the desirable lady of courtly romance takes on the role of physician to attend to the suffering of the wounded knight.[5] Just as

---

useful to compose this aphoristic doctrine.' Wherefore Galen says in his commentary, speaking of this science that this book has proven extremely helpful to those desirous of learning a long art in a short time. Another aspect of the same thing is that it is of prime usefulness in committing to memory those things that one has learned and in recalling those things that one has, after learning them, forgotten" (409). In *Medieval Medicine: The Art of Healing, from Head to Toe*, Luke Demaitre notes that this aphorism has "spawned countless interpretations and profound commentaries.... A single lifetime is no match for the Art of medicine. Mastering this vast and complex art requires the combination of knowledge with skill, reason with experience, and method with intuition" (2). "Art" and "craft" were often interchangeable in Latin, but the two terms could be understood as marking the difference between theory and practice or artful creativity and technical skill.

[5] Marion Turner, *Chaucer: A European Life* (Princeton, NJ: Princeton University Press, 2019), 72.

the dejected subject of the *Consolation* reveals his psychic distress to the Lady who would set his mind at ease and is urged to speak of his suffering ("If you seek the physician's help, you must uncover the wound" [Book 1, chapter 4]),[6] the grieving knight exposes his sorrow to enable its healing. The aphorism that launches the *Parliament* equating poetry and medicine thus captures the ethos of a time ravaged by the pestilence that has come to be known, perhaps coincidentally, as the Black Death. Life is indeed short, and the craft of treating some of its more dire effects can be a lengthy and painful process, filled with grief and sorrow.[7]

Yet there is a relative absence in Chaucer's work of a plague narrative equivalent to Boccaccio's presumably eyewitness account of the event in Florence in the *Decameron's* prologue, his description of the Florentines' responses and actions: some sequestered themselves in homes filled with juniper smoke or reveled uninhibitedly in the streets, while others, such as his select storytellers, escaped to a rural villa to avoid the miasma engulfing the city. While Boccaccio records this experience in explicit detail, and despite the skepticism such an "eyewitness" recounting has received, Chaucer by way of comparison does not speak directly to the epidemic unfolding in London and surrounding environs but rather alludes to it obliquely, as if to dwell upon it might be lethal to his poetic enterprise and his personal sense of calm. Nonetheless, as several critics have demonstrated, the Chaucerian literary corpus embodies the language of health and illness, pointing to the significance of what it means to be alive in the middle of a disease event. While Boccaccio's storytellers leave Florence to tell their tales in the "delectable gardens" of a country house, Chaucer's pilgrims share narratives on the way to Canterbury in search of a remedy for ostensibly more trivial ills at the shrine of St. Thomas: "the hooly blisful martir for to seke, / That hem hath holpen whan that they were seeke" (ll. 17–18). They tell their tales, not wholly in prose, as Boccaccio does (the "Tale of Melibee" being an exception in the Canterbury collection), but rather in rhyme and meter, early

---

[6] P. G. Walsh, trans. *Boethius: The Consolation of Philosophy* (Oxford: Oxford University Press, 1999).
[7] Anthony Goodman, *John of Gaunt: The Exercise of Princely Power in Fourteenth-Century Europe* (New York: Routledge, 1991), 46-7. This suggestion had been refuted by Marjorie Anderson in "Blanche, Duchess of Lancaster," *Modern Philology* 45.3 (1948): 152-9 (156). Regarding the birth of a son, Edward, who died in infancy: "The tentative date of his birth is given by Armitage-Smith as 1368 (table, p. 94); but, unless this is a sixth child, that date should be amended to 1367. It is also relevant to mention that Blanche's father and sister Maud also died of the plague, though there was a rumor of Maud's sudden death as having been a result of poison. Also worth noting here is the death of Princess Joan, the daughter of Edward III, allegedly of plague in 1348" See Rosemary Horrox, ed. and trans., *The Black Death* (Manchester, UK: Manchester University Press, 1994), 250.

iambic pentameter, decasyllabic couplets, and rhyme royal, all of which breathe life into their narrations especially when read aloud.[8]

Like the stories of patients so necessary for a comprehensive reading of the body as noted by Rita Charon in her theory and practice of narrative medicine, Chaucer's pilgrims offer tales that speak to the effects of disease on the human body. Like narrative medicine, narrative poetry in Middle English embodies the medical histories of pilgrims at the center of a public health crisis. Reading in the way that Charon suggests for medical practitioners enables us to see aspects of the experience of illness that even the chroniclers and physicians of Chaucer's time were unable to convey. While Chaucer does not acknowledge the plague as directly as Boccaccio or a select group of physicians and chroniclers have, he nonetheless offers a body of evidence that requires the interpretive skills of readers being asked to discern fact from fiction, fantasy from reality, and irony from straight talk for the purpose of understanding patients and their narratives as fully as possible.

Going to the shrine at Canterbury for the purpose of remedying illnesses of both body and soul underscores the significance of the role that pilgrimage played in Chaucer's world, to be sure, but so too does this ritualized journey provide a useful framework for narratives that reveal something more about the experience of an epidemic. Medieval pilgrimage provided a way in which individuals could unburden themselves, seek a holy remedy for their illnesses, both physical and psychological, and refocus their lives. Used as a signifier for the transience of human life and the eternality of the afterlife as well as being a literal road trip to a place where miraculous healing was believed to occur, pilgrimage was the means by which people of all estates and occupations could participate in a communal activity that promised to reinstate their health and well-being. In terms of the symbolic and literal significance of pilgrimage, it is worth noting that the cathedral at Canterbury was not only the site at which the relics of St. Thomas (Becket) were preserved but it was also a hospital that welcomed pilgrims and others in need of medical treatment. Established shortly after the death of Thomas Becket, St. Thomas the Martyr at Canterbury, or Eastbridge Hospital as it came to be known, was committed to admitting the

---

[8] As noted by John A. Alford, "Medicine in the Middle Ages," *The Centennial Review* 23.4 (1979): 377-96. "Peter of Abano (d. ca. 1316) argues that pulse rates conform exactly to certain musical proportions, and that the pulse beats in different meters at different ages. The 'normal' meter of infants is trochaic; for adults, spondaic, and for the aged, iambotrochaic" (381).

sick, the weak, and the infirm.[9] By Chaucer's time it appears that everyone who was willing and able to provide health care was welcome into service there.[10]

While it would be a commonplace to say that illness and suffering are notable motives for pilgrimage in the *Canterbury Tales*, such tropes point to an emerging medical discourse with a specialized lexicon that could be understood oftentimes both literally *and* figuratively. More than simply a means by which to convey medical information, the introduction of medical terminology, embedded oftentimes in descriptions of persons, places, and things, underscores the poet's recognition of the necessity for enfolding a technical vocabulary into his work.[11] Influenced by the language of the humoral concept of medicine as well as the philosophical understanding of the healing arts as modeled by Lady Philosophy in Boethius' *Consolation*, the poet uses words that make it possible to see how the macrocosm of the known universe—its planets, its elements, its movements—could have an effect on the microcosm—understood to be the human body.[12] As when Dante in his "Letter to Can Grande" urges exegetical modes of interpretation to be applied to readings of the *Commedia*, Chaucer encourages his audience to read the literal and the symbolic simultaneously in the manner of a palimpsest, one might say, layered and at the same time integrally related. Like Dante, who creates an eponymous persona as an avatar for his journey from hell to paradise, Chaucer invents Geffrey the Pilgrim to travel with the others, participate in the storytelling, record the stories told, and describe the other storytellers in vivid detail.

---

[9] Also relevant: according to Martha Carlin, "St. Thomas's Hospital, dedicated to St. Thomas Becket, originally formed part of the Augustinian priory of St Mary in Southwark, itself founded or re-founded in 1106. The circumstances of the hospital's foundation are unknown. It seems to have been in existence before c. 1180, and later tradition claimed it had been founded by Becket himself, in honour of the Holy Trinity…. The actual care and feeding of the patients were the responsibility of the hospital's sisters; the function of the brothers was purely religious" (20). See "The Medieval Hospital of St. Thomas the Martyr in Southwark," *Society for the Social History of Medicine Bulletin* 37 (1985): 19-23.

[10] Derek Ingram Hill, *The Ancient Hospitals and Almshouses of Canterbury* (Canterbury: Canterbury Archaeological Society, 1969).

[11] Bryon Lee Grigsby, *Pestilence in Medieval and Early Modern English Literature* (London: Routledge, 2004). See also Siegfried Wenzel, "Pestilence and Middle English Literature: Friar John Grimestone's Poems on Death," in *The Black Death: The Impact of the Fourteenth-Century Plague*, ed. Daniel Williman (New York: Center for Medieval and Renaissance Studies, 1982); Celia Lewis, "Framing Fiction with Death: Chaucer's *Canterbury Tales* and the Plague," in *New Readings of Chaucer's Poetry*, ed. Robert G. Benson and Susan J. Ridyard (Cambridge, UK: D. S. Brewer, 2003), 139-64.

[12] According to the theory popularized by Galen from ideas he attributed to Aristotle and Hippocrates, the body is composed of these four elements, which correspond to the four humors (bodily fluids): blood, phlegm, choler (yellow or red bile), and melancholy (black bile). "The blood is hot and moist to the likeness of the air; phlegm is cold and moist after the kind of the water; choler hot and dry after kind of fire; melancholy cold and dry after kind of earth" (*Secretum Secretorum*, EETS, e.s. 74, 219-20; modernized).

Such an approach to the telling of tales is pertinent to the theory and practice of narrative medicine. Just as Chaucer's pilgrims tell their stories, whether from personal experience or selected from other sources, so too patients are encouraged to reveal the circumstances of their illnesses, their medical histories, as well as the thoughts and emotions that present themselves during the course of their narration. The health-care provider's role is to listen attentively, produce a parallel narrative in writing, and engage in dialogue both with the patient and with other medical personnel involved in the case. The process helps both novitiate and experienced clinicians to acquire dialogic dexterity and an ability to write about individuals from an empathic point of view. Just as narrative medicine requires a community of others for support and guidance in the process of evaluating and treating a patient, Chaucer's *Tales* addresses an audience actively seeking remedies of their own. When his pilgrims are understood to be the subject of concern (patients, in other words), the audience becomes part of a diagnostic community, interpreting the stories being told and assessing the health of the individuals who tell them. Like a practitioner of narrative medicine, the poet teaches his audience the close reading skills necessary for a comprehensive understanding of each taleteller. The poet and his persona transform him into a supervising practitioner equivalent to Charon's mentor/physician as well as the medical student charged with writing parallel charts, while we, as audience members, participate in the diagnostic process.

Physician, Heal Thyself

Especially apt for beginning a discussion of how narrative medicine functions more specifically in the *Canterbury Tales* is the description of the Physician in the General Prologue. In its length and detail, the portrait creates a vivid characterization of the doctor through its verbal imagery. Written by the poet's chronicler and personal avatar, Geffrey, this is the impression offered for interpretation:

> With us ther was a Doctour of Phisik;
> In al this world ne was ther noon hym lik,
> To speke of phisik and of surgerye,
> For he was grounded in astronomye.
> He kepte his pacient a ful greet deel
> In houres by his magyk natureel [science]
> Wel koude he fortunen the ascendent
> Of his ymages for his pacient.

He knew the cause of everich maladye,
Were it of hoot, or coold, or moyste, or drye,
And where they engendred, and of what humour.
He was a verray, parfit praktisour;
The cause yknowe, and of his harm the roote,
Anon he yaf the sike man his boote.[remedy]
Ful redy hadde he his apothecaries
To sende hym drogges and his letuaries,
For ech of hem made oother for to wynne—
Hir frendshipe nas nat newe to bigynne.
Wel knew he the olde Esculapius,
And Deyscorides, and eek Rufus,
Old Ypocras, Haly, and Galyen,
Serapion, Razis, and Avycen,
Averrois, Damascien, and Constantyn;
Bernard, and Gatesden, and Gilbertyn.
Of his diete mesurable was he,
For it was of no superfluitee,
But of greet norissyng and digestible.
His studie was but litel on the Bible.
In sangwyn and in pers he clad was al,
Lyned with taffata and with sendal.
And yet he was but esy of dispence; [spending]
He kepte that he wan in **pestilence**,
For gold in phisik is a cordial,
Therefore he lovede gold in special.

(ll. 411-44)

Acknowledged for his expertise in medicine (called "phisik" at the time),[13] his preference for astronomy and science over Bible study, his ability to diagnose accurately, prescribe therapeutic drugs, forge liaisons with apothecaries, recite famous contributors to the history of medicine, and recount details of the Hippocratic-Galenic system of four humors, the Physician is presented as a model of medical perfection, a practitioner with a sartorial flare for fashion, and a connoisseur's appreciation for gold. Presented to his audience as a "verray, parfit

---

[13] The many meanings of "physik" as noted in the *MED*. Chaucer's uses include a medical science or theory; a book dealing with medical science or theory ["Parson's Tale," ln. 913]; his translation of Boethius, 2.pr.6.108. "Man of Law's Tale," B. 1189; as a natural science "Boece" reference to Aristotle's book of physic. In his description of Doctor of Physic in GP as medical treatment, KnT l. 2760.in NP as healthful regimen, 4028, in GP gold in phisik is a cordial, 443.

praktisour," he appears to be upstanding and knowledgeable, an exemplar of a credible, conscientious, and experienced doctor. Yet the critical assessment of his character has often been negative, skeptical, and suspicious primarily because of his overly close association with apothecaries, his attraction to precious metal, expensive clothes, and the remuneration he receives from treating plague-stricken patients. Doctors, then as now, were expected to instill confidence in their patients, to serve altruistically and in accordance with the Hippocratic Oath, as humanitarian acts done preferably without monetary reward but rather for the love of the art of healing. Those perceived to fall short of this ideal were roundly criticized.

When we consider Chaucer's penchant for irony or that his poetry can be read in several registers at once, however, the Physician takes on a more ambiguous form, not only as a literary representation of a doctor but as historically realistic and as capable of a range of behaviors as any human practitioner. As Carol Rawcliffe notes, much of the Physician's portrait accurately depicts the university-educated physician conversant in the history of medicine, its theories and practices, its ethical principles, and modes of care.[14] Dressed in the garb of the medical professional, Chaucer's Physician is familiar with the pharmaceuticals provided by the apothecaries with whom such practitioners forged collegial if not pragmatic alliances. He is a doctor who appears to wear the clothes of his profession with a certain *esprit de corps*, an enthusiasm he also shows in his apparent love for gold. That he is also fastidious about his diet and habits is also noteworthy since such a description echoes the regimens of health becoming so popular at the time: in the humoral medical system, food was considered to be therapeutic, the body the means by which such life-sustaining substances were processed and eliminated. Medical practice thus involved not only caring for the sick and despondent but preventing illness by recommending a balanced diet, practicing moderation, exercising regularly, and getting enough sleep.[15] In other words, dietetic medicine and healthy living were as important to medical practice as were patient treatment and care.

While several scholars seem to take pleasure in the negative critique of this character, for Rawcliffe the Physician is something of a hero who "risks his own safety by treating the sick in plague time and sets a fine example to his patients by adopting the spare diet and abstemious lifestyle recommended by the medical

---

[14] See Carole Rawcliffe, "The Doctor of Physic," in *Historians on Chaucer: The "General Prologue" to the Canterbury Tales*, ed. Stephen H. Rigby and Alastair Minnis (Oxford: Oxford University Press, 2015), 297-318.

[15] Christopher Bonfield, "The First Instrument of Medicine: Diet and Regimens of Health in Late Medieval England," in "*A Verray Parfit Praktisour": Essays Presented to Carole Rawcliffe*, ed. Linda Clark and Elizabeth Danbury (Cambridge: Boydell & Brewer, 2017), 99-119.

authorities to whom he is so devoted. By the standards of the age even his dress appears restrained."[16] Nonetheless, the Physician's description registers as more proscriptive than prescriptive performance rather than authentic medical knowledge and clinical expertise. That several medieval physicians are among the fifteen medical authorities cited by the Physician suggests that he knows what he's talking about, and, as some scholars suggest, marks an attempt to overcome skepticism associated with the profession.[17] From Apollo, the ancient god of medicine and other art forms, to practitioners of Chaucer's own time, the Physician's recitation demonstrates his comprehension of medical authorities and practices reaching back to the ancients.[18] His name-dropping may be seen as an attempt at establishing credibility on the subject that may ultimately be proven false.[19] Yet clinical experience seems not to be an overly familiar concept, perhaps even nonexistent, since the Physician's bedside manner and empathetic engagement with actual patients are not on display in this portrait.[20] For a fuller picture of who and what he is, the illustration in the Ellesmere manuscript offers an aspect of his character absent in the verbal description but significant in what it adds to the perception of his credibility and medical authority. In a stand-alone image drawn in the margin, the Physician is depicted on horseback, holding a urine sample up to the light (Figure 2). The large container (or jurdon) at which the doctor gazes intently is half-filled with a fluid of golden color, translucent and devoid of floating particles, made visible by the light shining through the transparent receptacle, qualities that tell the observant practitioner something about the internal health of his patient.[21] The color of urine was important: there

---

[16] Rawcliffe, "Doctor of Physic," 317.
[17] J. Pearn, "Two Medieval Doctors: Gilbertus Anglicus (c1180–c1250) and John of Gaddesden (1280–1361)," *Journal of Medical Biography* 21 (2013): 3–7. See also J. Pearn, "Bernard Gordon (fl. 1270–1330): Medieval Physician and Teacher," *Journal of Medical Biography* 21 (2013): 8–11.
[18] Rossell Hope Robbins, "The Physician's Authorities," in *Studies in Language and Literature in Honour of Margaret Schlauch* (Warszawa: Polish Scientific Publishers, 1966), 335–41. Carole Rawcliffe's reading suggests that the physician is less a charlatan than "a dedicated student of medicine who took seriously the maxim that 'the exercise of bokes worshippeth a leche' [Arderne, *Treatise of Fistula in Ano*]. Unlike the Summoner, who employs a few Latin tags to hoodwink the credulous, he is a genuine scholar" (311).
[19] See Kirk L. Smith, "False Care and the Canterbury Cure: Chaucer Treats the New Galen," *Literature and Medicine* 27.1 (2008): 61–81. Smith argues that the Physician is ethical and pointing out the problem with corruption in the legal system, especially in relation to Apius as judge.
[20] Jamie McKinstry and Corinne Saunders, "Medievalism and the Medical Humanities," *postmedieval: a journal of medieval cultural studies* 8.2 (2017): 139–46. They argue that clinical examination of a patient did not obtain until the eighteenth century.
[21] The beginning of internal medicine according to J. Pearn. See also Jake Walsh Morrissey, "Anxious Love and Disordered Urine: The Englishing of Amor Hereos in Henry Daniel's *Liber uricrisiarum*," *The Chaucer Review* 49.2 (2014): 161–83. "Uroscopy was practiced so widely in the Middle Ages, both by empirics and university-educated physicians, that the vessels used to examine urine came to symbolize the medical profession in the popular imagination…. The practice of uroscopy depends on the theory that the properties of urine can be interpreted as evidence of health or sickness. This

Figure 2 Chaucer's Physician holding up a "jurdon" to inspect a urine sample. MS Ellesmere, f. 133r, Huntington Library.

were, in fact, illustrated charts that showed nineteen or twenty different hues, accompanied by explanations of each variant, and what that color indicated about an individual's overall health.[22] A golden color, as illustrated in Figure 2, was read as a sign of well-being and humoral balance, perhaps the reason the golden urine is presented as a "cordial," a word rhymed with "special," calling

means of diagnosis is possible because, in medieval medical thinking, urine is produced from the blood during the second phase of digestion, at which time it acquires perceptible clues about the circumstances of its production, including factors such as the body's natural heat and the state of the live, life-forces (*spiritus*), and humors" (165-8).

[22] In medieval medicine the analysis of urine enabled the detection of disease in the entire body, while in modern practice the findings speak more specifically to urinary tract illnesses.

attention to the equation: "For gold in phisik is a cordial / Therefore he loved gold in special" (ll. 443–444). That the rhyme links the color of gold with the Physician's love of the precious metal draws attention to the connection between the two, but not necessarily in a negative way since gold could be ground into particles, mixed with other substances, and used as a medicinal drink.[23] That the urine sample is of a golden color suggests the relative health of the patient. When compared with other shades of urine—from green to black—which indicate a range of illnesses from mild to deadly, this is an important feature of the illustration, especially since "cordial" could signify "a substance which stimulates or invigorates medicinally" or "an object or action that gladdens or uplifts the heart."[24] There is something to be said about the depiction of the Physician in the General Prologue, in other words, and whether an audience *should* diagnose him as suspect and untrustworthy, honest and conscientious, or realistic and ambiguous.

That Chaucer's Doctor of Phisik keeps what he earns from his treatment of "pestilence"—a reference used not without significance here—suggests that he may have attempted to treat the disease. Reading the bodies of pilgrims in conjunction with their tales and historical contexts, as a twenty-first-century physician would "read" the body of her patient, offers another way to look at the Physician not only as an honest and knowledgeable medical practitioner but also as a doctor in search of a remedy for the disease spreading like wildfire around him. It is also not without significance that of the few references Chaucer makes to "pestilence" in the entirety of his work, one of them occurs in the General Prologue's description of the Physician, while another appears in the tale he tells.[25]

---

[23] While the *MED* cites the use of gold as a drinkable substance in the work of Guy de Chauliac as well as Lydgate's "How the Plague was Ceased in Rome," addressed in Chapter 3, its use in Chaucer's work suggests that the substance used as medicine was known much earlier and is perhaps the aim of the Canon's Yeoman's experiments.

[24] *MED*, s.v. cordial, n. In his chapter on the "Black Death and Medieval Medicine," Joseph P. Byrne adds this: "To counteract the poison [in the air and from other sources] directly, gold, in some drinkable form, was commonly prescribed. According to the author Solemnis Medicus, gold contained the power of the incorrupt sun itself, and could purify any poison, which by nature was corrupted. Gentile (of Foligno) suggested rose water or barley water (for the poor); Friar Giovanni da Rupescissa advocated strong distilled alcohol with gold in it" (47-8).

[25] Skeat dated the Scogan poem to 1393 because of the flood that occurred around Michaelmas that year. The fifth outbreak of the plague occurred between 1390 and 1393. This is often referred to as the plague of children as documented in Thomas Walsingham's *Historia Anglicana*, see Horrox, *Black Death*, 91.

Charting "Pestilence"

One way to acknowledge the presence of the plague in the poet's work is to chart his use of the word "pestilence" and its verbal contexts, especially in terms of medicine.[26] While one scholar claims Chaucer's usage constitutes "a rhetorical device urging readers to reflect upon their mortality, spiritual health and prospects of salvation,"[27] the reference appears more complex than this would suggest, emerging under varying circumstances often referring to the health and well-being of the spirit to be sure, but not consistently. That the term could also refer to the dis-ease of widespread social and political disruption, unforeseen climate events, and the presence of other diseases such as leprosy as well as human transgression needs to be taken into consideration as well.[28] "Pestilence" is deployed in a number of ways and in a number of verbal contexts that have an impact on its meaning, sometimes emphasizing disease as a metaphor for morality, while other times concerned primarily with ailments of the physical body. Writings of contemporary practitioners and specialists such as those mentioned in the description of the Physician contribute to Chaucer's understanding of medicine and his deployment of medical terminology.

The portrait of the Physician read alongside advice written by physicians of the time reveals something about the realities of medical practice in the middle of an epidemic. In addition to caring for or counseling the sick, one of those realities for practitioners was to earn enough money to answer the needs of everyday life, to retain a state of wellness during a time of intense need, or simply to maintain professional credibility.[29] As Henri de Mondeville, physician

---

[26] A number of technical terms and more broadly construed medical language emerge in the *Canterbury Tales*, including those cited by Julie Orlemanski, "veine-blood," "ventosynge," "expulsif," "lacerte," and "animal" (as an adjective for *anima*). See also Juhani Norri, *Names of Sicknesses in English, 1400-1550: An Exploration of the Lexical Field* (Helsinki: Suomalainen Tiedeakatemia, 1992).

[27] Tom Lawrence, "Infectious Fear: The Rhetoric of Pestilence in Middle English Didactic Texts on Death," *English Studies* 98.8 (2017): 866–80 (871).

[28] Found in "The Knight's Tale," "The Nun's Priest's Tale," "The Pardoner's Tale," "The Wife of Bath's Tale," and the short poem, Chaucer's "Lenvoy to Scogan," such a range of meaning indicates an underlying, thematically related, lexical network. In the Knight's Tale the word "pestilence" is spoken by Saturn, "the fader of pestilence," in a description of his destructive power; in the Nun's Priest's Tale Chauntecleer directs the fox to call out to the pursuing mob: "turneth again ye proude cherles alle, / A verray pestilence up on yow falle"; in the Wife of Bath's Tale it indicates Alisoun's curse of stingy old men: "olde and angrey nygardes of dispence, / God sende hem soone verray pestilence"; in the letter to Henry Scogan, the poet cites his friend's renunciation of Love as having caused Venus to weep a "diluge of pestilence"; and in the Pardoner's Tale, to which I will return shortly, the speaker refers to Death as having "a thousand slayn *this* pestilence."

[29] John of Arderne supported the charging of fees based on patients' ability to pay, that is, more for rich people and less or nothing for the poor.

and surgeon at Montpellier and Paris (c. 1315), suggests, patients should pay in accordance with their ability to do so, and, if possible, surgical procedures should be paid in advance.[30] According to Michael McVaugh, de Mondeville understood "the difficulties faced by surgeons if they wished to share in that status [i.e. academically trained practitioner] and to gain acceptance along with physicians, as learned professionals."[31] What better way to convey the efficacy of a procedure as well as the credibility of a physician/surgeon than to bequeath it monetary value? De Mondeville's comments, in McVaugh's view, provide a basis for Chaucer's Physician to be read with suspicion.[32]

But there is also another reality to uncover here and one that may explain in part the disturbing and seemingly incongruous tale the Physician tells. In a narrative moment that calls attention to what is to come, and one in which "pestilence" is spoken aloud, the Physician advises parents on how to raise their children:

> And taketh kep of that that I shal seyn:
> Of alle tresons **sovereyn pestilence**
> Is whan a wight bitrayseth innocence.
> Yet fadres and ye moodres eek also,
> Though ye han children, be it oon or mo,
> Youre is the charge of al hir surveiaunce,
> Whil that they been under youre governaunce.
> Beth war, if by ensample of youre lyvynge,
> Or by your necligence in chastisynge,
> That they ne perisse; for I dar wel seye
> If that they doon, ye shul it deere abeye.
> Under a shepherde softe and necligent
> The wolf hath many a sheep and lamb torent.
>
> (ll. 90-102)

While "sovereyn pestilence" is glossed in the *Riverside Chaucer* as "supreme wickedness," the phrase performs double duty here in view of the current disease crisis lurking in the background. Given its verbal context especially in relation to children, the reference accrues another dimension of meaning. As Rosemary Horrox has noted, children were more likely to succumb to the disease: "The

---

[30] Michael R. McVaugh, "Bedside Manners in the Middle Ages," *Bulletin of the History of Medicine* 71.2 (1997): 201–23.
[31] McVaugh, "Bedside Manner," 221.
[32] Ibid., 220.

disproportionate death rate among children in later outbreaks was taken by one writer as evidence of, and punishment for, children's disobedience to their parents... for which parental indulgence was held partly responsible."[33] One of the many theories circulating about the causes of the plague was the presumed culpability of human sin and the divine vengeance it incited. There was historical precedent for this assumption, of course, since biblical history enshrined plague stories that were invoked when the need arose: presumably, this is the "litel" part of the Bible the Physician knows. Yet as an educated individual he would have been exposed to religious texts, commentaries, and contemporary treatises that promulgated such a theory. In a contemporary sermon on the Ten Commandments the speaker reminds his audience: "it is in vengeance of this sin of dishonouring and despising fathers and mothers that God is slaying children by pestilence, as you see daily."[34] One of the items in the *Decalogue* from which this speaker is drawing—Honor thy father and mother—prefaces the edict by reminding readers that they are subject to a jealous God who will punish the children for the sins of the fathers to the third and fourth generations. Since the disobedience of children was considered to be one of the triggers for the plague, at least in the text cited here, the response is, for the Physician and others like him, to remind parents to assert their authority over their offspring in an effort to prevent a punitive divine response.[35] As is frequently the case, whether then or now, children become the locus of debate when disaster strikes, their suffering and death used to capture the attention of adults as justification for going to war, giving to charity, or warning the world of imminent apocalyptic demise.[36] Within the context of the Physician and his tale, however, the admonition appears to refer to something far more immediate when it echoes the thoughts of contemporary physician, John of Burgundy, who describes the outbreak of the early 1360s as the *pestis puerorum*.[37] The Physician's admonition to parents may also be read as emerging from a tradition of parenting that falls on the side of indulgence rather than discipline, too much care rather than not enough, an excess for which the Physician recommends balance. In an approach to health care based on the equanimity of bodily humors, this makes sense.

---

[33] Horrox, *The Black Death*, 98.
[34] Ibid., 134. The original text is in BL, Harleian MS 2398, ff. 93-4.
[35] That this idea is also posited by Reason in Langland's *Piers Plowman* underscores the widespread belief in the role of children in the plague.
[36] See anonymous poem in Horrox, *The Black Death*, 126.
[37] Lister M. Matheson, "John of Burgundy: Treatises on Plague," in *Sex, Aging, & Death in a Medieval Medical Compendium: Trinity College Cambridge MS R. 14.52, Its Texts, Language, and Scribe*, 2 vols. ed. M. Teresa Tavormina (Tempe, AZ: Arizona Center for Medieval and Renaissance Studies, 2006), vol. 2.

If we understand Chaucer's perfect practitioner not to be an ironic figure, suspected for narcissism and greed, but as a conscientious doctor faced with an unprecedented health crisis, how do we read him and what do we make of the shocking tale of child murder he tells? Is he recounting the tale simply to win a dinner at the Tabard Inn, or is there something to be gained when his story is understood as a warning to parents in Chaucer's immediate audience to keep their children away from possible harm? The narrative is about how the innocent maiden Virginia suffers death as a consequence of the desires of a judge named Apius, a scenario in which her parents participate—her mother by exposing her to the judge's lascivious gaze and her father for urging her to accept an "honorable" death. Rigorous discipline as in the biblical aphorism noted by the Physician himself—"to spare the rod is to spoil the child"—is presented as a requirement for raising children willing to consent to the desires of the adults governing them. Is the Physician's advice given to protect the child, the honor of the family, or as an indictment of a corrupt system of adjudication? That the tale is met with a strong visceral response from Harry Bailly indicates how the audience might be expected to react. After noting that the Physician is "lyk a prelate," he exclaims, "I kan nat speke in terme [technical language] / But wel I woot thou doost myn herte to erme [grieve] / That I almost have caught a cardynacle [a heart attack] for which he will seek a triacle [miraculous remedy]" (ll. 311-13), which for him is "a draughte of moyste and corny ale" (l. 315). The story is arresting enough to provoke a near heart attack in the Host and drive him to seek out his own mode of medication. The beheading of an innocent child is a wound that cannot be repaired by anything other than a miracle or magic, and the Physician is incapable of either. To the Host he is "lyk a prelate," trained as a cleric who narrates the exempla of sermons without understanding their meaning, a physician knowledgeable in the theory of medicine who falls short of having developed a bedside manner.[38]

The Wounded Child

As astonishing as this story is, the "Tale of Melibee" about the grievous wounding of a five-year-old girl named Sophie during a home invasion is even more so. As may be inferred from the remarks made by Prudence, Melibee's wife, surgeons

---

[38] Virginia Langum, "'The Wounded Surgeon': Devotion, Compassion and Metaphor in Medieval England," in *Wounds and Wound Repair in Medieval Culture*, ed. Larissa Tracy and Kelly DeVries (Leiden: Brill, 2015), 269-90.

and physicians, among the most respected members of the community, are asked to provide a prognosis for the wounded child as well as counsel about how best to respond to the perpetrators who carried out the attack. In the surgeon's advice, another dimension of the craft of medicine emerges, not on the treatment of disease, which would more likely have been the job of the physician, but on the healing of bodily wounds:

> A surgien, by licence and assent of swiche as weren wise, up roos and to Melibeus seyde as ye may heere: "Sire," quod he, "as to us surgiens asperteneth that we do to every wight the beste that we kan, where as we been withholde, and to oure pacientz that we do no damage, / wherfore it happeth many tyme and ofte that whan twey men han everich wounded oother, oon same surgien heeleth hem bothe; / wherfore unto oure art it is nat pertinent to norice were ne parties to supporte. / But certes, as to the warisshynge of youre doghter, al be it so that she perilously be wounded, we shullen do so ententif bisyness fro day to nyght that with the grace of God she shal be hool and sound as soone as is possible."
>
> (ll. 1010-1015)

The surgeon's iteration of the Hippocratic Oath—that medical practitioners should first and foremost do no harm—is presented here as a credential, evidence that this practitioner is who he says he is. The explanation the surgeon offers about surgeons doing the best they can, which seems at odds with the circumstances of the moment, underscores the need for such practitioners to assess the situation, do what needs to be done, and remain apolitical: when two men have wounded each other and there's only one surgeon to heal them both, that surgeon cannot play favorites, but rather must treat each combatant equally and without bias. In the end surgeons do whatever is necessary to heal wounds done to the physical body, but ultimately God determines the outcome. Here, of course, the body is not of a wounded combatant but that of a five-year-old child.

Especially notable in this gathering of medical professionals is that the physicians do not collectively address the primary concern—treatment of the child's wounds—but rather respond to the request for their counsel on how Melibee should react to the perpetrators: "that right as maladies been cured by hir contraries, right so shul men warisshe [cure] werre by vengeaunce" (ll. 1016-1017), they say in unison. In contrast to the surgeon and in keeping with standard practices, the physicians treat symptoms by the application of contraries. If a patient exhibited symptoms both hot and dry, the first line of action would be to apply something cold and moist to the area. The treatment, of course, would necessitate examination of the patient's body and a gathering of information about the circumstances surrounding the injury. There appears in this case to have been no such examination, but only a response to Melibee's request for counsel. What differentiates the surgeon's response from that of the physicians appears to be their differing approaches to medical problem solving.

Differences in the training of physicians and surgeons are relevant here since there is a distinction to be made between the surgeon as a spokesperson for his craft and the physicians who speak as a group. One of those realities was that physicians were university trained and expected to know the medical authorities of the past—as does the Physician in the General Prologue—to gain a sense of the historical tradition and ethical principles of medical practice. Surgeons, on the other hand, "required a university education and [were] provided apprenticeship for practical experience."[39] They also learned the "rights and duties of the practitioner as regards his patient" as well as how best to establish a working relationship with patients.[40] The resemblance of Geffrey the Pilgrim's surgeon to John of Arderne, a well-known practitioner of the time, is worth mentioning here, since unlike others in his field, he advocated the need for talking with patients to assure confidence in the course of treatment and in the person carrying it out. Storytelling from the perspective of the surgeon, according to Arderne, was crucial in earning the trust of the patient. "Comforting words could give a patient 'gret hert', and this 'maketh a man harde and strong to suffer thingis and grevous.'"[41]

Just as the Physician's familiarity with pestilence makes it clear that he derives monetary sustenance from his practice so too does it challenge the ethical principles of medicine of the Hippocratic-Galenic tradition. There are, in other words, grounds on which to criticize the Physician for taking payment for his services. At the same time, in another tale in the *Canterbury* collection there is an indication that as respectable members of the community, physicians and surgeons *should* be paid for their expertise and good counsel. This is a point of view offered in the "Tale of Melibee" by Prudence, who speaks to the veracity of the advice Melibee has received regarding their grievously injured child.

---

[39] Virginia Langum, "The Wounded Surgeon," 269-90.
[40] Peter Murray Jones, "The Surgeon as Story-Teller," *Poetics* 72 (2009): 77-91 (86). Surgeons are given credit for forging "a new genre of medical writing, the Latin *Chirurgia* or *Surgery*" that was "original to the Latin west, unlike other forms of medical writing that had a long history. The authors of *Chirguriae* were surgeons themselves, specialists who made large claims for what had hitherto been regarded as the business of a manual craft" (78). Writers of medical treatises, according to Orlemanski, "were well aware of the power of narrative simultaneously to convey truths and to shape reality rhetorically…. In the deonotological prefaces that often appeared at the start of *practicae*, caregivers are advised about how to talk to patients," to gain their trust and lift their spirits. See *Symptomatic Subjects*, 126.
[41] Bonfield, "The First Instrument of Medicine," 119.

Surgeons and physicians, she says, should be "heighly and sovereynly gerdoned for hir noble speche, / and eek for they sholde do the moore ententif bisynesse in the curacion of youre doghter deere / For al be it so that they been youre freendes, therfore shal ye nat suffren that they serve yow for noght, / but ye oghte the rather gerdone hem and shewe hem your largesse" (ll. 1271-1274); that is, they should get paid for their medical expertise and experience in the world.

Whether we read the words of the surgeon and the physicians as medically reliant depends upon our willingness to accept the veracity of the practitioner. The more credible the practitioner's presentation, the more likely the audience will be to listen and follow instructions. In the comparison between the singular surgeon and the many physicians, the need for trust based on ethical principles sincerely invoked becomes increasingly clear. But trust in this scenario must be mutual, and just as the patient must be able to trust the doctor, the doctor must be able to trust the truth of the patient's story. Here, that is not possible since Sophie is a young child egregiously harmed and unable to speak for herself.

Diagnosing the Summoner and the Friar

While the "Summoner's Tale" is not the first of Chaucer's stories to come to mind when the topic is mutual responsibility during the process of medical diagnosis, there are certain motifs that speak to these matters more directly. The first is the recurring theme of trustworthiness; the second is the need for the practitioner to remain unbiased and attendant to the patient's needs. This is the tale told by the Summoner about a Friar whom he characterizes as corrupt, prone to anger, hypocritical, an all-around fraud who disregards the ethics of his chosen profession: he is a mendicant Friar who visits an ailing parishioner named Thomas to persuade him to continue tithing despite the debilitating effects of his illness. The Friar enters an abode in which the head of household (Thomas) is afflicted with an undisclosed ailment, but there is also a child who has recently died. That the tale teller himself is described as exhibiting *saucefleume* (glossed in the *Riverside* as pimples or boils) renders his appearance disturbing enough to scare little children to death.[42] While leprosy is often the first disease mentioned

---

[42] As noted in John of Burgundy's *Treatise*, "First, you should avoid over-indulgence in food and drink, and also avoid baths and everything which might rarefy the body and open the pores, for the pores are the doorways through which poisonous air can enter, piercing the heart and corrupting the life force. Above all sexual intercourse should be avoided" (Horrox, 186).

in relation to the Summoner, signs of pestilence were also registered on the skin in the form of buboes. St. Roche, the patron saint of the plague, is often shown with the sign of pestilence on his inner thigh, insinuating disease located in the testicles.[43] But also worth noting here is that the "Summoner's Tale" is about a friar who neglects his duties as a mendicant. The tale not only literalizes the begging dimension of mendicancy but casts it as a deliberate extortion of a disabled man. The Friar violates his duties as a cleric whose house call should provide consolation to a parishioner in need. In this sense, he may be more akin to a *"frater medicus,"* practitioners who drew the criticism of monastics such as Thomas Walsingham.[44]

Diagnosing the Pardoner: "This" Pestilence

While it is challenging to make a case for the Pardoner as an ethical individual, he is nonetheless truthful about his shortcomings, confessing that he is a "ful vicious man" and even describing his multiple transgressions to convince his immediate audience of his credibility. Like the Physician, whose tale triggers a cardiac episode in the Host, the Pardoner provokes another strong emotional response from Harry Bailly. The tale recounts how revelers in a tavern in Flanders learn about the demise of one of their friends and launch a search for Death only to find a pile of gold that enables the attainment of their goal. While the older revelers plot the murder of their younger companion, the youth visits an apothecary and brings back not a bottle of wine as requested but rather a bottle of poison. This is the tale in which the reference to "pestilence" is especially revealing.

> Ther cam a privee theef men clepeth Deeth,
> That in this contree al the peple sleeth,
> And with his spere he smoot her herte atwo,
> And wente his wey withouten wordes mo.
> He hath a thousand slayn this **pestilence**.
> And, maister, er ye come in his presence,
> Me thynketh that it were necessarie
> For to be war of swich an adversarie.
>
> (ll. 675-82)

---

[43] Buboes also appeared in the armpits, in the groin, and joints of the limbs, or wherever the contagion-carrying flea decided to bite.

[44] Peter Murray Jones, "The Survival of the *Frater Medicus*? English Friars and Alchemy, ca. 1370-ca. 1425," *Ambix* 65.3 (2018): 232-49.

That Death has "a thousand slayn *this* pestilence" is indeed a necessary detail, and while the speaker locates the collective event "in this contree," which the audience has been given to understand as Flanders, the reference nonetheless signals an awareness of the presence of the disease in England. As Boccaccio notes for the Florentines, some ignored the contagion or tried to protect themselves by sheltering in place or not breathing the corrupt air; others fled the city and, as Peter Beidler observed years ago, "engaged in riotous living."[45] While the moralists of the time sounded the alarm in terms of human sinfulness, Chaucer addresses the matter in more indirect terms, in this case, enabling his rhetorically skillful Pardoner to line his pockets in the act of fundraising for a charitable cause. That he is "associated with the hospital of St. Mary Ronceval at Charing Cross, a hospital that had been particularly hard hit by the Black Death at mid-century" is no coincidence.[46] Rather, St. Mary Ronceval, considered by the English to be an alien presence, a place over which conflicts of interests were ongoing, seems an appropriate site.[47] Chaucer's matching of the Pardoner with this institution, if only for the opportunities it offered for irony, is no doubt deliberate. Making this the home of the Pardoner enables the merging of the literal with the figurative, actual death with its abstract personification.[48] What the Pardoner reveals about himself is how easily corrupt individuals could take advantage of the social and political chaos brought on by this unexpected health emergency. Whether wholly fictional or partially factual, his actions and his words ring true in a document dated 1382 wherein "fundraisers" accused of having "collected alms in the realm as proctors of the Hospital, and converted the same to their own use," were to be identified and brought to justice.[49] Even in the General Prologue, the Pardoner is constructed in such a way as to indicate

---

[45] Peter G. Beidler, "The Plague and Chaucer's Pardoner," *The Chaucer Review* 16.3 (1982): 257-69.

[46] This particular institution was established a century earlier as a daughter house of the Augustinian monastery located in the Pyrenees on the pilgrimage route to Santiago de Compostela; that the original institution was also the "famous site of the defeat of Charlemagne and the death of Roland, memorialized and fictionalized in the *Song of Roland*" (Turner, *Chaucer: A European Life*, 110), also plays into the authority of the speaker whose home he declares to be Ronceval. One would imagine then that this facility, made famous by its connection to a renowned battle and the epic poem that emerged from it, would need little financial support. Yet that was not the case.

[47] James Galloway, "The Hospital and Chapel of Saint Mary Roncevall at Charing Cross," *Journal of the Royal Society of Medicine* 6, Sect. Hist. Med. (1913): 191-232.

[48] Carole Rawcliffe, "The Hospitals of Later Medieval London," *Medical History* 28 (1984): 1-21. "The fall in land values consequent upon the Black Death severely affected many institutions, as did over-ambitious building schemes that proved a virtual guarantee of financial ruin. The underlying problem lay, however, in the precarious nature of hospital funding, since only part of the income necessary for survival came from land or rents, the rest being totally dependent upon public charity" (15).

[49] Galloway, "The Hospital," 213.

his bilking of the poor and gullible by selling them a bill of goods about the authenticity of the relics he carries in his bag.

But what does the Pardoner's tale tell us about his experience of the plague? Is he, like the revelers, drunk with inhibition and driven to mindless greed?[50] When Beidler calls our attention to the specificity with which this character refers to the pestilence, not as an epidemic that may have occurred sometime in the distant past but *this pestilence*, it points more specifically to conditions in England, where Death has slain "man and womman, child, and hyne, and page" (l. 688). Like the Physician, whose arresting tale immediately precedes his own, the Pardoner offers a narrative that captures the attention of his auditors in its dramatic urgency. When he directs the pilgrims and the Host to offer donations to needy institutions such as St. Mary Ronceval, all those present learn how suspicious Harry Bailly is of the Pardoner's enterprise: "I wolde I hadde thy coillons in myn hond / In stide of relikes or of seintuarie. / Lat kutte hem of, I wol thee helpe hem carie; / They shul be shryned in an hogges toord!" (ll. 952-55).[51] As many critics have suggested, such a response marks the homophobia so firmly embedded in late medieval culture, here embodied in the Host, whose imaginative surgical procedure is quite the opposite of what any credible practitioner would do. At the very least, the threatening nature of Harry's sharp-tongued ejaculation demonstrates how violent traditional societies could be toward those unlike themselves. While there is no question that the Pardoner is constructed in such a way as to provoke this vehement response, it is also the case that, like the Physician, he tells a tale that says something about his own need to find the "special" gold, to drink the "cordial," and, in this case, to die of its effects. And perhaps this is one reason he alerts his audience to the epidemic unfolding around them. While his methods for collecting funds on behalf of charities such as St. Mary Ronceval appear to be suspect, the Pardoner tells the truth about the deadliness of the pestilence to an audience aware of Death's presence. His story is a confession in search of atonement.

---

[50] See Johannes Nohl, *The Black Death: A Chronicle of the Plague*, trans. C. H. Clarke (New York: Harper & Row, 1969), 212.

[51] Galloway, "The Hospital," 227. David K. Maxfield, "St. Mary Rouncivale, Charing Cross: The Hospital of Chaucer's Pardoner," *The Chaucer Review* 28.2 (1993): 148-63. Maxfield offers this three-part conclusion: 1) "Even if Chaucer's pardoner was a genuine representative of St. Mary Rouncivale, Charing Cross, his pardons almost certainly were based on forged papal bulls. 2) His hospital may have deserved a bad reputation in Chaucer's time. 3) The poet chose this institution to be the sponsor of his Pardoner mainly because it offered a plenitude of ironical possibilities" (159).

Wounded Knight / Wounded Storyteller

As I have been suggesting throughout this chapter, there are signs of pestilence in the *Canterbury Tales* that are often so obscure as to be missed entirely, invisible until corpses begin to pile up in cautionary tales such as that told by the Physician and the Pardoner.[52] Once alerted to these allusions, however, we begin to recognize the presence of plague by other means, in a passing reference or descriptive phrase, as part of some weather event such as a flood or signaled by a geological disturbance such as an earthquake. This last example appears in the "Knight's Tale" in the identification of Saturn as the "fader of pestilence," and in the action he sets into motion. Told by a veteran knight weary of battle, and "meek as a maid," the tale pits Palamon against Arcite in a tournament to determine who will win the hand of Emelye. Like a knight wounded in the tumult of battle, Arcite incurs a grievous set of injuries not as a result of the impact of a weapon but rather from an earthquake. In a passage recently commented upon by Turner and Orlemanski,[53] the Knight narrates the condition of Arcite's body: "His brest tobrosten ... blak as he lay as any cole or crowe / So was the blood yronnen in his face" (ll. 2691-2693) to underscore the serious nature of his wounds and the need for immediate medical attention. This sets up the narrative moment, as Orlemanski and others observe, that contains many medical terms that appear for the first time in English.

> The clothered [clotted] blood, for any lechecraft,
> Corrupteth, and is in his bouk ylaft,
> That neither veyne-blood, ne ventusynge; [cupping]
> Ne drynke of herbes may ben his helpynge.
>
> (ll. 2745-2748)

Neither "veyne-blood, ne ventusynge, / Ne drynke of herbes may ben his helpynge," and the attempt to treat him medically is abandoned soon hereafter. Arcite's death, set in motion by Saturn, the self-described "fader of pestilence" in the form of an earthquake, finds resonance in the disease ravaging England, since one of the causes was believed to have been this natural phenomenon. Displaced from its fourteenth-century reality to a pre-Christian, Theban context, the epidemic is characterized as a seismic event designed by Venus to prevent a marriage between Arcite, a knight too closely aligned with Mars, and Emelye, a devotee of

---

[52] See Rossell Hope Robbins, "Signs of Death in Middle English," *Medieval Studies* 32 (1970): 282-98.
[53] Turner, "Illness Narratives"; Orlemanski, *Symptomatic Subjects*.

the goddess Diana. The erotically driven combatants are given a remedy for their lovesickness in this scenario of events: while one acquires the hand of the lady in question, the other dies, but only after having graciously relinquished his claim to her. As the medical emergency described above indicates, there is no cure for the internal injuries done to Arcite in his fall; instead, the doctors concede their defeat in their final pronouncement: "Fare wel phisik! Go ber the man to chirche!" (l. 2760). There is something to be said about the limitations of medicine, especially in relation to foreordained life events. When the poet links medicine to love, as he does in much of his work, it reveals how the language of illness can be used to indicate emotional as well as physical trauma. Whether the language of illness speaks from a bodily injury or a wound to the heart metaphorically inflicted, the two zones of human experience—physical and emotional—are integrally related. Remedies like the one Saturn, the "fader of pestilence," devises are extreme, yet demonstrate how courtly love has the capacity to engender rivalries, disrupt friendships, and end in someone's death.

Medicinal Barnyard

Strange as it may seem, the "Nun's Priest's Tale" brings many of the presumptions and expectations for effective medical treatment together. In what is most often described as a beast fable or mock epic, the comedic story is about chickens in a barnyard overseen by a poor widow and her two daughters. One of those chickens, a rooster named Chauntecleer, is responsible for protecting his domain by announcing the coming of the dawn and any intruders who might be lurking outside its boundaries. His other occupation is to produce another generation of chicks, a task for which he is given seven hens, one of whom is his favorite, a hen named Pertelote.[54] When Chauntecleer has a troubling dream, Pertelote springs to action to diagnose his ailment and provide remedies and a treatment plan, thus launching another of Chaucer's scenes of medical treatment, this one based on herbal remedies known to "wise women." Pertelote, contrary to her husband's belief that dreams have significance, reads his symptoms as a humoral imbalance caused by too much choler both yellow and black. Her treatment plan is as follows:

---

[54] Pertelote's name differs from the tale's analogues where the hen is called "Pinte," and signifies "one who confuses someone's lot or fate." See note for line 2870 in *The Riverside Chaucer*, 937.

> ... taak som laxatyf.
> Up peril of my soule and my lyf,
> I conseille yow the beste—I wol nat lye—
> That bothe of colere and of malencolye
> Ye purge yow; and for ye shal nat tarie,
> Though in this toun is noon apothecarie,
> I shal myself to herbes techen yow
> That shul been for youre hele and for youre prow
>
> (ll. 2943-50)

The purgatives she prescribes, as identified by Corinne Kauffman years ago, are suspect in several ways, however: they would have been unavailable at that time of year, dangerous, inappropriate for the ailment, and/or downright poisonous.[55] For Linda Voigts, Pertelote's prescription is not to be taken seriously since the tale is "a joke about a hen who thinks she is knowledgeable on the subjects of humoral physiology and herbal therapy,"[56] while for Marion Turner, Chaucer shows us how "medical language ... terms such as 'fevere terciane,' 'agu,' and 'digestyves'" (ll. 2959-61) are features of an "imperfectly understood jargon."[57] That Pertelote is discredited by Chauntecleer in Latin—*mulier est hominis confusio* (woman is man's confusion)—a language she does not understand, underscores differences in the gendered perspectives inside the barnyard. At the same time the disparity and ridicule mirror the increasing hostility of male physicians toward female practitioners in the human world outside the enclosure.[58] While women were heavily involved in the practice of medicine, over time "they were gradually restricted to a role as subordinate and controlled assistants."[59] Women healers were marginalized or subordinated to nursing roles or, in the case of Pertelote, contained within a "yeerde" supervised by her domineering husband.[60]

There is more to be said about the position of women in medicine and their dispensing of herbal remedies, many of which are contraindicated for Chauntecleer's ailment. Like a "wise woman" without the benefit of a formal

---

[55] Corinne E. Kauffman, "Dame Pertelote's Parlous Parle," *The Chaucer Review* 4.1 (1970): 41-8.
[56] Linda Voigts, "Herbs and Herbal Healing Satirized in Middle English Texts," in *Herbs and Healers from the Ancient Mediterranean through the Medieval West: Essays in Honor of John M. Riddle* (Farnham, UK: Ashgate, 2012), 217-30 (228-9).
[57] Turner, "Illness Narratives," 72.
[58] Carole Rawcliffe, *Sources for the History of Medicine in Late Medieval England*, TEAMS Documents of Practice Series (Kalamazoo, MI: Medieval Institute Publications, 1995). An English widow petitioned the king for support, arguing that she "had nothing to live off except the physic which she had learnt" (119). John of Arderne also disparaged the "medycines of ladies" (120).
[59] Green, "Women's Medical Practice."
[60] Roberta Magnani, "Chaucer's Physicians: Raising Questions of Authority," in *Medicine, Religion and Gender in Medieval Culture*, ed. Naoë Kukita Yoshikawa (Cambridge, UK: D. S. Brewer, 2015), 45-64. In 1421 a petition demanding that "no Woman use the practyse of Fisik" came before Parliament.

medical education and no apothecary in the immediate vicinity, this resourceful hen seeks a remedy for her husband's medical emergency. This would seem a heroic gesture, an honest attempt to alleviate the rooster's anxiety, a condition that could affect the entire barnyard community given the importance of his clarion call. Yet the disparagement shown to her by the very patient she is attempting to treat seems wholly unwarranted especially when Chauntecleer's insulting remarks are read as representative of the prevailing attitudes of physicians toward women's involvement in medicine. The answer to the insult may reside in the occupation of the Nun's Priest as teller of the tale as well as his physical and mental status, or humoral balance. As one of three priests accompanying the Prioress, he literally has a vested interest in a story that discredits a woman healer and evinces a bias consistent with the attitudes of an emerging medical establishment. So too are his biases in alignment with ecclesiastical views that considered women empirics to pose "a threat to the religious messages they preached and to the formal medical licences that were issued by the Church to university-trained doctors. The more successful the 'peasant healers' were, the more the Church feared people would become less reliant on prayer."[61]

That the Nun's Priest is left unnamed and undescribed in the General Prologue provides a modicum of anonymity that shields him from criticism, especially from the Prioress or the verbally aggressive Alisoun of Bath, whose curse against stingy old men could easily be aimed at a priest who disparages women, even those disguised as barnyard hens. To suggest then that like Chauntecleer the priest is fearful of all that lurks outside his domain no less than the Prioress whom he serves seems quite reasonable; and since the narrative he tells is a beast fable to be read allegorically, he aligns with the rooster, while the fox becomes a figure for the pestilence, the silent intruder who steals the lives of the unsuspecting. Even those attuned to the signs of nature as Chauntecleer presumably is could not see the pestilence coming. Neither priests nor physicians nor the most astute cockerel could have anticipated its effects or produced an effective remedy once recognized. Perhaps that is one reason there is such a proliferation of regimens of health that outline a strategy for self-care and a reminder to the vernacular audience to "see the writing of Jeremy the prophete, that a man ought to forsake evyl things & doo gode dedes & mekely to confesse his sinnes. For why it is the hyest remedie in time of pestilence, penaunce & confession to be preferred [to] al other medicynes."[62]

---

[61] Laura Jefferson, Karen Bloor, and Alan Maynard, "Women in Medicine: Historical Perspectives and Recent Trends," *British Medical Bulletin* 14.1 (2015): 5-15.
[62] J. P. Pickett, "A Translation of the Canutus Plague Treatise," in *Popular and Practical Science of Medieval England*, ed. L. M. Matheson (East Lansing, MI: Colleagues Press, 1994), 270-81.

In a medieval genre that resonates even now, the regimen contained advice on how to stay healthy through diet, exercise, and modest living. The Nun's Priest's description of the widow captures the elements of such a regimen:

> A povre wydwe, somdeel stape in age,
> Was whilom dwellyng in a narwe cotage,
> Biside a grove, stondynge in a dale.
> This wydwe, of which I telle yow my tale,
> Syn thilke day that she was last a wyf
> In pacience ladde a ful symple lyf,
> For litel was hir catel and hir rente.
> By housbondrie of swich as God hire sente
> She foond hirself and eek hir doghtren two.
> Thre large sowes hadde she, and namo,
> Three keen, and eek a sheep that highte Malle.
> Ful sooty was hire bour and eek hir halle,
> In which she eet ful many a sklendre meel.
> Of poynaunt sauce hir neded never a deel.
> No deyntee morsel passed thurgh hir throte;
> Hir diete was accordant to hir cote.
> Repleccioun [overeating] ne made hire nevere sik;
> Attempree diete was al hir phisik,
> And exercise, and hertes suffisaunce.
> The goute lette hire nothing for to daunce,
> N' apoplexie shente nat hir heed.
> No wyn ne drank she, neither whit ne reed;
> Hir bord was served moost with whit and blak—
> Milk and broun breed, in which she foond no lak,
> Seynd bacoun, and somtyme an ey or tweye
> For she was, as it were, a maner deye.
> A yeerd she hadde, enclosed al aboute
> With stikkes, and a drye dych withoute,
>
> (ll. 2821-2848)

That the Nun's Priest offers an extensive description of the widow, her habits, her habitat, and her self-sufficiency suggests that she appeals to him in some way. After all, the widow has the kind of agency that the Nun's Priest lacks: she lives independently, and she's able to support her daughters and her domestic animals in the modest space of a barnyard "enclosed al aboute / With stikkes, and a drye dych withoute" (ll. 2847–2848). Even without a husband to do the heavy labor (plowing fields and harvesting crops) and protect her barnyard, the widow is successful in producing the food necessary to support herself and her daughters. She consumes a modest diet of milk and brown bread, accompanied by an occasional slice of smoked bacon and an egg or two; her meals are meager without wine, either white or red; she governs the operation of a small farm—chickens, pigs, cows, and a sheep named Malle—free from the constraints of oversight and protected from intrusion not by a knight errant but rather by a self-righteous rooster. She is the very model of the wise woman whose daughters will surely acquire empirical knowledge of medicine and husbandry from her regimens. The protracted nature of the Nun's Priest's description suggests that he admires this woman and is holding her up as an example of how a widow facing the prospect of life without a husband manages to thrive. It is not until the priest states that "No deyntee morsel passed thrugh hir throte" (l. 2835) that we are reminded of his position as the priest of a nun whose table manners (not wanting to spill anything on her wimple [like the Prioress]) seems out of place for her station. One need only think of women such as Julian of Norwich or any authoritative religious woman of the time to expose these incongruities. The priest has succeeded in disguising his resentment as he sets the stage for a tale that reveals something more about himself than he may have intended. Not unlike male ecclesiastics, the widow practices the daily regimen prescribed by certain religious orders and recommended by medieval physicians. Regimens of health regulated a person's daily habits just as an order's Rule controlled the quotidian routines of its members. Nutrition, fresh air, exercise, and time for contemplation formed the core of a simple, disciplined life designed to maintain both physical and spiritual well-being.[63] Regimens such as these were thought to maintain humoral balance in such a way as to ward off disease before it could take hold of any individual or threaten the larger community.

Medicinal Gardens and the *Hortus Conclusus*

The enclosed space of the barnyard where Pertelote makes medicinal remedies from plants, however ineffectual they are claimed to be in the "Nun's Priest's Tale," contrasts with another sort of enclosure more regulated and cultivated than the widow's "yeerde." Such spaces are the medicinal gardens belonging

---

[63] Pedro Gil Sotres, "The Regimens of Health," in *Western Medical Thought from Antiquity to the Middle Ages*, ed. Mirko Grmek (London: Wellcome Trust Centre for the History of Medicine, 1998), 291-318.

to religious orders, horticulturalists and botanists who set the standard for expertise on effective remedies for a wide range of illnesses. Monastic gardens were symbolic spaces as well as literal places in which to cultivate plants, and memories of Eden were certainly implanted in the idea of a garden. Likewise, though in different ways, the *hortus conclusus* depicted in so many romances of the time captured the idea and its associations with courtship and desire. We need only be reminded of Chaucer's translation of the *Roman de la Rose* and its tropes to see the influence of this allegory on his understanding of the kinship between love and medicine. Roses were included in the horticulturalist's garden both for medicinal purposes and for their symbolic value, as emblems of love both human and divine.

Like those who recognized the health benefits of plants and the spaces that contained them, according to Carole Rawcliffe, "medical authorities devoted considerable space to advice about the value of gardens as places of relaxation, whose physiological benefits included the preservation of sight and memory, the invigoration of the vital spirit and the opportunity to exercise in pleasant surroundings."[64] The gardens of the Benedictines were especially effective in this regard since they contained a variety of medicinal plants that factored into the making of remedies used for a number of ailments. And since monasteries were known as repositories of useful information, no doubt medical books named for flowers known to have therapeutic value such as Bernard Gordon's *Lilium* and John of Gaddesden's *Rosa Medicina* could also be found there.

Toward a Healing Philosophy

Toward the end of his life, Chaucer rented a house at Westminster Abbey in which there was a medicinal herb garden for treating the physical illnesses of the brothers in residence. There was also a Lady Chapel on the premises for meditation and prayer and the healing of their spirits. The poet, of course, was not a Benedictine monk nor did he take religious vows of any kind as far as anyone knows, yet being in close proximity to such a sanctified place and within a monastic environment would surely be of benefit to a poet of Chaucer's interests and proclivities. Not only could he sequester himself from the madding crowd but so too would he retain access to the marketplace and all its activities. The

---

[64] Carole Rawcliffe, "The Concept of Health in Late Medieval Society," in *Le interazioni fra economia e ambiente biologico nell' Europa preindustriale secc. XIII–XVII*, ed. Simonetta Cavaciocchi (Florence: Firenza University Press, 2010), 321–38 (323).

Lady Chapel was, of course, dedicated to the Virgin Mary, whose intercessory powers were proven effective for those experiencing a personal crisis of some sort. That she factors into Chaucer's poetry at critical moments in his storytelling demonstrates the efficacy of her consolation: Constance in the "Man of Law's Tale," who prays to the Virgin for protection when she is sent into exile with her infant son, is but one example. Another example is evident in the poet's earliest work, *An ABC*, in which the Virgin is presented as integral to the basics of language taught to every child. As Marion Turner reminds us, this is the poem that when juxtaposed to Chaucer's last—"Complaint to His Purse"—forms a framework for his life: "it is instructive," she says, "to put these two poems side by side: the first focusing on the image of the Virgin Mary, the second written when Chaucer lived in the shadow of the Lady Chapel of Westminster Abbey. They frame Chaucer's adult life … a poetic career driven by an interest in subject, mediation, and identity, as both poems illustrate."[65]

The Lady Chapel is a significant place in this regard, dedicated as it was to the Virgin Mary. As the figure identified honorifically by the narrator in *An ABC* as "Almighty and al merciable queene," "glorious mayde and mooder," "ladi bright," "Temple devout," "quene of comfort," and "the verrey light of eyen that ben blynde," among others, she stands not only as a lady of consolation addressing those in distress but as a healer of wounds both physiological and psychological. She is not the Mater Dolorosa as so often depicted in Pietà images or weeping at the foot of the Cross or even a theological replica of Boethius's Lady Philosophy but rather, as Roberta Magnani suggests, "a woman of great authority," whose mode of comfort bridges the gap "between medical practice and spiritual care/cure."[66] Positioned within a larger context of actual women healers, as Diane Watt has argued, she may be regarded not simply as the Mother of God, or nurse to the *Christus medicus*, but as Mary the Physician, the iconic symbol for "the role of the woman as healer" in late medieval England.[67]

As Arthur Frank notes in his book, *The Wounded Storyteller*, wounded people are storytellers who turn illness into a narrative that forges a "common bond of suffering that joins bodies in their shared vulnerability."[68] Drawing upon Rita Charon's advice to physicians including herself to "allow our own injuries to

---

[65] Turner, *Chaucer: A European Life*, 502.
[66] Magnani, "Chaucer's Physicians," 47.
[67] Diane Watt, "Mary the Physician: Women, Religion and Medicine in the Middle Ages," in *Medicine, Religion and Gender in Medieval Culture*, ed. Naoë Kukita Yoshikawa (Cambridge, UK: D. S. Brewer, 2015), 27-44.
[68] Frank, *The Wounded Storyteller*, xix.

increase the potency of our care of patients, to allow our personal experiences to strengthen the empathic bond with others who suffer" (xx), he expresses the heart of the patient-physician relationship. Chaucer, in this sense, is also a wounded storyteller whose tales call his audience to attention, to decide how to read the stories being told and how to interpret the individual doing the telling. He gives us tales that admonish, instruct, entertain, lift our spirits, as well as remind us of the shortness of life and the length of time it takes to master the craft of living. As Turner suggests, Chaucer reminds us "to take responsibility and interpret our own lives"; his last work "reminds us that it is the job of readers, not writers, to interpret poems. He imagines poetry as a conversation that reaches across doorways and blurs boundaries between social estates and genders, genres, and styles, interiors and exteriors, readers and writers."[69] There is something else to be said about exchanges across so many boundaries that rings true to the Hippocratic aphorism with which I began this chapter: "Lyfe is short, the craft so long to lerne." Love and medicine equate, and it takes a lifetime to understand why. Life is indeed short, and the craft of documenting some of its more dire effects can be a lengthy and painful process.

[69] Turner, *Chaucer: A European Life*, 504.

2

Gower and Langland: Therapeutic Dialogue and Intersubjective Medicine

[I]t spedeth that a leche kunne talke of god talegh [good tales] and of honest that make the pacientes to laugh, as wele of the bible as of other tragedieys.[1]
—John of Arderne

[H]ere after folowen the remedies for the pestylence: First, see the writing of Jeremy the prophete, that a man ought to forsake evyl thinges & doo gode dedes & mekely to confesse his sinnes. For why it is the hyest remedie in time of pestilence, penaunce & confession to be preferred [to] al other medicynes.
—Canutus[2]

John Gower and William Langland are keenly aware of the shortness of life and the effort it takes to craft a work that speaks to a culture in the middle of a health crisis. Living at a pivotal historical moment beset by recurrent outbreaks of the plague, they are witness to a disease phenomenon with the potential to alter the structure of society as they knew it. While neither author responds directly to the events unfolding before their eyes as Boccaccio does (or appears to do) so famously, their vernacular writings, Gower's *Confessio Amantis* and Langland's *Piers Plowman*, signal their awareness of what would later be called the Black Death.[3] While each poet is demonstrably unlike the other, there are notable similarities in the themes of their work as well as their efforts to alert their readers

---

[1] John Arderne, *Treatises of Fistula in Ano, Haemorrhoids, and Clysters*, ed. D'Arcy Power, EETS, o.s. 139 (London: Kegan Paul, Trench, Trübner, 1910), 8. 10-12.

[2] This is a fifteenth-century plague treatise based upon the earlier work of Johannes Jacobi. See J. P. Pickett, "A Translation of the Canutus Plague Treatise," in *Popular and Practical Science of Medieval England*, ed. L. M. Matheson (East Lansing: Colleagues Press, 1994), 263-82.

[3] The B-text is the primary source for this study, though the C-text has also been consulted. *William Langland, Piers Plowman: A Parallel Text Edition of the A, B, C, and Z Versions*, ed. A. V. C. Schmidt (Kalamazoo: Medieval Institute Publications, 2011). *Piers Plowman by William Langland, an Edition of the C-Text*, ed. Derek Pearsall (Berkeley, CA: University of California Press, 1978).

to the urgency of an unprecedented confluence of disease and disruption: both are strong proponents of institutional reform, both use confession as a means by which to expose systemic disruption, both structure their poems around a penitential system infused with medical language, both understand the human body as a psychophysiological organism, and both demonstrate their medical consciousness in the deployment of specialized terminology.[4] Yet the question remains: why is there such concern about the dissemination of medicine and medical knowledge at this particular historical juncture when so many other disruptions are present at the time? Is it the fear of an impending apocalypse that provides extra incentive for producing poetry with the potential to heal the social body and change human behavior? Perhaps these two poets thought their work could provoke an increasingly literate vernacular audience into engaging in social reformation and preventative health-care practices or to practice their faith more often. The Hippocratic aphorism enunciated at the beginning of Chaucer's *Parliament of Fowls*, as noted in the previous chapter, applies to Gower and Langland as well. In medicine as in poetry life is short and the craft is long to learn, even for a skillful practitioner.

While structural and thematic similarities resonate in the poets under consideration in this chapter, there are also significant differences. They speak in different dialects: they travel in different social circles; they write in different styles and forms; they have different personal experiences; they speak to differing segments of the audience, all of which puts each writer in a category of his own.[5] Neither poet deploys the trope of pilgrimage as Chaucer does, but highlights instead the search for an ethical way to exist in an unethical world, a healthy way to live a productive life threatened by an epidemic. For Gower, the plague (or "pestilence," as he calls it) becomes a marker of the species of social disruption (or dis-ease) that affects the equanimity of the body politic as well as the humoral balance of the body human.[6] For Langland, the plague (also referred to as "pestilence") is an existential crisis lurking just beneath the surface in the subtext of the poem ready to break out at any moment given the right triggering mechanism. Many of the symptoms of epidemic disease in these works are exposed through the dialogic process of confession and treated by the

---

[4] Virginia Langum, *Medicine and the Seven Deadly Sins in Late Medieval Literature and Culture* (New York: Palgrave Macmillan, 2016).

[5] Whereas Gower appears to be more focused on appealing to the *literati*, writing in Anglo-French and Latin as well as English, Langland is firmly anchored to an English-speaking world. The difference is in how they talk about therapeutics and treatments, whether they use allegorical or literal modes of speech or both at once.

[6] See Kara McShane, "Social Healing in Gower's *Visio Angliae*," *South Atlantic Review* 79.3-4 (2014): 76-88.

therapeutic exchange that follows.[7] In the *Confessio*, the lover, Amans, listens to tales told by Genius (and sometimes Venus herself) that provide an entrée into an audience's understanding of how storytelling and dialogue undertaken by such commanding figures contribute to a young man's healing. In *Piers Plowman*, Will, Langland's equivalent to Amans, listens and learns from a series of interlocutors who alert him to the disequilibrium affecting his well-being both internally and in relation to the world around him. Not unlike talk therapy or a friendly data-gathering consultation between a physician and her patient, the exchange between these two figures and the authority figures who guide them enables us to see how the treatment of illness transpires through intersubjective modes of communication.

The diagnostic process of narration so central to the theory and practice of narrative medicine is made manifest through this species of dialogic exchange. In Gower's work confession is the means by which an internal search for a sense of equilibrium and self-definition is not only made possible but sustained throughout the poem.[8] In Langland's work the healing process unfolds through the advice and counsel of a number of "confessors" with whom Will interacts. That each poet's persona represents an abstract concept obtains in both works: Will and Amans, whose names literally signify the human "will" and the abstract "lover," respectively, have something in common in their kinship to the poets who have made them into literary avatars. Just as they listen and learn from their mentors, the audience also listens and learns from what they say and how they act. They too become readers and diagnosticians made privy to the efficacy of storytelling and the otherwise inaudible introspection operating within the therapeutic dialogue of confession.

Reading is a "powerful medicine," says Russell Peck, with "provocative implications in Middle English. It connotes engagement of the reader through sight and (especially in a culture where books were commonly read aloud) hearing, as we might expect, but it likewise signified engagement of the mind in a broad range of interior activities, such as learning, teaching, interpretation of riddles, dreams and parables."[9] Just as a modern patient's story may have several layers of meaning waiting to be uncovered and related to observable symptoms,

---

[7] As cited in Raymond St. Jacques, "Langland's Christus Medicus Image and the Structure of *Piers Plowman*," *Yearbook of Langland Studies* 5 (1991): 111-27. The B text used for the reading here contains a prologue and twenty passus; eight major dreams, two others (Visio and Vita), figures named Dowel, Dobet, and Dobest, the eponymous Piers, and Will the Dreamer.
[8] Katherine C. Little, *Confession and Resistance: Defining the Self in Late Medieval England* (Notre Dame, IN: University of Notre Dame Press, 2006), esp. chapter 4.
[9] Russell A. Peck, ed. Andrew Galloway, trans., *John Gower, Confessio Amantis*, TEAMS Middle English Texts Series, 2nd edition (Kalamazoo, MI: Medieval Institute Publications, 2006), 6.

so too do these poems tell us something of the realities of those experiencing catastrophic dis-ease of individuals and the larger community. Whether their tales are framed within a dialogue, spoken in a monologue or simply described in expository fashion, stories about how to assuage the Seven Deadly Sins enable certain truths to emerge. The moralization of medicine vis-à-vis a penitential system predicated upon transgressive human actions provides structure and an organizing principle for these poetic and ultimately therapeutic narrations. Designed to prompt self-assessment and altered behavior by alerting an audience of that necessity, such writings not only deliver information about medicine and its practice but link disease to an ethical and moral framework. What better way to encourage a newly literate vernacular audience to pay attention to the medical challenges unfolding before their very eyes in the form of a contagion for which there was no known cure than through storytelling? The Seven Deadly Sins—Pride, Envy, Wrath, Avarice, Sloth, Gluttony, and Lechery[10]—are helpful not only for creating categories for multiple tales within a dialogic framework but also for rendering visible the deleterious effects of willful human desire. Scholars such as Bryon Lee Grigsby separate the sins into categories of spiritual and carnal, those that threaten "the stability of the community," with those manifested outwardly and visible to the discerning eye.[11] In these categories, the "sins of the flesh" included Sloth, Gluttony, and Lechery, while the other four—Pride, Envy, Wrath, Avarice—were relegated to the spiritual realm and its broader implications. Such groupings can be differently construed by others, of course: for Virginia Langum, the sins "closer to the body" include Wrath because of its ability to make the blood boil and the skin to register the effect.[12] One could say something similar about Envy, since it was so often linked to leprosy and read as a visible sign of an inner defect.[13] As such determinations suggest, the condition of the body was presumed to be integrally related to the condition of the soul; when one was sick, the other exhibited symptoms. To attain optimum health to this way of thinking

---

[10] This is the order typically followed by late medieval writers. In Latin they are: Superbia, Invidia, Ira, Avaritia, Acedia, Gula, and Luxuria.

[11] Bryon Lee Grigsby, *Pestilence in Medieval and Early Modern Literature* (London: Routledge, 2004), 79. See also Richard Newhauser, ed. *The Seven Deadly Sins: From Communities to Individuals* (Leiden: Brill, 2007).

[12] Langum, *Medicine and the Seven Deadly Sins in Late Medieval Literature and Culture*, 119. There is a darkening effect on the skin.

[13] In the *Miroir de l'Omme*, Gower links envy to leprosy and anger to heart disease: "Anger is completely described in the swelling that inflames her, for she does not consider herself and pays no attention to anyone else. Her malady is comparable to heart disease, for it results in a sad life and soon dries up the heart so that no one is capable of curing it. Not only does she ill the body, but she also perverts the soul to her will" (*Miroir de l'Omme [The Mirror of Mankind]*), trans., William Burton Wilson (East Lansing: Colleagues Press, 1992), 74.

required the practice of moderation in all things, a lesson to be learned from the health regimens of the time.[14]

The process of narrating that I am claiming for these poets and these particular works focuses on the means of communication and dialectical engagement between Will of *Piers Plowman* and Amans of the *Confessio Amantis* and their interlocutors, as well as by the medical language used throughout. Specialized terminology, as noted in the previous chapter, contributes to the making of a medical discourse composed of disparate genres, many of which are not often considered to be medically informed. References to physicians and surgeons or empirics, to medicine and medical practice, maladies of the psychophysiological body, as well as a variety of medicaments—gemstones, plants, and organic substances—used as remedies are present in both poets' work to a greater and lesser extent. That one of the key terms for both poets is "pestilence" speaks to their growing awareness of the disease lurking in the background.

Pestilence and Penitence

Langland's poem introduces its medical themes in the very first passus when Holy Church proclaims that "Mesure is medicine" (B. I. 35),[15] a statement that addresses the need for a "moral, psychological, and social remedy, a deterrent for a natural inclination and defense against siege," according to the *MED*.[16] The pronouncement is given additional significance soon hereafter when Holy Church proclaims that "Trewth telleth that love is triacle of Hevene" (B. I. 204). Love, in this context, equates with Caritas, charity writ large, the divine medicine that includes communal consciousness and compassion for others, lessons that Will needs to assimilate for the sake of his own reformation. Spoken during

---

[14] Keywords common to both, based on listing in the *MED*, are "pestilence" and "fisik" or "phisik," "physique," "medicine," and "surgerie." Both use the term "fisik" (in modern English, medical practice) in multiple iterations. A text: (1376) "Fisik shal... be fayn... his fesik to leten, And lerne to labouren with lond." "Fisik shal his furrid hood for his foode selle." B text: (1378) "Surgerye ne Fisyke may noughted a myte availle to medle agein elde." "The Frere with his phisik this folke hath enchaunted, and plastred hem so esyly thei dred no synne." "Lyf fleigh for fere to fysyke after helpe, and besought hym of socoure." C text: (1387) "Ich praye yow... syre hunger, gyf ye can other knowe eny kynne thynge of fysk?" [A. XVI.105-106]. Gower uses the term and its multiple meanings throughout the *Confessio Amantis*.

[15] Roseanne Gasse, "The Practice of Medicine in *Piers Plowman*," *The Chaucer Review* 39.2 (2004): 177–97. The rest of the quote is as follows: "love is triacle of hevene (1.148). The love of his subjects is the king's "tresor... and tryacle at [his] nede" (5.49), according to Reason. Triacle and salve are pharmaceutical preparations. Triacle is the equivalent of theriac, an expensive compound imported from the Mediterranean thought to be effective in preventing the plague.

[16] See *MED*, s.v. medicin(e).

an epidemic threatening to undermine the status quo and the fundamental structure of medieval society, which the actual plague succeeded in doing, such lessons accrue additional authority. That Langland uses the term "pestilence" is important to note, in this regard, since such references situate the poet in the midst of the outbreak: "Persons and parisshes preestes pleyned hem to the bisschop / That hire parisshes weren pouere sith the pestilence tyme" (B. Prol. 83-84). When he says, "sith the pestilence tyme," it not only refers to the plague events captured in biblical history and histories of the ancient Mediterranean world but also to the epidemic of the present moment. Likewise, in a prelude to the confession of the Seven Deadly Sins in Passus V, when Reason is said to have "preved that thise pestilences was for pure synne" (B. V. 13), "thise pestilences" indicate the several outbreaks that occurred after 1348, the year the plague was thought to have struck England. The same may be said for the reference to "pokkes and pestilences, and muche peple shente" in Passus XX (B. XX. 98). Parish priests, no less than the poets and physicians who assume the voices of prophets like Jeremiah, complained to their bishops that their parishes were poor since the time the pestilence began in England. Witness the advice of the plague doctor in the epigraph at the beginning of this chapter:

> [H]ere after folowen the remedies for the pestylence: First, see the writing of Jeremy the prophete, that a man ought to forsake evyl thinges & doo gode dedes & mekely to confesse his sinnes. For why it is the hyest remedie in time of pestilence, penaunce & confession to be preferred [to] al other medycynes.[17]

The doctor's recommendation is to be knowledgeable about medicine and apply preventative remedies for the plague: repentance, confession, and foregoing evil things are the medical treatments of preference.

Like Langland, Gower refers to "pestilence" in the historical present when he critiques the institutional Church in the prologue of the *Confessio* for having failed to maintain the health of society as a whole: "that scholde be the worldes hele (health) / Is now, men sein, the pestilence / Which hath exiled pacience / Fro the clergie in special" (Pro. 278-81).[18] Like Langland, Gower situates much of his commentary in cotemporaneous England, the temporal epoch he describes as having devolved from the Edenic golden past featured in his well-known statue of time.[19] Like Langland, Gower uses medical language to underscore the gravity

---

[17] See Pickett, "A Translation of the Canutus Plague Treatise." This is an anonymous fifteenth-century treatise based upon the earlier work of Johannes Jacobi.

[18] This may also apply to the split in the papacy in both Avignon and Rome that accrues added significance in the time of pestilence. Gower's criticism of the Great Schism is well known.

[19] A description of the statue as having a head of gold, torso of silver, legs of brass, and feet of clay is understood hierarchically starting from the top as the best of times to the worst of times.

of a widely disruptive health crisis (socially, politically, and economically) indicated by terms such as "medicine," "disese," "fisik," "phisik," "physique," words for various medications, as well as "pestilence" to remind readers of that fact at strategic points in the work.[20] Like Langland, Gower is critical of the clergy for not addressing the needs of their constituents more conscientiously. Like Langland, Gower is no slouch when it comes to social and political satire: in the earlier *Mirour de l'omme* and *Vox Clamantis*, he exposes the institutional corruption around him, voicing harsh critiques along the way. The lack of common profit, whether from Gower's purview or Langland's vision, warns society of the need to diagnose accurately the illnesses of the body politic to enact a return to collective well-being. In the process of telling and listening so central to narrative medicine, both works reveal a range of experiences that necessitate a comprehending audience willing to engage actively in the reading and listening.

Confession and the Seven Deadly Sins

For both poets, confession in its traditional form provides a framework for exposing the insidiousness of the Seven Deadly Sins. As a means by which the transgressions of penitents could be made manifest to prompt a dialogue that would raise the consciousness of that person and alter that person's purview, confession was therapeutic and potentially life changing. It required every person to look inward, acknowledge the illicitness of the behavior, feel contrition for enacting such behavior, speak such transgressions aloud, accept the consequences, and make the necessary adjustments. Confession proved to be an effective remedy for individual ills and a means by which to convey those illnesses to a wider audience when recorded in a poem. Langland puts an unusual spin on the process when he has one of his allegorical characters, Repentance, confess the personified Sins themselves. Pride, Lust, Envy, Wrath, Avarice (Covetousness), Gluttony, and Sloth take turns in confessing not only the activities in which they have engaged but their understanding of themselves as morally flawed. As personifications of the human sins accused of having caused the pestilence, they render public what would otherwise be relegated to silence. The medicalization of their flawed character links morality to medicine in a way made manifest to an audience becoming increasingly health conscious.

---

[20] "[M]edicine" is used in books 1, 2, 4, and 5.

Gower not only uses the Seven Deadly Sins as an organizing principle for his poem but constructs his multi-tale narration around lovesickness, an illness taken seriously by medical practitioners as a form of melancholy. One might say, in fact, that the *Confessio* is driven by the desire to find a remedy for the Lover's malady, to alleviate debilitating symptoms—insomnia, depression, listlessness, sloth, and a general lack of ambition—associated with the illness.[21] The malady finds a place in the history of medicine from Hippocrates and Galen through the translations of Arabic doctrines of love done by Constantinus Africanus. Both lovesickness and stylized approaches to courtship such as those found in Andreas Capellanus' *Art of Courtly Love* and popularized in medieval romance, according to Mary Wack, "offered techniques for constraining and yet indulging in potentially disruptive erotic impulses."[22] Amans' interlocutors, Venus and her priest, Genius, are appropriately charged with examining, diagnosing, and treating the Lover's ailment. The outcome of the remedy is left to the poem's ending with its stunning revelation that John Gower has been in the guise of Amans all along.

Medical Consciousness and the Psychophysiological Body

The medical consciousness that I am claiming for these poets is underwritten by two basic assumptions: (1) that individual human bodies and the body politic are integrally connected, and (2) that the human body and its soul (or psyche) constitute an integrated organic unity. The question to be asked of this pre-Cartesian understanding of the body-soul dyad, however, is where a nonbiological concept such as the soul might reside? Not surprisingly perhaps there exists a longstanding debate inherited by medieval thinkers about whether the soul was located in the brain or the heart, two of the most important organs of the body and identified consistently as such throughout the Middle Ages. Medical writers who were influenced by Aristotle's preference for the heart as the soul's primary locus assumed it to be the site of intelligence, motion, sensation, and even the source of the breath of life—or, put another way, as Avicenna later claimed, the "root of all faculties."[23] In her study of the medieval heart, Heather Webb notes

---

[21] Ellen Shaw Bakalian, *Aspects of Love in John Gower's Confessio Amantis* (New York: Routledge, 2005).

[22] Mary Frances Wack, *Lovesickness in the Middle Ages: The "Viaticum" and Its Commentaries* (Philadelphia: University of Pennsylvania Press, 1990), 30.

[23] As quoted in Heather Webb, *The Medieval Heart* (New Haven: Yale University Press, 2010), 33.

that this Aristotelian concept as understood by Albertus Magnus and other medieval thinkers underscores that organ as "the source of power for the body because it is uniquely positioned to spread its strength into all the members."[24] This is an attribution for which the late medieval physician Pietro Torrigiani provides further explication: "the heart is the principle of all the faculties and the source of pneuma.... The soul is in the heart, and therefore the heart is the principle of the most important bodily functions, and therefore the soul must be located there."[25]

Given the authority of Aristotle and the testimony of practicing physicians like Torrigiani, it is not surprising that this line of thinking gained considerable credibility by the fourteenth century, though not without competition from the other side of the debate, the one that favored the brain as the soul's home base. As depicted in Edwin Clarke and Kenneth Dewhurst's *An Illustrated History of Brain Function*[26] and found originally in an early fourteenth-century trilingual compendium of texts, in this system (and its several variations), the brain was divided into ventricles or cells imagined to house faculties such as *sensus communis* (common sense), *imaginativa* (image formation), *estimativa* (judgment), and *memorativa* (memory) (Figure 3).[27] Inherited from the ancient Greeks and incorporated into the thinking of patristic writers such as Augustine, this notion of brain function was endorsed from its early beginnings by medical luminaries such as Hippocrates and Galen. The many illustrations and diagrams produced to render these complicated brain theories, in what became known as "Cell Doctrine," into visual images over the course of the Middle Ages suggest the intensity of interest not only in the structure and function of the brain but its relation to the rest of the body. Figure 3 shows five cells (or ventricles) labeled from anterior to posterior in the inscription above the head. The two anterior cells are connected to the eyes to enable the operations of common sense and image formation; the next two cells function as judgment and cognition, while the posterior cell is set aside for memory. One of the most distinctive features of this diagram, dated to circa 1310, is the "worm" whose function was to open

---

[24] Webb, *The Medieval Heart*.
[25] Ibid., 21.
[26] By way of contrast, in John of Trevisa's translation of Bartholomaeus Anglicus' *De Proprietatibus Rerum*, the brain is divided into three cells marked from anterior to posterior imagination, reason, recollection and mind: "for the brayne hath thre holowy places that phisicians clepen *ventriculus* 'smale wombes.' In the formest celle and wombe is ymaginacioun conformed and imaad; in the middle, resoun; in the hindemest, recordacioun and mynde." *On the Properties of Things* (Oxford: Clarendon Press, 1975), Book V, p. 173.
[27] MS Gg. 1.1, f. 490v, Cambridge University Library.

Figure 3 Cells of the brain as an exemplum of the Doctrine of Cells. Early fourteenth century. MS Gg. 1.1. item 52, Cambridge University Library. Reproduced by kind permission of the Syndics of Cambridge University Library.

or close "the channel between the middle and the posterior cell according to the needs of the thought processes."[28] While such a dynamic gatekeeping device suggests that only certain thoughts were worth remembering, Peck notes that the worm functions in a dual capacity presumably (it would appear) to enable the recovery of thoughts as well as their storage.[29]

---

[28] Edwin Clarke and Kenneth Dewhurst, *An Illustrated History of Brain Function* (Oxford: Sanford Publications, 1972), 29.

[29] Russell A. Peck, "The Materiality of Cognition in Reading, Staging, and Regulation of Brain and Heart Activities in Gower's *Confessio Amantis*," in *John Gower: Others and the Self*, ed. Russell A. Peck and R. F. Yeager (Cambridge, UK: D. S. Brewer, 2017), 7–31.

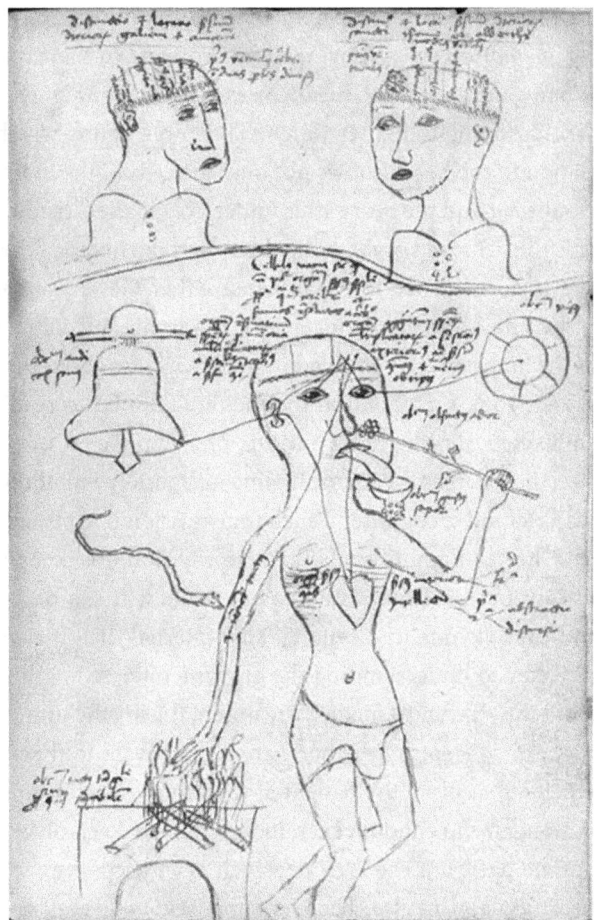

Figure 4 The connections between the heart and other senses. *De Sensu*, Gerard de Harderwyck's *Epitomata seu reparationes totius philosophiae naturalis Aristotelis*. Courtesy of the Wellcome Historical Medical Library of London.

One of the more distinctive illustrations of the pathway that connects the brain, the ears, and the heart for a reading of Gower and Langland is a "crude drawing" found in the *Epitomata* of Gerard de Harderwyck in the 1496 print version of the *De Sensu* (Figure 4). In this illustration are two examples of the construction of the brain with its various cells underneath showing lines that connect the ears, the brain, and the heart. Reading from the top down, the head on the left, which represents the theories of Galen and Avicenna, contains four compartments—the *sensus communis* (common sense), *phantasia* (image formation), *cogitativa* (thought), and *memorativa* (memory). The head on the right shows five parts of the brain, locating two—the *sensus communis* and *imaginativa*—in the first compartment with the other three—*estimativa*, *phantasia*, and *memorativa*—occupying compartments of their own. This is a diagram drawn in accordance with the theories of Albertus Magnus and Thomas Aquinas in writings done well after Galen. The lower figure, which is of most interest in relation to the heart, shows not only the cells of the brain but also its connections to the ear and the heart, thus underscoring the Aristotelian concept that the heart is the principal organ of the body and the home of the soul.[30]

While there is no evidence to suggest that either Gower or Langland was fully cognizant of these varying concepts of the brain and its relation to the other parts of the body, or even engaged in public debates about the organ most likely to house the soul, such medical theories are relevant to readings of their work.[31] The links between the heart and the brain provide a two-way path of communication that enables the intermingling of emotion with thought. In what Russell Peck calls "emotive cognition," such transmission is applicable to Gower's use of the term "herte's-thoght," enabling us to envision this complex exchange between the heart and the brain as well as to see how it can be influenced by what Langland calls "kynde knowyng."[32] This internal dialectic in the bodies of individuals is key to understanding the growing interest in self-care and the skepticism about the efficacy of medical treatment during the time of pestilence.

Such premodern concepts of the body are also relevant to the procedures of narrative medicine that place the patient at the center of a community of like-minded practitioners who conduct examinations, make keen observations, and gather appropriate data, not the least of which is an accounting of vital signs, including a heartbeat and a pulse. There is something to be said, in other words, for cardiocentrism as a concept that applies to premodern practitioners, their modern counterparts, and these two poets, especially when each of their poems focuses on the concept of Love. Whether related directly to the material body or presented as an abstract notion of Caritas, the idea of the heart as the "root of all faculties" obtains.

The cardiocentric model that I am suggesting here is applicable to readings of both Gower and Langland, especially since they address the individual body as well as the social body. Both poets are aware of how compassion plays out in a Christian community predicated upon a penitential system of introspection

---

[30] Clarke and Dewhurst, *An Illustrated History of Brain Function*, 17. A brief introduction to this phenomenon appears in *Accessus: A Journal of Premodern Literature and New Media*, vol. 7.1. See Eve Salisbury, "Gower's 'Herte-Thoght': Thinking, Feeling, Healing," 1-16.
[31] Peck, "The Materiality of Cognition," 7-31.
[32] Ibid., 18.

and self-reformation. At the center or heart of the mystic body of Christ there resides the ideal practitioner—the *Christus medicus*—against whom all human practitioners are measured. As recorded in the synoptic gospels the metaphor signified that Christ's healing abilities were of the miraculous sort—blind men could see, and lame men could walk—simply at His behest or the laying on of hands; there were neither failures of diagnosis nor an inability to provide the most effective remedy for the ailments identified and treated by this exemplary healer.[33] The standard of care set forth in these New Testament accounts is, of course, impossible for ordinary practitioners to achieve, even those whose university training included the study of religion. Nasoë Kukita Yoshikawa's observation that many physicians "went on to seek a higher degree in theology" and that "[m]edical knowledge was disseminated outside the universities primarily through learned clerics who had come to appreciate the important connection between medicine and religion"[34] widens the scope and expectations for medical practitioners, many of whom served the royal courts. William of Exeter, Queen Philippa's physician, a practitioner who earned a "double doctorate," is one such example.[35]

Practitioner and Priest

The intersectionality between doctoring and ministering in a world confronted by bubonic plague was ostensibly designed to enable the physician to hear a patient's confession and provide last rites should that be required. While this suggests that practitioners could be fallible and simply wrong in their diagnoses and treatments, the expectations for them were that they be accurate at all times: healing and faith go hand in hand in various ways and for various reasons, but especially so in the face of a pandemic imagined by many to be divine punishment for human sin.

I mention the equivalency of priest and physician to suggest not only that the standard of care was exceptionally high in the late Middle Ages but that there

---

[33] The passage in Lk. 4: 21-24 is also relevant here in that it cites the ancient aphorism, "Physician, heal thyself," spoken by Jesus to hometown skeptics: "No doubt you will quote the proverb to me, 'Physician, heal yourself,' and say, 'We have heard of all your doings in Capernaum; do the same here in your own hometown.'" *The New English Bible with the Apocrypha* (New York: Oxford University Press, 1976), 74.

[34] Nasoë Kukita Yoshikawa, "Holy Medicine and Diseases of the Soul: Henry of Lancaster and *Le Livre de Seyntz Medicines*," *Medical History* 53.3 (2009): 397-414.

[35] Faye Getz, *Medicine in the English Middle Ages* (Princeton, NJ: Princeton University Press, 1998), 66.

was an assumption that sickness and sin were related. Witness the statement from the Fourth Lateran Council:

> Let the priest be discreet and cautious so that, in the manner of a skilled physician, he may pour wine and oil over the wounds of the patient, diligently inquiring into both the circumstances of the sin and of the sinner, by which means he may wisely understand what advice he should give to him and what remedy he should employ, making trial of various remedies to heal the sick man.[36]

Christopher Page's response to this decree is illuminating:

> At first, we might read this as a figure of speech in which priests are advised to think admiringly of physicians and to imagine themselves in a comparable role. This cannot be. Since the soul is more precious than the body, priests, who care for souls, are more important than physicians, who care for flesh. A physician from Salerno or Montpellier might be learned in his craft, but care of souls was the art of all arts: *ars artrium regimen animarus*. Fourth Lateran requires every physician to advise his patient that treatment does not truly begin with a physician's work, but with a priest's.[37]

The presumption that physicians could (or should) also be priests explains in part the suspicion that both poets have about ordinary human practitioners. As Gower says in the *Mirour*,

> Physicians are glad of sickness and surgeons of hurt people, when they can thus earn something.… And very often, just as the physician cunningly delays the restoration of his patient's health, and sometimes (in order to earn more money from the patient) even aggravates and makes the malady worse than it was at the beginning, likewise (to the good observer), the men of law obtain their delays and put their client in fear, in order to get more of his money.[38]

Gower also talks about the fancy potions used by physicians and made for them by fraudulent apothecaries: "The physician, wherever he may go about his business in the cities, always gets acquainted with an apothecary; and then they do things that will place many a life in the balance. For he who, on their

---

[36] The Latin reads as follows: Sacerdos autem sit discretus et cautus ut, more periti medici, superinfudat vinum et oleum vulneribus sauciati, diligenter inquirens et peccatoris circumstantias et peccati, per quas prudenter intelligat quale illi consilium debeat exhibere et cujusmodi remedium adhibere, diversis experimentis utendo ad sanandum aegrotum. As quoted and translated in Christopher Page, "Music and Medicine in the Thirteenth Century," in *Music as Medicine: The History of Music Therapy since Antiquity*, ed. Peregrine Horden (New York: Routledge, 2000), 116. See also Jeremy J. Citrome, *The Surgeon in Medieval English Literature* (New York: Palgrave Macmillan, 2006).

[37] Christopher Page, "Music and Medicine," 116.

[38] Wilson, *John Gower, Mirour de l'Omme*, 318.

prescription, regularly uses syrup or electuary, may languish greatly in hope of getting better, for their prescriptions are most contrary to nature."[39]

Likewise, when Langland conflates doctors of physic with theologians, he bridges a presumed gap between fields of expertise and authority. His skepticism on the role of the physician becomes legible in this regard during the conversation toward the end of the poem between the Doctor of Divinity and Sir Penetrans Domos, the friar-physician considered to be a figure for Satan himself. "The bitternesse that thow hast browe, now brouke it thiselve; / That art doctour of deeth, drynk that thow madest! / For I that am lord of lif, love is my drynke, / And for that drynke today, I deide upon erthe" (B. XVIII. 364-67). As Roseanne Gasse notes,

> These dramatic words spoken to Satan by Christ during the Harrowing of Hell episode highlight the cosmic opposition between these two physicians. The drink of the one is bitterness; the drink of the other, love. The one brings death to humanity; the other, life.... Satan's poisonous medicinal brew most importantly kills the soul in damnation; yet of course it was through Satan's trickery in the Garden of Eden that physical death and disease first entered the world.[40]

To understand these "medications" as juxtaposed within this good-versus-evil binary system of signification enables a fuller comprehension of how thin the line between poison and therapeutic medication could be. While one produces certain physical death, the other promises the extension of physical life, and assuming the patient is also a willing believer, life after death. To understand the nature of the Fall in Eden in terms of a "poisonous medicinal brew" rather than divisive Satanic rhetoric and the mindless gullibility it depends upon changes the perception of that event from one based on language to one focused on medicine.

Reading the Cardiocentric Body: Langland

While one might argue that the negative view of physicians and surgeons is simply used as a "mesure of medicine" to make visible the parallels between Piers the Plowman and the *Christus medicus*, there are other ways to look at the analogy. For Raymond St. Jacques, "the *Christus Medicus* image provides Langland with a structural device more powerful and more dramatic than do

---

[39] Wilson, *John Gower, Mirour de l'Omme*, 336.
[40] Gasse, "The Practice of Medicine in *Piers Plowman*," 182.

most, if not all other, images in the poem."[41] And while the poet is not innovative in his use of this trope, the claims made here are valid and convincing. Certainly, the figure of Piers embodies a mode of apostolic devotion that functions as an ideal in a poem in which poverty, community, and labor are valued over the accumulation of personal wealth, social status, and political power. The notion that Piers the Plowman is Langland's "parfit practisoure" sets the humble laborer up as the model of effective doctoring, both physical and spiritual. Witness the following:

> And Piers the Plowman parceyved plener tyme
> And lered hym lechecraft his lif for to save,
> That, though he were wounded with his enemy, to warisshen [heal] hymselve,
> And dide hym assaie his surgerie on hem that sike were,
> Til he was parfit praktisour if any peril fille.
>
> (B. XVI. 103-107)

What I find most intriguing about Langland's use of the *Christus medicus* and other medical tropes is how well they support the notion of cardiocentrism and the integral relation between Love and medicine, especially within the context of the healing aspect of the sacred. Here there is compassion expressed by Piers, the human replica of the *Christus medicus*, toward his enemies whose wounds he sutures together to save them. "Lechecraft" can be learned even by those most humble and poor for the purpose of preserving their own lives as well as the lives of others.

The intersubjective medicine indicated in this passage finds expression in other parts of the poem, including its very beginning when we are introduced to Holy Church, who announces that "mesure is medicine":

> For Treuthe telleth that love is triacle of hevene.
> May no synne be on hym seene that that spice useth.
> And alle his werkes he wroughte with love as hym liste.
> And lered it Moyses for the leveste thyng, and moste lik to hevene,
> And also the plante of pees, moost precious of vertues:
>
> (B. I. 148–52)

> And for to knowen it kyndely, it comseth by myghte,
> And in the herte, there is the heed, and the heigh welle.
> For in kynde knowynge in herte ther [coms]eth a myghte.
>
> (B. I. 163-65)

---

[41] Raymond St. Jacques, "*Christus medicus*," 112.

Then later:
Love is leche of lif and next Oure Lord selve,
And also the graithe gate that goeth into hevene.
Forthi I seye as I seide er by sighte of thise textes
Whan alle tresors ben tried, treuthe is the beste.

(B. I. 204-07)

Love and Truth are embodied in Christ in this context, and the *Christus medicus* provides remedies to all those in need of physical and spiritual healing. Love is the force that is the great gate of heaven that will open when of "alle tresors," Truth is recognized as the best. The medications offered, such as the "plante of pees" (plant of peace) and the "triacle of hevene," resonate in both metaphorical and material ways, applied on the one hand to the spirit, and on the other, quite literally, to the physical body. Not only is a "triacle" a medicinal compound used for a variety of ailments and lauded for its extraordinary efficacy but it is also a remedy that specifically draws out or neutralizes the poison that comes of infections.[42] Such antidotes, including one called the "drink of Antioch," recall both the poisonous bite of a venomous snake and the venomous poison of the archetypal Serpent. Antidotes for the former (the snake) may be transformed into antidotes for the latter (the Serpent) within the context of any reference to this species of reptile. "[T]o knowe it kyndely" acknowledges a mode of comprehension that comes from a natural assimilation of knowledge rather than by the words of others.

Of the Seven Deadly Sins represented in *Piers Plowman*, all of whom are confessed by Repentance in Passus V, Envy is one of those closest to the body and described in the most explicit terms of physical ailments. While many authors, Gower included, associate Envy with visible signs of leprosy, one of the most dreaded of diseases in the Middle Ages aside from the plague, for Langland, Envy embodies other sorts of illnesses, including heart trouble, digestive difficulties and the flatulence resulting from that condition. One might also include arrogance, in this regard, since Envy considers himself to be more knowledgeable than any physician when he comes up with his own diagnosis and treatment plan, one that calls for a costly "sugar stick" medication. "As might be expected," notes Virginia Langum, "this material cure is ineffective. Sugar will not alleviate Envy's internal swelling nor will the pharmaceutical 'diapenidion' relieve his gas."[43]

---

[42] See *MED*, s.v. triacle. See Christiane Nockels Fabbri, "Treating Medieval Plague: The Wonderful Virtues of Theriac," *Early Science and Medicine* 12.3 (2007): 247-83.

[43] Langum, *Medicine and the Seven Deadly Sins*, 112. The pharmaceutical named here is thought to be rare. Diapenidion is "a sweet drug in the form of a twisted thread, used to relieve coughing." See *MED*, s.v. diapenidion.

Also revealing about Envy's physical symptoms are the many references he makes to the "false tonge" with which he spreads lies about others, engaging in backbiting and duping the gullible. These are some of the activities that Envy recognizes as the cause of his "body bolneth [blow up] for bitter of my galle" (B. V. 118), a condition mitigated only when he laughs at another's loss "that litheth [lifts] myn herte" (B. V. l. 113), he says.

One of the more vivid stories of illness in Langland's poem is recounted in Hawkin's complaint about melancholy caused by excessive bile, a physical condition that emerges when no one expresses love for him: "For tales that I telle no man trusteth to me" (B. XIII. l. 332). Like Envy his habits of life are cloaked in falsehood and guile, backbiting and slander, lacking empathy, compassion, or general concern for others. He literally embodies the pestilential-like ills of society and those individuals whose approach to life is wholly self-centered and consumed by the desire to control others through whatever means necessary. His obsession is made manifest in the many physical symptoms described in his tale:

> And when I may noght have the maistrie, swich malencolie I take,
> That I cacche the crampe, the cardiacle som tyme,
> Or an ague in swich an angre, and som tym a fevere,
> That taketh me al a twelvmonthe, til that I despise
> Lechecraft of Oure Lord and leve on a wicche,
> And seye that no clerc ne kan—ne Cryste, as I leve—
> To the Souter of Southwerk or of Shordych Dame Emme.
>
> (B. XIII. 334-40)

Symptoms described as "malencolie" "crampe," "cardiacle," "ague in swich an angre, and som tym a fevere" in the middle of a dialogue with Conscience expose Hawkin's physical ailments to an exemplary specialist well-suited to aid in his recovery. The diagnosis is not the sugar-stick or pharmaceuticals known to provide relief from pain and anguish but rather a confessor's advice to remedy his patient's symptoms with the holy medicine confession is claimed to be.[44] In his turning away from the "lechecraft of Oure Lord" and seeking out the charms of witchcraft from a local practitioner, Dame Emme of Shordyche, Hawkin has exposed the extent of his diseased soul. Along with Contrition and Faith, Conscience is one of the "surgienes" noted for his ability to excise sins that, like

---

[44] This claim is most evident in the *Book of Holy Medicines* of Henry de Grosmont cotemporaneous with both Langland and Gower. See Catherine Batt, *The Book of Holy Medicines by Henry Lancaster* (Tempe, AZ: ACMRS, 2015).

malignant cancers, eat away at the soul. While Hawkin's list of symptoms needs to be treated as representing a genuine physical illness, he also needs to practice a level of faith that would affect his psychic well-being. As Rebecca Krug observes,

> Hawkin's problem is that his focus on physicality encourages him to ignore the power of the spiritual.... The poem does not dismiss physical concerns or reject bodily healing, but instead draws attention to the importance of understanding that God is the source for both physical and spiritual recuperation. Hawkin's confusion is underscored by both over-reliance on physical medicine and under-reliance on spiritual remedies. He insists, early in his self-analysis that, were it up to him, he would end the plague by writing to the pope for a pot of "salve" to provide universal healing.
>
> (B. XIII, 249)[45]

Reading the Cardiocentric Body: Gower

As noted earlier, one of the premises of the *Confessio* is that the Lover is lovesick and in need of a remedy to overcome his malaise. The narrator introduces the trope in Book I on Pride when he says, "For yet was nevere such covine, / That couthe ordeine a medicine / To thing which God in lawe of kinde / Hath set, for ther may no man finde / The rihte salve of such a sor" (I. 29-33). In this ailment Amans embodies the world around him, evoking the image of the microcosm at the center of the macrocosmic universe; just as all the elements are contained within the human body, so too are the poet's elemental themes contained within the body of Amans. Just as the absence of love has exacerbated divisions in the outside world, so too does the lover exhibit signs of dissemblance and discord within himself. There is a discernible disconnect between his heart and his brain that has affected his abilities to process the advice he is being given, to recognize the difference between Truth and falsehood, genuine love and naked desire. He is the human embodiment of a world in which "love is falle[n] into discord" (Prol. 121), a walking emblem of the confused and divided self. How appropriate then that Venus and her Genius priest engage him in a diagnostic conversation, both figures assuming the role of physician to Amans' role as patient. Venus asks him to describe his illness so that she might help him:

---

[45] Rebecca Krug, "*Piers Plowman* and the Secrets of Health," *The Chaucer Review* 46.1-2 (2011): 166–81 (175-6).

> Sche seide, "Tell thi maladie:
> What is thi sor of which thou pleignest?
> Ne hyd it noght, for it thou feignest,
> I can do thee no medicine."
>
> (1. 164-67)

To which Amans eventually replies:

> I am destourbed
> In al myn herte, and so contourbed,
> That I ne may my wittes gete,
> So schal I moche thing foryete.
> Bot if thou wolt my schrifte oppose
> Fro point to point, thanne I suppose,
> Ther schal nothing be left behinde.
> Bot now my wittes ben so blinde,
> That I ne can miselven teche.
>
> (Prol. 221-29)

Because Gower "brings together ecclesiastical treatises on confession, courtly love poems, and contemporary medical understanding of lovesickness" that explore "how love as a sickness serves as a nexus wherein love literature, medicine, and confession come together," according to James Palmer, the figures of Venus and Genius take on additional meaning, both acting as priestly figures as well as physicians.[46] Neither measures up to the *Christus medicus* described earlier in relation to Langland's work, but they are significant nonetheless in their suitability for treating the lover's ailment, at least at the beginning of the poem. Venus initiates a dialogue taken up more extensively by Genius, whose storytelling abilities create distractions that capture Amans' attention most of the time and change his mood some of the time. What happens in this opening salvo sets the stage for the kind of exchange at the heart of narrative medicine. As Kathryn Hunter notes, "[m]edicine is fundamentally narrative… and its daily practice is filled with stories. Most important are the opening stories patients tell their physicians. These are not the vivid, repetitive stories told outside the medical encounter… but the opening stories of a malady that gains them admission and good standing in the world of the ill."[47]

---

[46] James M. Palmer, "Bodily and Spiritual Healing through Conversation and Storytelling: Genius as Physician and Confessor in the *Confessio Amantis*," in *Approaches to Teaching the Poetry of John Gower*, ed. R. F. Yeager and Brian W. Gastle (New York: Modern Language Association, 2011), 53.

[47] See Kathryn M. Hunter, *Doctors' Stories: The Narrative Structure of Medical Knowledge* (Princeton: Princeton University Press, 1991), 5.

The Constantine and Sylvester exemplum in Book II on Envy seems not to apply to Amans' malady at first; he indicates that he is not subject to this particular vice, especially since Constantine's illness is most often equated with the physical symptoms of leprosy as well as lechery, a transgression that does not necessarily pertain to courtly lovers like Amans. In the *Mirour de l'Omme*, Gower himself seems to support this conflation of physical disease and unchecked desire when he claims leprosy to be "so virulent that it corrupts the air together with all the wind that blows by its side, and in this respect stands for Lechery."[48] Yet Constantine's sin turns out to be a divine punishment for the emperor's persecution of Christians without mention of lechery or any other sexual behavior thought to be deviant. Instead, the tale Genius tells underscores the emperor's pre-conversion aggression; his cruelty toward those practicing the new religion for which he contracts leprosy is to be read as the outward manifestation of God's punishment for the emperor's heterodoxic actions. The question is, however, why Envy is the designated vice here and not, say, Wrath or some other aspect of violent aggression? Of the Seven Deadly Sins, Envy is neither overtly harmful nor pleasure producing, but rather unrewarding in that respect, producing, as Chaucer's Parson explains, "angwissh and sorwe" instead of these more aggressive emotions. As Jessica Rosenfeld observes, "[e]nvy thus took formal shape as a simultaneous emotional and behavioral refusal of the command to love one's neighbor, a refusal that could only be remediated by the feeling of compassion."[49] Clearly, Constantine has refused to love his neighbors as prescribed by tradition, but there appears to be more to his illness than that. As the exchange between Genius and Amans suggests, Envy needs to be interpreted correctly to produce an accurate diagnosis and an appropriate remedy to be effective. To Genius, his priestly doctor-confessor, Amans says:

Min holy fader, reson wolde
That I this vice eschuie scholde.
Bot yit to strengthe mi corage,
If that ye wolde in avantage
Therof sette a recoverir [remedy]
It were to me a gret desir,
That I this vice mihte flee.

(II. ll. 3155–61)

---

[48] Grigsby, *Pestilence*, 81.
[49] Jessica Rosenfeld, "Compassionate Conversions: Gower's *Confessio Amantis* and the Problem of Envy," *Journal of Medieval and Early Modern Studies* 42.1 (2012): 83-105 (84).

To which Genius replies:

Now understond, my sone, and se,
Ther is phisique for the seke,
And vertus for the vices eke
For as the water of a welle
Of fyr abateth the malice,
Riht so vertu fordoth the vice.
Agein Envie is Charité,
Which is the moder of Pité,
That makth a mannes herte tendre,
That it mai no malice engendre
In him that is enclin therto.

(II. ll. 3162-64; 3170-77)

To this scene of dialogic exchange so closely akin to the procedures of narrative medicine, as noted by Pamela Yee, I would suggest not only that the tale exemplifies some of the challenges to accurate interpretation but that it defines a treatment explicitly located in the heart, the organ that serves as a site of emotion as well as cognition.[50] The tale itself models a doctor-patient relation when Sylvester, an exemplary empiric who later becomes Pope, heals Constantine by means of holy medicine, that is, full-body immersion in "clean" water. There is a miraculous dimension to this gesture of healing when a debilitating disease such as leprosy is instantaneously cured by virtue of what appears to be a purification ceremony or baptism. As to be expected in a scene presented as miraculous, the leprous scales covering Constantine's body instantly fall away, underscoring both the efficacy of the treatment of this particular malady and the exemplary status of water made "clean" by a sanctified healer.

As with any such miraculous recovery, the event needs to be contextualized, in this case, in relation to the genre of hagiography to which it belongs. In Jacobus de Voragine's *Legenda Aurea*,[51] the probable source of the tale for Gower, Sylvester is described as the holy man whose name combines the green in contemplation of heavenly things (*silvas*) with the richness of the earth (*terra*); made into a product of Nature, the saint is further portrayed by the hagiographer as a wild man who flees into the woods when the occasion calls for it, here, when a newly

---

[50] Pamela M. Yee, "'So schalt thou double hele finde': Narrative Medicine in the 'Tale of Constantine and Sylvester,'" *South Atlantic Review* 79.3-4 (2014): 89-104.

[51] Jacobus de Voragine, *The Golden Legend: Reading on the Saints*, trans. William Granger Ryan, 2 vols. (Princeton, NJ: Princeton University Press, 1993), 62.

installed emperor begins to persecute Christians. As the story goes, Constantine is punished by God for the fierceness of his aggression, given a disfiguring and contagious disease that marks him as inwardly disturbed. This is the condition for which he seeks medical advice from his court physicians; the treatment they recommend—a bath made of the blood of 3,000 slain children under the age of seven—is literally a bloodbath made of slaughtered innocents. That this is an echo of Herod's actions against infants, one of whom was prophesied to supplant him, is perhaps less ironic than it seems in its unveiling of the destructive effects of this sin. Constantine's violent desire is driven not out of envy of opposing forces or even of someone whose achievements are greater than his own but rather his envy of the innocence embodied in the thousands of infants whose blood he needs to heal his condition. In something of a miraculous epiphany, he responds to the display of love by the mothers who so strenuously object to the slaughter of their innocent children. As if collectively invoking the Virgin Mary, whose tears were understood by penitents to be the medical equivalent of sanctified breast milk and to remind the emperor of his own mother, whose discovery of the buried Cross elevated her to sainthood, he is compelled to desist.[52] As if to recuperate his own childhood and return to a state of infancy, he responds with a genuine change of heart. When confronted by the abjection of these women, Constantine expresses pity and remorse, giving charitably to those he has so brutally traumatized. Charity, as Genius tells Amans, is the antidote to Envy.

While many readers would understand this tale as a moral exemplum recounted simply to make a point, the story also underscores the healing power of saints. As intercessors between the human and the divine, they demonstrate an unwavering mode of faith that lifts the spirits of the sick in such a way as to advance the healing process. While Constantine's conversion to Christianity includes the ill-effects of his subsequent "donation" to the Church, the story also reveals an important feature of everyday medical practice. The patient must trust the practitioner and have confidence in the treatment, a regimen that elevates the spirit and encourages the acceptance of the prescribed medication.[53] If we return to the epigraph at the beginning of this chapter and the statement

---

[52] Henry de Grosmont, in his *Book of Holy Medicines*, refers frequently to the efficacy of the Virgin Mary's breast milk as he meditates on sacred scenes of maternal nurture. Relevant here too is Augustine's nostalgia for his mother, Monica, as expressed in his own confession.

[53] This is, of course, the way in which placebos work even in medical experiments today. That this word in Latin means "I shall please," and has been used in the Office of the Dead since the Middle Ages, is relevant here, since the pleasing effect necessitates a willingness to believe in the treatment and its efficacy.

attributed to John of Arderne, what becomes clear is that instilling trust in the patient, even to the point of making that patient "laugh," is another way to increase the efficacy of both practitioner and treatment.[54]

Gower's Physique and the "Parfit Practisour"

Gower uses the term "physique" in ways that both overlap with Langland's usages and differentiate with them at the same time. The semantic variation in the *Confessio* underscores the importance of context in the determination of meaning in terms of the line in which the word appears as well as in the overall themes of the narrative. Etymologically related to the Latin *physicus* as well as the Old French *physique*, the word can refer to medical science or theory, an ancient medical authority such as Hippocrates, a medical treatment, a regimen for daily life, a healing medication or remedy, or even Aristotle's work on natural philosophy known as the *Physics*.[55] In Book 4 of Gower's *Confessio* on Sloth, Genius uses the word to extol the benefits of sleep done judiciously and in moderation ("whan it is take be mesure," the "it" referring to physique). In Book 6, he uses it to talk about non-naturals that are therapeutic and that Hippocrates should be credited with founding medicine as a field; in Book VII, he uses it to talk about the Four Servants of the Heart—the liver, lungs, gall bladder, and spleen—in an anatomy lesson that comes after his disquisition on the four elements, the four humors, and his explanation about how the psychophysiological system works. Despite this range of usages throughout the poem, it is the poet's use of "physique" in Book VIII, to mean "physician," that I turn to now since the medical practitioner indicated here comes as close to representing a "parfit practisour" as there is in Gower's entire oeuvre.

Found in the last book of the *Confessio* in the story of Apollonius of Tyre, the scene of note focuses on the loss and recovery of Apollonius' wife, who, after the birth of a daughter onboard a ship, is pronounced dead, placed in a coffin, and set adrift in a turbulent sea. When the casket washes up on shore near Ephesus, where it is discovered by a physician and his students, the description tells us that the doctor is a "worthi clerc, a surgien, / And ek a gret phisicien, / Of al that lond

---

[54] Peter Murray Jones' "The Surgeon as Story-teller," *Poetica* 72 (2009): 77-91 is useful for making the analogy between confessor and Amans, *clericus* and penitent, surgeon and patient. Arderne's text contains case histories or *experimenta* as they were called that resonate with Charon's idea of parallel texts as well as notions of exempla.

[55] As per the *MED*, s.v. phisik. See note 13.

the wisest on, / Which hihte Maister Cerymon" (VIII. 1163-66). Cerymon has an already established reputation as a master physician, an experienced doctor who teaches medicine and its many techniques to medical students. When they take the casket back to Cerymon's household to examine its contents, they find what seems to be a lifeless corpse wrapped "in cloth of gold" and accompanied by a letter that explains the circumstances surrounding the death of a "kings doghter"; they soon begin to prepare the body for burial, but when the woman is determined to be "of youthe," Cerymon decides to look more specifically for "a signe of lif": the body is henceforth removed from the coffin, laid on a couch, and covered with a "scheete warmed ofte." Soon "hire colde brest began to hete, / Hire herte also to flacke and bete" [flutter] (VIII. 1195-96), and Cerymon begins to massage the comatose body with "certein oile and balsme enoignt," after which he "putte a liquour in hir mouth / Which is to fewe clerkes couth, / So that sche coevereth ate laste" (VIII. 1197-1201). When Apollonius' queen awakens wondering where she is, what had happened, and where her husband and newborn child might be, Cerymon assures her that she is in a safe place and in good hands: her near-death experience is never articulated from her point of view. Rather, she is led to believe that both husband and child have drowned in the storm, a tragic happenstance that prompts her to consent to enclosure in a religious community devoted to the virgin goddess, Diana.

There are many points to make about this remarkable scene of rescue and recovery, especially from a medical perspective. Not only does Apollonius' queen seem dead but her body exhibits certain signs that would lead a casual observer to concur with that diagnosis. Cerymon demonstrates his powers of observation, however, one of the hallmarks of an exemplary physician, to arrive at another conclusion when he reads the silent body as if it were a medical chart speaking on behalf of a speechless patient. That he observes the youth of the body, as presumably his students do also, leads him to the next step: the rubbing of a "certaine" oil and balsam into the lady's joints, and the administering of a "liquour" known "to fewe clerkes." Such medical action and expert selection of efficacious oils and liquids may seem insignificant at first, but decisive moves such as these speak volumes about Cerymon's diagnostic skills.[56] By wrapping

---

[56] According to G. C. Macaulay, "In the original it is not Cerimon himself, but a young disciple of his, who discovers the signs of life and takes measures for restoring her. She has already been laid upon the pyre, and he by carefully lighting the four corners of it succeeds in liquefying the coagulated blood. Then he takes her in and warms her with wool steeped in hot oil" (vol. 3, pp. 540-1). While Gower identifies his source as the Godfrey of Viterbo's *Pantheon*, there are a number of variations that indicate his use of another source, i.e., the *Historia de Apolloniii*. Another change imposed by Gower is the addition of Cerymon's daughter as the liaison to the religious community (Diana's

the body in a "scheete warmed ofte," the blood assumed to have coagulated as a result of the drop in body temperature is warmed enough to detect a viable pulse and a heartbeat. The application of a "certain oile" and balsam, substances of miraculous healing power in biblical literature, factors into the physician's knowledge and expertise. So too the "liquour" is worthy of note since the scene's location in Ephesus with its regional proximity to Antioch reminds us of the incestuous king whose actions set Apollonius' journey into motion in the first place. This is the substance that may well be a reference to the ancient antidote for poison mentioned earlier called the "drink of Antioch." Used ironically here, it recalls that episode and launches a treatment plan designed to prevent Antiochus's sin from infecting Apollonius' nuclear family. After all, one of the central features of the narrative is to resolve this family diaspora in a reunion that not only provides a sharp contrast to Antiochus's poisonous approach to household governance but remedies it.

Apollonius' queen begins a process of sanctification from the moment she is resuscitated to the moment she is reunited with her husband and child at the tale's end. Made abbess of the local religious community, which Cerymon's daughter makes possible, the queen is assured that she will be safe, her chastity protected, her status as wife and mother not only preserved but sanctified by her presence in Diana's temple. If the association with the Greco-Roman goddess recalls images of the Virgin Mary, it is probably intended to do just that since for medieval writers like Gower, mapping pre-Christian ideology onto the historical present was routine. Moreover, because Ephesus is a well-known site for the veneration of Diana, the religious community into which Apollonius' queen is integrated accrues the identity of a medieval convent, a place of holy sanctuary for women. The attention paid to her "fluttering" heart is also significant in relation to the cardiocentrism I am claiming to be the driving force of the poem; it is the organ that provides the evidence that alerts the master physician to the presence of life after a death has been presumed. As the organ in which the soul is located, according to the authorities cited previously, the heart is the locus of compassion and the "root of all faculties." Cerymon is clearly not the *Christus*

temple) to which Apollonius' wife has been assigned. She looks after Apollonius' queen like a nurse practitioner. This varies from the *Historia* and *Pantheon* according to Thari Zweers and shifts the focus to the role of women in medical treatment. That both women put on the black clothes to indicate their new status, i.e., dead to the world, is also significant. See "Godfrey of Viterbo's *Pantheon* and John Gower's *Confessio Amantis*: The Story of Apollonius Retold," in *Accessus: A Journal of Premodern Literature and New Media* 5.1 (2018). https://scholarworks.wmich.edu/accessus/vol5/iss1/3. See also, Elizabeth Archibald, *Apollonius of Tyre: Medieval and Renaissance Themes and Variations* (Cambridge, UK: D. S. Brewer, 1991). In Shakespeare's *Pericles*, Cerimon brings the fire of life to the "o'verpressed spirits" and uses a vial of unknown medication to revive his patient.

medicus and his students clearly not disciples in the original sense of the word. Rather, they are human practitioners whose skills come as close as possible to that ideal, at least in Gower's tale.

Health in an Unhealthy World: Langland

The popularity of the Pseudo-*Secretum Secretorum*, attested to by multiple scholars, plays a significant role in both Gower's and Langland's work: "[h]elthe is the most precious thing that longith to man, for it passith alle ricchesse,"[57] proclaims the *Secretum*, in an expression of great significance in both poems. As noted earlier, however, bodily health is not all that is at stake in these works, but rather the health of the entire psychophysiological organism. In *Piers Plowman* the notion of the body's health is expanded and redefined as a "tresor" that includes the health of the soul. The poet, as Rebecca Krug observes, "redefines the association between physical bodies and *treasure* in order to find a means to acknowledge the value of health while at the same time affirming the paramount importance of the soul."[58] The rather straightforward advice offered to Piers by Hunger in Passus VI initiates the process of body-soul symbiosis. Redefining the meaning of "tresor" in this context is crucial to the enfolding of an abstract concept of health into a literal understanding of how dietary habits serve that purpose. Over the course of the narration Will and his constituents begin to revalue the food that feeds the body and nourishes the soul. The dual meaning of this dietary regimen begins to unfold, appropriately enough, in the dialogue between Piers and Hunger, when Piers presses Hunger for an explanation:

> Yet I preie yow, quod Pieres, "*pur charite*, and ye konne
> Any leef of lechecraft, lere it me, my deere.
> For some of my servauntz and myself bothe
> Of al a wike werche noght, so oure wombe aketh."
> [I pray you, for charity's sake! Teach me and some of my followers [servants] any aspect of the craft of medicine. We've done no work all week [because] our stomachs ache.]

---

[57] See Robert Steele, ed. *Three Prose Versions of the Secreta Secretorum*, EETS, e.s. 74 (London: Kegan Paul, Trench, Trübner, 1898), 21-2.
[58] Krug, "*Piers Plowman* and the Secrets of Health," 169.

To which Hunger responds:

"I woot wel," quod Hunger, "what sikenesse yow eyleth."
"Ye han manged over muche: that maketh yow grone.
Ac I hote thee," quod Hunger, "as thow thyn hele wilnest,
That thow drynke no day er thow dyne somwhat.
Ete noght, I hote thee, er Hunger thee take
And sende thee of his sauce to savore with thi lippes;
And keep som tyl soper tyme and sitte noght to longe;
Arys up er appetit have eten his fille.
Lat noght Sir Surfet sitten at thi borde;
Leve hym noght, for he is lecherous and likerous of tonge,
And after many maner metes his mawe is afyngred.
And yif thow diete thee thus, I dar legge myne eris
That Phisik shal hise furred hodes for his fode selle."

(B. VI. 252-68)

The message from Hunger is this: do not imbibe before eating, and don't eat too much, or when you're not hungry; when you do eat, do not expect to savor the taste. If you follow this advice, you will not need the services of a physician, and he will have to sell his fancy, furred hood for his own food. As pointed out in the explication, the disdain for physicians is palpable in this exchange; Hunger even goes so far as to call them "frauds." But the fact that the dialogue takes place between Piers, Langland's figure for the *Christus medicus*, and Hunger, more often the purveyor of illness than its remedy, paves the way for the transformation of wholly human medicaments into holy medication.

Health in an Unhealthy World: Gower

Interest in the practice of medicine has been said to be largely absent in Gower's work despite his inclusion of education on the basics of the humoral system in Book VII of the *Confessio*. In his recent article on Gower's cosmological knowledge, for instance, Seb Falk asserts the following: "It should be noted that Gower shows little practical interest in the medical implications of this cosmic interconnectedness: although he discusses the four complexions (CA: VII. 393–462), he does not name the humours and makes little reference to diseases or medical authorities: his concern is rather to emphasise that 'man... is made upon divisoun'"

(Pro. 974-76).[59] Other scholars concentrate on the ethical and sociopolitical aspects of the dialogue and the well-known fictional exchange between Aristotle and Alexander the Great from the Pseudo-*Secretum Secretorum*.[60] Yet, as noted above, Gower conveys the medical knowledge of the time not only by describing the four complexions and their embodiment of the four humors but by noting their qualities, what he considers to be the principal organs of the body, and their functions: "The livere makth him for to love, / The lunge gifth him weie of speche, / The galle serveth to do wreche [harm], / The splen doth him to lawhe [laugh] and pleie, / Whan al unclennesse [disease] is aweie" (VII. 470-74). Each of the four organs is responsible for providing something essential to the heart, not the least of which is the ability to speak by virtue of that organ's production of the breath of life. All these bodily functions, Genius goes on to say, would be impossible without the sustained support of the stomach and digestive process.[61] The importance of eating a healthy diet was believed to protect the body from disease. Likewise, by practicing moderation in the routines of daily life, essentially enacting Aristotle's Golden Mean in the most literal way possible, was to follow a prescription for living a balanced life and maintaining the humoral homeostasis necessary to stave off disease. Perhaps the goldenness of the mean accounts for Gower's interest in the potability of gold made possible through the transformative powers of alchemy. As Stephanie Batkie notes,

> Alchemy in Gower is the parfite medicine (*Confessio*, IV, ln. 2624) in a material and in the spiritual sense. Materially, the bodies and spirits of metals are cured of their imperfections through the contagious purity embodied in the Philosopher's Stone; commensurately, human perfection, indicated by health, improved sensory perception and even immortality, is accomplished through the same basic principle of exposing a corrupted material, the human body, to a hyper-perfect material, a potable form of the Stone known as the Elixir of Life.[62]

---

[59] *Historians on John Gower*, Stephen Rigby, ed. with Siân Echard (Cambridge, UK: D. S. Brewer, 2019), 494. See Seb Falk, "Gower and the Natural Sciences," in *Historians on John Gower*, ed. Stephen Rigby, with Siân Echard (Cambridge, UK: D. S. Brewer, 2019), 491-525. "[H]is aim was to educate and entertain more than to inform" (524). "Magic and medicine, alchemy and astrology: all were popular parts of late medieval learning" (523). While these statements are truthful, there is much more medicine than meets the eye.

[60] See Peter Nicholson, ed. *An Annotated Index to the Commentary of John Gower, Confessio Amantis* (Binghamton, NY: Center for Medieval and Early Renaissance Studies, 1989), 423-6.

[61] See Christopher Bonfield, "The First Instrument of Medicine: Diet and Regimens of Health in Late Medieval England," in "*A Verray Parfit Praktisour*": *Essays Presented to Carole Rawcliffe*, ed. Linda Clark and Elizabeth Danbury (Cambridge, UK: Boydell & Brewer, 2017).

[62] Stephanie L. Batkie, "'Of the parfite medicine': *Merita Perpetuata* in Gower's Vernacular Alchemy," in *John Gower, Trilingual Poet: Language, Tradition, and Translation*, ed. Elisabeth Dutton, John Hines, and R. F. Yeager (Woodbridge, UK: Boydell & Brewer, 2010), 157-67 (165).

The ingestion of this transformative substance rids the body of its impurities and returns it to a state of prelapsarian Edenic form. This is an education in how to achieve overall health in a medically efficacious way, a lesson Amans needs to assimilate and literally internalize.

At the end of Book VI, Amans asks Genius to tell him about Aristotle and Alexander and the advice the Philosopher was thought to have written in a letter to the impetuous young king. As if echoing the counsel of John of Arderne noted in the epigraph at the beginning of this chapter, Amans' request is for "strange tales" that might distract him from his malaise. It is the query that provides a segue into a protracted explanation of the knowledge of the time, an explication of four-fold creation, the planets and stars, the signs of the zodiac, plants, stones, and essentially all of Nature and the known world.[63] Genius articulates, in as much detail as possible, the correspondence between the macrocosm and the microcosm, the universe and the human body, from the four elements—air, water, earth, fire—their relation to the four complexions—melancholic, phlegmatic, choleric, sanguine—the location of each humor in the body—spleen, lungs, liver, gall [bladder]—and how these four organs serve the heart. What appears to be quite clear from Genius' anatomy lesson is that the heart is the center of the body just as the microcosm is the center of the universe.

Diagnosing the Storyteller's Illness

One of the principal features of narrative medicine is attentiveness to the patient's story, the tale that provides entrée into the inner life of the storyteller. How do we as audience members read the works of Langland and Gower, diagnose them, and bring them into conversation with other communities of readers or listeners? What may we infer about Langland or Gower through narratives mediated by personas that bear a strong resemblance to their creators yet differ from them in significant ways? Like the relation of Geffrey the Pilgrim to Chaucer, Will and Amans embody some aspects of Langland and Gower animated and drawn upon to participate in their respective stories and register their experiences in the material world around them. Will is neither exclusively a figure for an aspect of the soul nor a generic name for a man from Malvern Hills, but rather an integral part of the writer's identity, a figment not of his imagination (or ours) but rather of his "heart's thought," to echo Gower's term. How do we connect this

---

[63] Gower's primary source for this knowledge is Brunetto Latini's *Tresor*.

persona and this narrative to the poet when there is so little known about him? One way might be to consider a passage in Passus V of the C-text taken to be an autobiographical portrait of the author as a young man:

> When Y yong, yong was, many yer hennes,
> My fader and my frendes foende me to scole,
> Tyl Y wyste witterly what Holy Writ menede
> And what is beste for the body, as the Boek telleth,
> And sykerost for the soule, by so Y wol contenue.
> And foend Y nere, in fayth, seth my frendes deyede,
> Lyf that me lykede but in this longe clothes.
> And yf Y be labour sholde lyven and lyflode deserven,
> That laboure that Y lerned beste, therwith lyven Y sholde.
>
> (C. V, 35–43)[64]

The description fits the picture of a pious youth whose talents prompt his father and friends to send him to school to learn holy scripture and "what is beste for the body... And sykerost for the soule" (ll. 38–39). In his edition of the C-text in which this passage is unique, Derek Pearsall says, "the tradition of Langland's life... is that he was the son, perhaps illegitimate, of Stacy de Rokayle... [who] paid for him to go to school... where... he was left half-trained for a clerical vocation to make a living as best he could."[65]

This, of course, raises the question of why the poet would take the name Langland, a question answered in part by the text itself: "I have lyved in londe... my name is longe wille" (B. XV. 152), an identity supported by a legal document of 1385 in which "William, called Long Will" (Willelmus vocatus Longwyll), is written.

In his challenge to the acceptance of such a nominal invention, even one supported by a legal document, however, Robert Adams agrees that the poet is a member (probably illegitimate) of the Rokayle clan, but suggests that he "may have sometimes preferred this nickname to any surname at all."[66] The inference is, in other words, that Will[iam] Langland is a "nickname" that provides a modicum of legitimacy for an illegitimate son of a prominent family. Whoever the historical Will was, however, is less important than the persona he creates to function in the narrative as a witness to the recurring outbreaks of pestilence

---

[64] Derek Pearsall, ed. *Piers Plowman by William Langland: An Edition of the C-text* (Berkeley, CA: University of California Press, 1978), 99. I've slightly modernized the orthography.
[65] Pearsall, *Piers Plowman*, 99.
[66] Robert Adams, "The Rokeles: An Index for a 'Langland' Family History," in *Cambridge Companion to Piers Plowman*, ed. Andrew Cole and Andrew Galloway (Cambridge, UK: Cambridge University Press, 2014), 85-96 (87).

he and his personified Self are living through. Like a patient who discloses his symptoms to a team of health-care providers, Langland's Will enables his audience to participate in and empathize with all those experiencing that pandemic event. At the same time, he is in conversation with another version of himself and in so doing benefits from a process of introspection that advances the healing of his own wounds made complete through the intersubjective dialogue with his priest/physician.

While we know much more about the life of John Gower, like Langland he also creates a persona to engage in the *Confessio*'s dialogue. That identification is made manifest in the revelation toward the end of the poem when Amans is asked by Venus to speak his name and he replies, "Ma Dame," I seide, "John Gower." The eye/I of the poem has been redirected toward the reader/listener to witness the healing of the lover's wound and the recuperation of Gower's personhood. He is old, "feble and impotent," he says, and awakened from his self-delusion, cured of his lovesickness at last, but *not* by an ordinary physician ("Of love and of his dedly hele, / Which no phisicien can hele") (VIII. 3155–56). Instead, the division between the persona and the person inventing it is healed by the epiphany of Self that results from the therapeutic dialogue that confession provides; this is the intra-subjective medicine that makes self-definition and a return to psychic wholeness possible.

What do the narratives offered by these poets convey to an audience experiencing the onslaught of the bubonic plague? What remedies do they offer for themselves and others? Certainly, one of the overall messages of both poems is that dis-ease can be defined in terms of social and political disruption, but also more literally identified as a threat to the psychophysiology of every person and treatable through the intersubjectivity confession provides. Just as the proverbial "physician, heal thyself" finds its way into Langland's poem to underscore the need for introspection and self-healing as practiced by a humble plowman, so too patients can recognize and remedy many of their own illnesses: "And Piers the Plowman parceyed plener tyme / And lered hym lechecraft his lif for to save" (B. XVI. 103-04).[67] The symptoms of dis-ease both private and public often speak for themselves through history and epidemic events. In these poems both individual and collective voices are given amplification and meaning in the stories they tell.

---

[67] See Stephanie Batkie, "'Of the parfite medicine,'" *passim* and Tamara O'Callaghan, "The Fifteen Stars, Stones, and Herbs: Book VII of the *Confessio Amantis* and Its Afterlife," in *John Gower, Trilingual Poet: Language, Translation, and Tradition*, ed. Elisabeth Dutton, et al. (Cambridge, UK: D. S. Brewer, 2010), 139-56.

3

Lydgate and Hoccleve: Dietetic Medicine and the Medicalization of Madness

> ... to be mery in his hertte yt ys a gret remedye for helth of the body. Also, another yt ys, that in the time of pestilence you shulde not be afferde, but caste halle maner of fantasyes away, and ette & drinke mesurabely with a glade & mery hertte, hoppyng & trustyng in God to lyve lenger.
>
> —Canutus[1]

The medical themes and language found in the works of Chaucer, Gower, and Langland, as noted in the previous chapters, underscore the therapeutic nature of dialogue as well as the necessity for developing effective methods of disclosure. Tales conveyed in the dialogic exchanges in a storytelling contest as among the pilgrims in the *Canterbury Tales*, or through confession and dialogue as in the *Confessio Amantis* and *Piers Plowman*, enable us to read both collective and individual experiences of illness despite the fictional status of the narratives. Given the urgency of the historical moment in which these authors found themselves, the recurrence of a disease event for which no etiology was certain, the attention to strategies for articulating the anxiety and fear provoked by spontaneous outbreaks of the pestilence provides a modicum of relief for those living through what can only be described as an urgent public health crisis. The literary works noted above not only reveal the experience of the illness but also provide some of the remedies and advice offered by practitioners of the time. Excerpted from the plague tractate known as the "Canutus," the epigraph above advocates casting "halle maner of fantasyes away," to eat and drink with a

---

The phrase "medicalization of madness" is borrowed from the title of an essay written by M. W. Bychowski, "Unconfessing Transgender Dysphoric Youths and the Medicalization of Madness in John Gower's 'Tale of Iphis and Ianthe,'" *Accessus: A Journal of Premodern Literature and New Media* 3.1 (2016): 1-38. https://scholarworks.wmich.edu/accessus/vol3/iss1/

[1] *Middle English Medical Texts*, ed. Irma Taavitsainen, Päivi Pahta, and Martti Mäkinen (Helsinki: John Benjamins Publishing, 2005).

"glade & mery hertte." And while prescriptive treatises such as the Canutus were far from the norm, guides to healthful living were as much a part of the medical milieu as the plague itself.[2]

The correspondence to narrative medicine as noted in previous chapters is evident in the ways in which the narrators of a body of poetry in Middle English disclose symptoms and enable reading audiences to engage with the stories and their tellers. As Rita Charon explains,

> the point of equipping doctors and medical students with the readerly skills to follow a narrative thread, to adopt multiple and contradictory points of view, to enter into the teller's narrative world and see how that teller makes sense of it, to identify the images and metaphors used, to recognize the temporal flow of events, to follow allusions to other stories, to tolerate stories' ambiguity, and to be imaginatively transported to wherever the story might take the one who surrenders to it. The result might be that patients would hear—both the said and the unsaid—and that doctors could use the self as a potent therapeutic instrument.[3]

Both the tale teller and the diagnostician gain something from the narration that contributes to a more comprehensive diagnosis than a clinical exam alone could provide. And just as Charon's methodology functions as a diagnostic reading tool, so too does narrative medicine provide a framework for understanding literature produced by poets and practitioners who found themselves living through a pandemic.

The two authors addressed in this chapter provide another aspect of the experience of disease and the ways in which any individual might respond to the anxiety engendered by its multiple threats.[4] For Lydgate and Hoccleve, immersion in reading and writing poetry, in addition to carrying out the duties of their respective occupations, appear to function as personal therapy for dealing with some of the emotions provoked by the presence of the disease around them. Yet there are more subtle indications that by the late fourteenth and early fifteenth centuries the pandemic had become normalized and accepted as the inevitable

---

[2] Both Joseph P. Byrne and Samuel Cohn characterize *consilia* (plague treatises) as a "literary genre." See Byrne, *The Black Death* (London: Greenwood Press, 2004), 36. Cohn, *The Black Death Transformed: Disease and Culture in Early Renaissance Europe* (Oxford: Oxford University Press, 2002), 66.

[3] Rita Charon, "The Self-Telling Body," *Narrative Inquiry* 16.1 (2006): 191-200 (194). See also Charon's, "Narrative Medicine as Witness for the Self-Telling Body," *Journal of Applied Communication Research* 37.2 (2009): 118-31.

[4] For the most part, this appears to be supported by the relative absence of references to the pandemic or description of the symptoms visible on the corpses of those who succumbed to the illness, even the miasma that Boccaccio describes as an everyday experience in Florence.

consequence of everyday life in England.⁵ Perhaps this is one of the motivating forces that moves writers to seek out remedies that do not require a doctor's oversight, preventative strategies that they or their readers might themselves implement. That folk medicine is considered to be as efficacious as its academic counterpart, a trend becoming more evident after England's initial series of outbreaks in the fourteenth century, helps explain the dissemination of medical recipes and practical advice written in English and incorporated into household codices as well as conduct and health manuals.

No two authors of the fifteenth century could be so unlike one another in terms of the lives they led, the vocations they pursued, or even the places they called "home." As a Benedictine monk of Bury St. Edmunds, said to be the richest monastery in England, Lydgate's life centered on the rules and practices established by St. Benedict in the sixth century. Members of the Order became known for their adherence to the humility and obedience demanded by the Rule as well as their Order's well-stocked libraries, medicinal gardens, and dedication to the care of the sick. By way of contrast Hoccleve was part of the secular world in his capacity as a clerk of the Office of the Privy Seal, "one of three writing offices (in company with Chancery and the Signet office) that formed the administrative center of government at Westminster."⁶ A bureaucratic scribe with a penchant for poetry, he lived most frequently in chill penury, ever in need of additional support despite his governmental affiliations. These were poets who traveled in different "professional" circles and faced different kinds of challenges to their lives and livelihoods. Nonetheless, there are notable similarities that bring the two together in striking ways: both had Lancastrian loyalties;⁷ both were influenced by Chaucer and Gower;⁸ both were conversant in medicines and medical practices; both created personas who spoke compellingly of illness.⁹

---

⁵ Robert S. Gottfried, *Epidemic Disease in Fifteenth Century England: The Medical Response and the Demographic Consequences* (New Brunswick, NJ: Rutgers University Press, 1978). Gottfried argues that neither Lydgate nor Hoccleve addressed the epidemic: "Lydgate and Hoccleve, probably the century's premier poets, seem to have been rather oblivious to epidemic disease. It is therefore necessary to turn to more obscure sources" (75).

⁶ Ethan Knapp, *The Bureaucratic Muse: Thomas Hoccleve and the Literature of Late Medieval England* (University Park: Pennsylvania State University Press, 2001), 22.

⁷ Paul Strohm, "Hoccleve, Lydgate and the Lancastrian Court," in *The Cambridge History of Medieval English Literature*, ed. David Wallace (Cambridge: Cambridge University Press, 1999), 640-61.

⁸ Katherine Little, *Confession and Resistance: Defining the Self in Late Medieval England*. There is a link between Gower and Hoccleve worth noting here: Not only did Hoccleve serve "as one of the scribes for the Trinity College Cambridge MS R. 3.2" but he also "contributed to the 'mirror for princes' genre which Gower had introduced (introduced into English vernacular, that is) with the seventh book of the *Confessio*" (350) [see Little, p. 169, n.1].

⁹ It is worth noting here that some of the works of Lydgate and Hoccleve appear together in several manuscripts that contain the *Series* as well as the "Danse Macabre" (c. 1426-9).

For Lydgate such knowledge appears in works that include "A Diet and Doctrine for the Pestilence," "How the Plague Ceased in Rome," the *Fabula Duorum Mercatorum* (The Story of Two Merchants), and the "Danse of Death," while for Hoccleve, medical matters appear discursively in the *Series*, which includes a complaint, a dialogue, a meditation on death, and two fables from the *Gesta Romanorum*.

While there are clear variations among these texts and the health perspectives offered by each poet, taken together they underscore the attention each writer paid to medicine and its practice. More importantly, when they do *not* seem to confront the plague directly, the recurrence of the disease during the fifteenth century prompts in them a continuation of the medical consciousness established during the previous century. According to Joseph P. Byrne fifteen outbreaks occurred after 1370, and many more thereafter during the lifetime of these poets: 1379-83, 1389-93, 1400, 1405-7, 1413, 1420, 1427, 1433-4, 1438-9, 1457-8, 1463-4, 1467, 1471, 1479-80, and 1485.[10] Added to the collective social and political trauma caused by the Hundred Years' War, which extended into the 1450s, the continued presence of the plague is no small concern either for the general population or for actively engaged poets.[11] Yet there appears at first glance to be little attention paid to such life-threatening circumstances as presumably an outbreak of the plague would urge. Instead, as Bryon Lee Grigsby observes, "[p]lague has become part of the medical warp and the literary weft of the social web rather than an apocalyptic sign."[12] Like Chaucer and Gower, who reveal their own impulses to turn away from the disease ravaging England before their very eyes, or even Langland, who provides an apocalyptic warning of the economic and social impact of the dis-ease[13] spreading around them in the form of economic destabilization and widespread hunger, Lydgate and Hoccleve seem to follow suit.

Whereas Chaucer, Gower, and Langland deploy dialogic strategies for addressing individual and collective health through their poetry, Lydgate and Hoccleve take these strategies to another level, giving voice to medical concerns

---

[10] Byrne, *The Black Death*, 60. The dates offered by Carole Rawcliffe in *Urban Bodies: Communal Health in Late Medieval English Towns and Cities* (Woodbridge, UK: Boydell & Brewer, 2013) expand the list after the initial outbreak in the late 1340s from the 1370s to 1429: 1374-5, 1377, 1378-9, 1380, 1383, 1384, 1387, 1389, 1390, 1391, 1399-1400, 1407, 1413, 1417-18, 1419, 1421, 1423, 1426-7, 1428, and 1429.

[11] R. D. Perry, "Lydgate's Danse Macabre and the Trauma of the Hundred Years War," *Literature and Medicine* 33.2 (2015): 326-47.

[12] Grigsby, *Pestilence*, 138.

[13] The first use of this word, *disese*, to mean "absence of ease, uneasiness, discomfort," according to the *OED*, occurs in Robert Mannyng of Brunne's *Chronicle*: "Go and mak his pes, or he do the more stoure, / And thou to this *dese* may haf the frute and floure" (emphasis mine).

through intersubjective and self-reflexive dialogues as well as by inserting their avatars into select narratives. Unlike those personae created by Langland (Will), Gower (Amans), and Chaucer (Geffrey), Lydgate animates multiple voices that demonstrate the poet's technical range and vocal dexterity; this is especially discernible when he inserts himself into the action of the *Siege of Thebes*, or ventriloquizes the voice of the physician in the *Fabula Duorum Mercatorum*, or speaks the words of the translator as well as the author in the "Danse of Death."[14] Perhaps even more dramatic than Lydgate's multifaceted deployment of authorial vocality is Hoccleve's self-reflexive persona in the *Series*, who speaks in such a realistic manner that modern critics have called his narration autobiographical.[15] Not unlike the relationship between author and persona presented to reading audiences by Chaucer, Gower, and Langland, as well as Lydgate, Hoccleve's narrator, a persona he calls "Thomas," is discernibly separate from "Hoccleve," the writer whose name appears in select holograph manuscripts. By splitting himself into the speaker on the one hand and the writer on the other, Hoccleve reveals his own (or what appears to be his own) ailments to an audience in need of learning something about the emotional, psychological, and physical experience of melancholy, a disease he diagnoses in himself. But first, Lydgate.

A Diet and Doctrine for the Pestilence

If the popularity of a text is any indication of the needs of an audience, then this text stands as evidence for a growing interest in plague medicine. With fifty-nine manuscripts in circulation, Lydgate's "Dietary" fills the gap in literary production at a time "when medical poems represented a small and dwindling subset of the corpus of Middle English medical texts."[16] The "Dietary" became so popular over the course of the fifteenth century, in fact, that it was incorporated into the London Thornton manuscript, William Caxton's *Governayle of Helth* in 1490, reprinted by Wynkyn de Worde, and "from 1506 until the time of the Commonwealth" found its way into the *Kalender of Shepherdes*, an almanac of

---

[14] For a discussion of this work, see Seeta Chaganti, *Strange Footing: Poetic Form and Dance in the Late Middle Ages* (Chicago: University of Chicago Press, 2018), esp. chapter 4.
[15] See J. A. Burrow, "Autobiographical Poetry in the Middle Ages: The Case of Thomas Hoccleve," *Proceedings of the British Academy* 82.3 (1987): 389–412.
[16] Jake Walsh Morrissey, "'To al Indifferent': The Virtues of Lydgate's 'Dietary,'" *Medium Aevum* 84.2 (2015): 258–78.

practical advice.[17] Despite the work's status as more unoriginal than not (it's a translation of the Latin *Dietarium* with, in some cases, a translation of Dechamps' ballad attached as a prologue), Lydgate's "Dietary" makes this medical poem accessible to an English audience for the first time. The fact that the poet adds the word "pestilence" to the work's incipit suggests that he recognized the need for advice on how to remain healthy in the face of the plague. As Glending Olson suggested years ago,

> [t]hat a poem specifically concerned with the plague could so readily fuse with a general regimen reveals both the pervasiveness of pestilence in fifteenth-century life and the widespread familiarity of the rules for dealing with it first announced in the plague *consilia*.[18]

That *consilia* became a genre in response to demands for pragmatic advice based on experiential observation rather than astrological medical theories marks a turn both toward the vernacular and toward the use of plain language, less artful and symbolic and certainly less jargon-ridden than other forms of contemporary poetry.[19]

> Who will been holle & keep hym from sekenesse
> And resiste the strok of pestilence,
> Lat hym be glad, & voide al hevynesse,
> Flee wikkyd heires, eschew the presence.
> Off infect placys, causyng the violence;
> Drynk good wyn, & holsom meetis take,
> Smelle swote thyng[es] & for his deffence
> Walk in cleene heir, eschew[e] mystis blake.
>
> (ll. 1-8)[20]

While neither the "Doctrine" nor the 124-line "Dietary" that follows in a select number of manuscripts is wholly original with Lydgate, the poet appears to have recognized the importance of its subject matter to his audience. Written

---

[17] Morrissey, "To al Indifferent," 258. For the work's incorporation into the London Thornton manuscript see Susanna Fein, "The Contents of Robert Thornton's Manuscripts," in *Robert Thornton and His Books: Essays on the Lincoln and London Thornton Manuscripts*, ed. Susanna Fein and Michael Johnston (York, UK: York Medieval Press, 2014), 13–65.

[18] Glending Olson, *Literature as Recreation in the Later Middle Ages* (Ithaca, NY: Cornell University Press, 1982), 174.

[19] Much criticism of this work is, in fact, based on aesthetics rather than pragmatics. See Morrissey, "To al Indifferent," 258-60.

[20] Henry Noble MacCracken, ed. *The Minor Poems of John Lydgate*, EETS, o.s. 192 (London: Oxford University Press, 1934; rpt. 1961), II.702-7. Also, Henry Noble MacCracken, ed. *The Minor Poems of John Lydgate*, EETS, e.s. 107 (London: Oxford University Press, 1962). All quotations derive from this two-part edition.

in three, eight-line stanzas in keeping with the poem that follows (i.e., the "Dietary" proper), the "Doctrine" echoes the advice in the Canutus (and other *consilia*) on maintaining a "mery herte" and voiding "al heynesse."[21] When the last line of the opening stanza is repeated, the recommendation to avoid "black mists" resonates with other *consilia*, while the "Dietary" itself echoes the health advice of narrative poems such as those noted in previous chapters.[22] Such an emphasis on the pragmatic aspects of medical care is, of course, responding to the needs of the physical body, which must be kept away from "bad air" and encouraged to engage in more pleasant sensory experiences. Readers are advised to "walk in sweet-smelling gardens," "drink good wine," "eat wholesome food in moderation," "get adequate sleep," and avoid "older, sensual women," who presumably represent temptations of the carnal sort,[23] to maintain humoral balance; such advice includes certain medications and their applications: "caraway is a good medicine"; "potable gold is good for chills or fever" (for the rich), or "watery gruel" (for the poor). In what amounts to a premodern equivalent of modern dietetic medicine, food is to be ingested according to one's complexion or temperament, "governed by the four humors—phlegm, melancholy, blood, choler."[24] So too behavior modification is necessitated and the activities of a contentious, discordant, or quarrelsome nature, especially aimed at one's betters, one's peers, or those over whom one governs, were to be avoided. In addition to remedies for the physical body are those advised for the soul: being on time for Mass, doing reverence to God, visiting the poor, having sympathy and compassion toward those in need. That the body/soul connection is integral in this text is made explicit in the last stanza, in which moderation in eating and charity go hand in hand:

> Thus in too thyngis stondith al the welthe,
> Of sowle & bodi, who so list hem sewe,
> Moderat foode yeveth to man his helthe,
> And all surfetis doth fro hym remewe,
> And charite to the sowle is dewe;

---

[21] See Jamie McKinstry, "Heaviness: Illness, Metaphor, Opportunity," *postmedieval* 8.2 (2017): 170–8. The notion of heaviness applies to Hoccleve as well, as McKinstry demonstrates.

[22] As Bryon Lee Grigsby notes, Langland's Hunger "describes a dietary regimen similar to that prescribed by doctors as a precaution against plague." See *Pestilence in Medieval and Early Modern English Literature*, 109.

[23] William Snell, "Lydgate's *Dietary* and *Doctrine for Pestilence* Re-examined," says that this is a peculiarity of Lydgate's text. MacCracken's edition lists these two works separately.

[24] Lydgate, or the original writer of the *Dietarium*, correctly conflates melancholy, a temperament, with black bile, the humor thought to cause its symptoms.

> This receiht bouht is of non appotecarie,
> Off Maister Antony, nor of Maister Hewe;
> To al indifferent richest dietarie!
>
> (ll. 161–68)[25]

Beyond the concerns of the corporeal body and its incorporeal spirit, there is another dimension to the recommendations of the "Dietary": to be glad of heart, free from worry and excessive pensiveness, to do everything in moderation, all to (a)void the debilitating effects of melancholy. This is advice given freely in a gesture of charity even to those "indifferent" and unwilling to listen.

All of this is instructive to an audience in need of medical advice at this pivotal moment in history, but there are certain passages that are especially significant when it comes to melancholy, its symptoms, its effects, and its treatment. When elaborating on overindulgence in eating, Lydgate writes:

> Greedi souper & drynkyng late at eve
> Causith of fflewme gret superfluyte;
> Colre adust doth the stomak greve,
> Malencolik a froward gest, parde!
> Off mykil or litel cometh al infirmyte,
> Attween thes too for lak of governaunce,
> Dryve out a mene, excesse or scarsete,
> Set thi botaill upon temperaunce.
>
> (ll. 73–80)

> And yiff so be leechis doth the faile,
> Than take good heed to use thynges thre,
> Temperat diet, temperat travaile,
> Nat malencolius for non adversite,
> Meeke in trouble, glad in poverte,
> Riche with litel, content with suffisaunce,
> Nevir grucchyng, mery lik thi degre,
> Yiff phisik lak, make this thi governance.
>
> (ll. 97–104)

The emphasis on moderation is, of course, reminiscent not only of the literary works of the previous century but also the Pseudo-Aristotelian *Secretum*

---

[25] According to Jake Walsh Morrissey, "'To al Indifferent,'" "these two masters may be Antonio Cermisone (died 1441) and Hugh of Siena (died 1439), after which time the reference would lose its topicality; the English translation, of course, dates to sometime before Lydgate's death in late 1449" (264).

Secretorum, a source of pragmatic advice written expressly for the nobility. Like the "Mirror for Princes," aimed specifically at the education of a king, Lydgate's "Dietary" offers practical ways to stave off illness should doctors fail in their medical treatments. In so doing the poet effectively brings a recipe for health and self-governance to ordinary folks at a time when the pestilence is literally in the air.

The broadening of focus in this text is significant in and of itself, but it is Lydgate's statement about "all infirmity" that returns me to an earlier assertion I made about the plague becoming something else, some other disease, its existence denied, displaced to another time, or altered in some way. "Infirmity" ranges in meaning from a generic disease or "bout of sickness" to "a plague, an epidemic," and while the *MED* lists the last meaning as occurring in the Wycliffite Bible, where it refers to the plagues in ancient Egypt, its use in this context becomes more ambiguous and expansive, enabling the poet to confront the pestilence in England by displacing it to another time and place.[26] Certainly, using narrative poetry as a form of entertainment is compatible with the advice to be merry and worry free, but "How the Plague was Ceased in Rome" seems more instructive than entertaining, more materially graphic than metaphorically uplifting. Is Lydgate distancing himself and his readers from the present-day disease event or is he simply displacing it to other genres, times, and places? The short work that follows is suggestive in all these ways.

How the Plague Was Ceased in Rome

Considered to be a "minor" poem and often undervalued by critics, "How the Plague was Ceased in Rome" refers to a time in the pre-Christian past when the presence of pestilence provided a challenge that even celebrated medical experts such as "Avicen, Ypocras, nor yet [or even] Galen, Cerapion ... nor Asculapius" (ll. 3-5) could not cure. Written originally in Latin and ostensibly from the "gestys of Lumbardy" during the reign of "kynge Gilberte," the poet describes: "a cruell pestilence, / An ugsom dethe environde Italy, / Where crafts cure coude make no resistence / As provyd was, by dredfull experience / In Rome and Pavy, to carefull Citees / Wher pestilence regnyng dyd tyrannes" (ll. 10-15). As if the

---

[26] This is especially significant when understood within the context of earlier episodes of the plague, especially the Justinian plague, the plague in sixth-century Gaul reported by Gregory of Tours, the plague of the seventh century spoken of by Bede, and into the "second" pandemic of the late Middle Ages known as the Black Death.

incipit were not enough to alert an audience to subject matter pertinent to their own time, the poet repeats the word "pestilence" during the course of this forty-three-line poem, referring to the disease as "pestilent," a "furious syknes" so lethal that "mo were dede / Then lefte on lyve" (ll. 17–18). No medicine was effective in curing this deadly illness, he says, not even "golde potable."[27] Rather, the only effective cessation came about through the intervention of a saint, in this case, St. Sebastian. The apparent source for this tale, which is a much longer version in the *Legenda Aurea*, clarifies some details missing in Lydgate's adaptation. That part, given in translation here, goes as follows:

> In the *Annals of the Lombards* we read that during the reign of King Gumbert all Italy was stricken by a plague so virulent that there was hardly anyone left to bury the dead, and this plague raged most of all in Rome and Pavia. At this time there appeared to some a good angel followed by a bad angel carrying a spear. When the good angel gave the command, the bad one struck and killed, and when he struck a house, all the people in it were carried out dead. Then it was divinely revealed that the plague would never cease until an altar was raised in Pavia in honor of Saint Sebastian. An altar was built in the church of Saint Peter in Chains, and at once the pestilence ceased. Relics of Saint Sebastian were brought to Pavia.[28]

The plague that rages in these two cities at the time of this king's reign provides the context for the miracle associated with Sebastian, the saint so famously martyred by being shot with multiple arrows. The story leading up to and including Sebastian's death precedes the excerpt cited above and is made into the focus of the story by Lydgate. The two angels who appear in this tale, one who gives the command to bring disease, and the other who carries out the deed, collaborate in inflicting the plague on select households. That Lydgate describes these figures as "pestiferous" suggests that they are demonic agents in disguise sent to carry out their orders on humanity and not God himself. As the legend would have it, the plague ceases when the altar to St. Sebastian is constructed, as recommended by a local holy man.

Why St. Sebastian? Important to note in Lydgate's version of this tale is that Sebastian was in Lydgate's time a "plague saint," intercessor on behalf of victims of the disease in real time as well as a commonly held belief in its

---

[27] This is an early reference to drinkable gold made from particles of the precious metal mixed with other substances and used as medicine— also understood to be the elixir of life in alchemy. Lydgate's use of the term is cited in the *MED* along with an earlier reference by Guy de Chauliac, who relates his recipe for a medicinal compound.

[28] Jacobus de Voragine, *The Golden Legend*, trans. William Granger Ryan, 2 vols. (Princeton: University of Princeton Press, 1993), 101.

divine sanctioning. As Joseph P. Byrne notes, Sebastian's "association with the pestilence stems from his having survived the shower of arrows. The association of arrows with divinely sent disease is ancient."[29] Byrne goes on to list biblical texts that support this reading: Deut. 32:23, Ps. 64:7, Ps. 7:12, Job 6:4, adding that "[c]lassical authors spoke of pestilence as arrows, as did Christian writers during the First Pandemic."[30] Also significant in this regard is that Sebastian is associated with the Justinian Plague, the pandemic that struck Constantinople and surrounding environs in the sixth century. This is the event recorded in the *Annals of the Lombards* cited by Jacobus de Voragine and adapted by Lydgate.

Fabula Duorum Mercatorum (The Story of Two Merchants)

Arrows shot into the body of a plague saint would in most instances be likely to evoke thoughts of the pestilence, yet there is something to be said about the trope and its link to the deleterious effects of Cupid's arrow. As noted in the previous chapter in relation to Gower's *Confessio*, lovesickness was an illness taken seriously by late medieval physicians. And while one could argue, as many have done,[31] that the *Fabula* is about neither pestilence nor lovesickness but rather about male friendship and a Boethian take on the vicissitudes of Fortune, the 900+ line poem features a scene of medical diagnosis, suggesting that one disease may not be mutually exclusive of any other. Certainly, succumbing to an illness is often as sudden a loss of material status and respectability as it could possibly be. Based upon the tale found in Petrus Alphonsi's *Disciplina clericalis*, a twelfth-century collection of Latin *exempla* often used in sermons, Lydgate provides an overview of the process of medical assessment and diagnosis in the voice of an exceptionally well-informed *medicus* like Petrus Alphonsi himself: the section on lovesickness with its protracted differential diagnosis by an "assembly of physicians" demonstrates something more than a passing knowledge of medicine. That Lydgate is a Benedictine monk presumably privy to medical

---

[29] Byrne, *The Black Death*, 94.
[30] Ibid.
[31] See Pamela Farvolden, *Lydgate's Fabula duorum mercatorum and Guy of Warwyk*, Middle English Texts Series (Kalamazoo: Medieval Institute Publications, 2016). See also Robert Stretter, "Rewriting Perfect Friendship in Chaucer's 'Knight's Tale' and Lydgate's 'Fabula Duorum Mercatorum,'" *The Chaucer Review* 37.3 (2007): 234-52; Lisa H. Cooper, "'His guttys wer out shake': Illness and Indigence in Lydgate's *Letter to Gloucester* and *Fabula Duorum Mercatorum*," *Studies in the Age of Chaucer* 30 (2008): 303-34.

books in the library of Bury St. Edmunds makes this text all-the-more relevant for his vernacularizing of medicine in the fifteenth century. That he echoes the advice of medical practitioners, many of whom are cited by Chaucer's Physician, suggests its currency.

> Assemblyd been of leechis many oon,
> The beste and wisest, that he coude ffynde;
> Unto the sike they been ecomen echoon,
> To taste his poorys [test his pulse]³² and for to deeme his kynde.
> Thei were ful besy to fynd out roote and rynde,
> Of what humour was causyd his dissese,
> And theron werke his accesse to appese.
>
> (ll. 267-73)

The physicians collaborate on diagnosing their patient—taking his pulse, assessing the nature of his fever, checking his urine—to discern the etiology of the illness. In what amounts to a medieval version of the modern-day physician's house call, they bring their medical supplies with them: syrups to make "dygestyves," pills and powders for purgation, and "confortatives" to have on hand for a timely cure. They check his fever to determine which kind it is, ephemeral ("effymora"), the short-lasting kind, a more long-lasting one caused by emotional trauma ("etyk"), or the fever called "putrida" thought to be caused by a putrefaction of the humors; they also consider the two kinds of "sinochus," diagnosed respectively, as Lisa H. Cooper notes, "as either the excessive 'quantite' or 'qualitie' of a single humor."³³ The point of such a detailed diagnostic procedure is to determine whether the malady is due to excessive food and drink, perturbed thoughts of various kinds, or an overabundance of one or more humors, in this case, blood and bile. When they examine the color of their patient's urine, it is to see whether this particular bodily fluid is pure or "unpure," "citryn or vitelline"; it is an observation that provokes an allusion to Giles de Corbeil, famous for his treatise on uroscopy subsequently translated

---

[32] Galen diagnosed lovesickness by testing the rate of the pulse. As noted in the *METS* edition, the word "poorys" may also refer to "pores"; this may be a scribal error or Lydgate's possible (con)fusion between theories for preventing pestilence (the opening of the pores of the skin by bathing) and lovesickness. In Lydgate's "Pageant of Knowledge," under the entry for "Phebus," the poet describes the classical god as the inventor of the "craft of medicine," in which diagnostic procedures included "touche of pounce veyne," the artery where a pulse could be detected. As is the case with Chaucer in his listing of medical authorities in the description of the Physician in the General Prologue, Lydgate refers to Aesculapius, the Greco-Roman god of healing, also considered to be the founder of medicine.

[33] See *METS* edition, note to lines 286-7; see also Cooper, "'His guts wer out shake,'" 319.

into English by Henry Daniel.[34] Only after an extensive and detailed description of their diagnostic process can the doctors conclude their patient's symptoms to be consistent with melancholy brought about by "thouht or love, that men calle / Amor ereos, that he was falle" (ll. 335-36). This is, of course, a diagnosis that readers of the tale have been made aware of several stanzas prior to the arrival of the physicians. *Hereos amor*, or "*amor ereos*" in Lydgate's rendering, is equivalent to lovesickness or "love-madness" with symptoms similar to melancholy—"sighing, weeping, swooning, pallor, loss of appetite, weakness"—that if left untreated lead ultimately to death.[35] Such physical symptoms and the emotional distress that accompanies them enable us to see how the metaphorical wounds of Cupid's arrow become associated with the anxiety and humoral imbalance of melancholy. As Corinne Saunders observes, "Love was commonly depicted as a force-like illness, striking unexpectedly from outside and often represented as a wound caused by the God of Love's arrow. Only the lady could cure this wound, and secular poetry repeatedly employs the image of the lady as physician."[36] Such a gendering of the physician may recall thoughts of Lady Philosophy in her capacity to heal the wounds of Boethius during his imprisonment, but there is something less philosophical going on in this scenario and one rather more focused on the material causes of a body in pain.

Unlike Lady Philosophy, the lady of "tender age" in the *Fabula* does not speak when the Syrian merchant sees her and claims he has fallen in love. As Lisa Cooper points out, the maiden is made into a commodity described in "commercial language," whose "value can be assessed and even overestimated" as the cure for the Syrian's malady.[37] Given the prominence of the lovesickness trope, it is probably no coincidence that this tale is often equated with Chaucer's "Knight's Tale" and the amorous triangle featuring Palamon, Arcite, and Emelye, as discussed in an earlier chapter. What is worth noting here is that just as the grievously wounded Arcite bequeaths Emelye to Palamon before the injured knight dies, the Egyptian merchant hands over his beloved lady to his esteemed

---

[34] Jake Walsh Morrissey, "Anxious Love and Disordered Urine: The Englishing of Amor Hereos in Henry Daniel's *Liber uricrisiarum*," *The Chaucer Review* 49.2 (2014): 161-83. Daniel's work marks a milestone in literature on uroscopy in England; his *Liber uricriarum*, "which Daniel drafted in Latin in 1375 or 1376 and revised in several English versions until at least 1379, is among the first and most widely disseminated of the specialized treatises in which learned medicine entered the English language" (166).

[35] Corinne Saunders, "'The Thoghtful Maladie': Madness and Vision in Medieval Writing," in *Madness and Creativity in Literature and Culture*, ed. Corinne Saunders and Jane Macnaughton (New York: Palgrave Macmillan, 2005), 67-87.

[36] Ibid.

[37] Cooper, "'His guttys wer out shake,'" 303-34.

Syrian friend.[38] In a gesture that seems to override the transactional nature of the friendship, the merchant maintains the bond made all the more meaningful in the exchange of the woman they both love.

Death and Its Dance

The bond between men forged over the love of a woman causes the pain and anguish needed to validate the courtly relation not between a man and a woman but between men. That the severity of the pain often leads to someone's death in this scenario seems to be the desired outcome, a fantasy given additional significance over time. Sickness caused by unrequited love and uncontrollable yearning for a presence that cannot be satisfied for one reason or another often leads to the death of lovers. One thinks immediately of the tale of Cupid and Psyche or the notion of Liebestod, so central to the Tristan story, or the soul's desire to return to its creator, so fundamental to Christian theology. Death is not an ending in these narratives but rather a teleological aspiration for the living. And perhaps this helps explain the popularity of the *danse macabre* in graphic images as well as in poetic form. The first known visualization is a wall painting at the Holy Innocents Cemetery in Paris which took years to complete after its initial groundbreaking in the summer of 1424. That Lydgate viewed this mural is given credibility by his acknowledgment in the poem—"like the example wiche that at Parys / I fonde depict oones in a wal" (l. 19-20)—in a translation that inspired the visual art and its later replication on the walls of Pardon churchyard at St. Paul's cathedral.[39] Image and text together, according to Megan Cook and Elizaveta Strakhov, were "designed to function like a mental 'image-text,' compelling the reader to imagine a set of visualizations organized around a single idea."[40]

When translated from image to text, there is something more to be said for how the idea of death is received by an audience experiencing recurrent outbreaks of the plague. Certainly, they felt the pain of the disease as well as the shock of how rapidly it took a life. In Lydgate's translation of the "Dance of Death," a seemingly

---

[38] Stretter, "Rewriting Perfect Friendship," 234-52.
[39] See Karen Smyth, "Pestilence and Poetry: John Lydgate's *Danse Macabre*," in *The Fifteenth Century XII: Society in the Age of Plague*, ed. Linda Clark and Carole Rawcliffe (Woodbridge, UK: Boydell & Brewer, 2013), 39-56.
[40] Megan L. Cook and Elizaveta Strakhov, eds., *John Lydgate's Dance of Death and Related Works*, TEAMS, Middle English Texts Series (Kalamazoo: Medieval Institute Publications, 2019), 3. See also Rossell Hope Robbins, "Signs of Death in Middle English," *Mediaeval Studies* 32 (1970): 282-98.

living, speaking personification repeatedly claims his power over life. Death is sudden and nondiscriminating, striking everyone from the highest status to the lowest or in Lydgate's version, from the Pope to representatives from all ages and occupations, including physicians.[41] Moreover, when Lydgate takes on the voices of both the translator and the author, as he does in his version of the tale, he is quite literally lending a vocal dimension to an otherwise static visual.[42] And while wall murals told stories to viewers aware of how to "read" them sequentially, poetic adaptations, especially those that could be read aloud,[43] spoke to them in another register. As we know from manuscript illustration and the texts they illuminate, the two forms of art speak not only to the viewing/reading audience but to each other, sometimes in harmony, and sometimes in dissonance.[44] By "shaping the reader's experience through the poem and by interacting with the reader's own sense of the visual tradition," a decidedly augmented full immersion becomes "something different: an untimely and irregular experience," according to Seeta Chaganti.[45] Yet there is another aspect of the poem to consider here, one that signals the aural dimension of the otherwise silent visual texts.

The first stanza from the A version in which Lydgate speaks in the words of the translator (*verba translatoris*) stands as an example of how a text could be made to speak to its readers. Lydgate's voice and the urgency he enfolds into his opening salvo are notable in this regard; as if he were sounding an apocalyptic alarm, he awakens his audience and alerts them to the warning message:

O yee folks harde-hertid as a stone,
Wich to the worlde have al your advertence,
Liche as it shulde laste evere in oone—

---

[41] As Karen Smyth notes, the majority of manuscripts list the following: "pope, emperor, cardinal, king patriarch, constable, archbishop, baron, princess, bishop, squire, abbot, abbess, bailiff, astronomer, burgess, canon secular, merchant, Carthusian, sergeant, monk, usurer, poor man, physician, lover, youthful squire, gentlewoman, man of law, Master John Rykill, fool, parson, juror minstrel, labourer, friar minor, child, young clerk and hermit. Lydgate makes six additions to his French source: the four women, a juror and a conjuror (Master Rykill)" (40).

[42] As Seegta Chaganti puts it, "In several danse macabre installations, vernacular poetic text visibly collaborates with the spectacle's other media of paint, architecture, and moving bodies, appearing as verse dialogues inscribed under the painted sets of partners." See *Strange Footing*, 145. There is also a song—"*Ad mortem festinamus*" —found in the *Libre Vermell de Montserrat* (1399); my thanks to Clifford Davidson for this citation.

[43] Claire Sponsler, "Text and Textiles: Lydgate's Tapestry Poems," in *Medieval Fabrications*, ed. E. Jane Burns (New York: Palgrave Macmillan, 2004), 28.

[44] Suzanne Lewis, *Reading Images: Narrative Discourse and Reception in the Thirteenth-Century Illuminated Apocalypse* (Cambridge: Cambridge University Press, 1995). See also Anne Laskaya, "The Feminized World and Divine Violence: Texts and Images of the Apocalypse," in *Domestic Violence in Medieval Texts*, ed. Eve Salisbury, Georgiana Donavin, and Merrall L. Price (Gainesville, FL: University Press of Florida, 2002), 299-341.

[45] Seeta Chaganti, *Strange Footing*, 144-5.

> Where is your witt, where is your providence
> To se aforn the sodeine violence
> Of cruel Dethe, that ben so wis and sage,
> Wiche sleeth, allas, by stroke of pestilence
> Bothe yong and olde, of lowe and hy parage?
>
> (ll. 1-8)

This is an audible interrogative, a rhetorical ploy designed to alert a "hard-hearted" audience to the unpredictable attack of Death; hard-heartedness echoes the resistance of the target audience identified in the "Dietary" "to al thos indifferent," in preparation for the jarring message: Death waits to pounce with "sodeine violence," to strike down both young and old, and to level the playing field by age, by status, by gender all "by stroke of pestilence." This is the sounding of an apocalyptic warning, a hue-and-cry emergency, a heavenly sign to prepare for the judgment to come. The virtual audibility of the series of actions taken by Death is difficult to dismiss even in written form.

Lydgate's opening gambit gives voice to the gravitas and fearsome countenance of the figure of Death depicted in an illustration called "Death and a Dying Man," in which the skeletal personification approaches the dying man with raised rod poised to inflict injury (Figure 5).[46] This is a fearsome contrast to the visual images of a skeleton that at first glance appears to be more comic than not, a human shape devoid of flesh, not frozen in coffin-like repose but moving to the rhythms of life, dancing or "hopping," as each candidate is escorted to the grave.[47] To augment the authority of the message in the words of the "translator," the poet follows up by animating the voice of the more authoritative *auctor* who, as the poem's creator, reminds his "creatures" that the eternality of the soul depends upon how conscientious life is lived in the material world. This is the voice of authority whose words carry greater weight than that of scribe, compiler, or commentator, if we look to Bonaventure's distinctions among the roles of those who produce texts, whose voice trumps that of the translator, whose work bridges one language community and another.[48] The image of the *Danse Macabre* is more than a mere *memento mori*, in other words, but rather

---

[46] The image is found in Oxford Bodleian Library, MS Selden supra 53, f. 118r.
[47] Sophie Oosterwijk, "Lessons in 'Hopping': The Dance of Death and the Chester Mystery Cycle," *Comparative Drama* 36.3/4 (2002): 249-87. See also Clifford Davidson and Sophie Oosterwijk, *John Lydgate: The Dance of Death, and Its Model, the French Danse Macabre* (Leiden: Brill, 2021).
[48] See *The Idea of the Vernacular: An Anthology of Middle English Literary Theory, 1280-1520*, ed. Jocelyn Wogan-Browne, Nicholas Watson, Andrew Taylor, and Ruth Evans (University Park: Pennsylvania State University Press, 1999), 4.

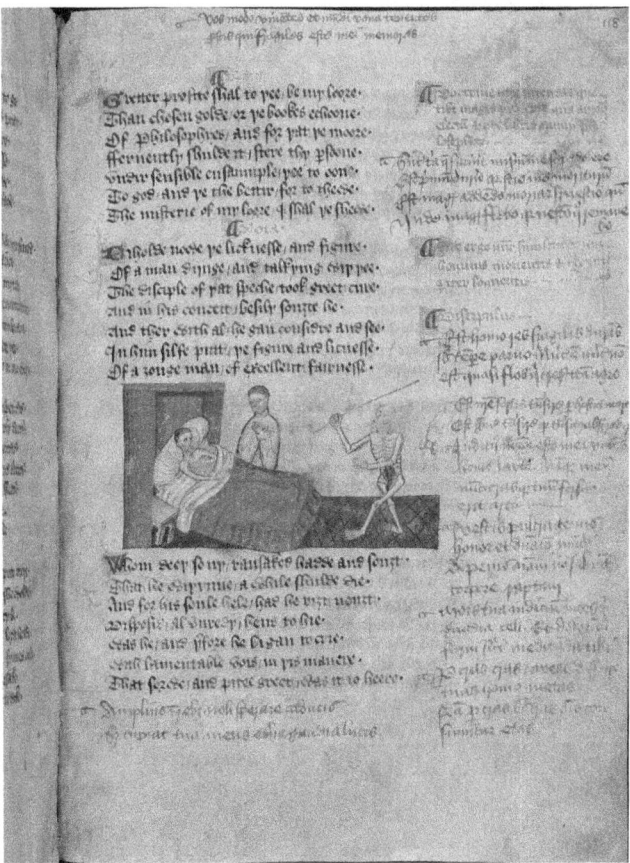

Figure 5 Death and a Dying Man. MS Selden Supra 53, f.118r. By permission of the Bodleian Library, Oxford.

a visual and textual prescription for living that enters the body through the ears and the eyes before it wends its way to heart and brain.

> *Verba Auctoris*
> O creatures ye that ben resonable
> The liif desiring wiche is eternal,
> Ye may se here doctrine ful notable,
> Youre lif to lede wich that is mortal,
> Therby to lerne is especial
> Howe ye shul trace the Daunce of Machabre,
> To man and woman yliche natural,
> For deth ne spareth hy ne lowe degré.
>
> (ll. 41–48)

In the authoritative voice of the author, Lydgate reinforces the message of the translator when he reiterates the necessity for his audience to heed the warning that life eternal is conditional and predicated upon a return to faith. As the great leveler of status, however that status is constructed, those of high degree are just as likely to succumb as those of low degree, and all humans, men as well as women and children, are subject to the same outcome, lest they change their attitudes and turn to God. This is an aspect of a poem filled with dialogues that render the conversation between Death and the Physician so significant.

Death and the Physician: A Dialogue

This is the dialogue that gets to the heart of the discontent and suspicion to which physicians are subject when uncertain about their remedies or their treatments fail entirely. Lydgate fills the gap in this portrayal, animating the voice of the "Fisician" to address his attempt to prevent or cure the pestilence decisively. Reminiscent of Chaucer's Physician, whose portrait in the margins of the Ellesmere manuscript depict him holding the jurdon up to the light for a better read of its fluid, Lydgate's Fisician also gazes upon the jurdon and the urine it contains "agein the sonne." As is the case with the other dialogues in the poem, each one designates the directionality of the spoken word in a way that echoes the liturgical call and response structure.

> Deeth to the Fisician:
> "Maister of phisik, wiche on youre uryne
> So loke and gase and stare agein the sonne,
> For al youre craft and studie of medicine,
> Al the practyk and sience that ye konne,
> Your lyves cours so ferforthe is ironne.
> Agein my myght youre craft may not endure
> For al the golde that ye therby have wonne.
> Good leche is he that can himsilfe recure."
> The Fiscian answerith:
> "Ful longe agon that I unto phisik
> Sette my witt and my dilligence,
> In speculatif and also in practik,
> To gete a name thorugh myn excellence,
> To finde oute agens **pestilence**

Preservatives to staunche it and to fine,
But I dar seie, shortly in sentence,
Agen Deeth is worth no medicine."

(ll. 417-32)

The dialogue is relevant to the Fisician's practice in relation to one of the most contentious medical issues of the time, that is, the inability of doctors to "cure" the pestilence. Death's opening statement is especially compelling in this regard: he summarizes the course of the Fisician's life, his acquisition of medical knowledge, his dedication to that enterprise, only to end by suggesting that his efforts were all for nothing. Given the dialogue's inclusion in a poem that repeats the inevitability of bodily demise, the reference seems to be quite literal in its depiction of a physician who has failed in treating a disease he cannot cure even in himself. That the reading is as allegorical as it is literal appears to be substantiated by the physician's response: he invests himself in the theory and practice of medicine only to discover that "agens pestilence / Preservatives to staunche it and to fine /... Agen Deeth is worth no medicine" (ll. 429-32). All the expertise and gold in the world (whether used as potable medication or as a means by which a doctor might support himself and his practice) are not enough to reverse the lethal effects of the plague, especially if the doctor is afflicted with the disease. As in the more positive reading of Chaucer's Physician provided by Carole Rawcliffe and discussed in an earlier chapter, Lydgate's medical man indicates neither indifference nor callous disregard, but rather acknowledgment of the challenges of an illness for which he knows no certain remedy.

Lydgate Meets Hoccleve Virtually

While Lydgate and Hoccleve are not likely to have met in person, themes such as those represented in the *Danse Macabre* and other works collectively designated "death poetry" can be found together in a single manuscript—Oxford Bodleian Library MS Selden Supra 53—in which the illustration noted above also appears. Both poets are clearly attuned to death as a silent art form used for distraction and entertainment as well as one that sounds an alarm in the souls of its readers, shocking them into reassessing their lives in preparation for mortal demise. That there was an art to dying is captured in the *ars moriendi* in which Henry Suso was a prominent author is attested to by Hoccleve's translation and inclusion of the piece in the collection of works that has come to be known as the *Series*.[49]

The useful art of dying (*Lerne for to Dye*) seems especially appropriate for the *Series* right from the start when Hoccleve's "Complaint" describes an illness he identifies as his "wilde infirmitee," a "thoghtful maladie," a condition induced, according to the narrator's nonmedical friend in the subsequent Dialogue, by too much studying. The friend's remedy for Thomas's illness is to write something that will counter his allegedly unflattering views of women as depicted in his translation of Christine de Pizan's *Epistre au Dieu d'Amours*. Despite Thomas's rejection of that allegation and what he believes to be his friend's inaccurate assessment, he nonetheless acquiesces and produces two fables from the *Gesta Romanorum*, following his translation of Suso's *Ars Moriendi*.

The "Complaint," which contains a detailed account of the narrator's debilitating illness, has encouraged contemporary critics to speculate on the poet's condition, even to the point of diagnosing it as a "nervous breakdown" or a "psychosomatic" ailment of some sort.[50] Clearly, the narrator exhibits symptoms that would indicate a level of anxiety, even to the point of a state of depression that affects his sense of self. Since medieval medicine made no distinction between the psychological and the physiological, the notion of a psychosomatic illness is more in alignment with the basic medical assumption that all illnesses originated in the body. "Since humours were seen as shaping individual temperaments," as Corinne Saunders notes, "it seemed unsurprising that their disorder was seen as potentially affecting the mind as well as the body."[51] Nonetheless, it is important to note that mental disorders were divided into categories that included not only melancholy but mania, phrenitis, and epilepsy. Of these maladies, Saunders observes,

> Most important was melancholy (caused by excess of black bile), which probably included the diseases now classified as depression, schizophrenia and paranoia, and which was often seen as the origin of other mental disorders. Melancholy was characterized by fear or suspicion, and by sadness of an enduring nature,

---

[49] According to Cook and Strakhov, "Among the A manuscripts, there is a strong association between the Dance of Death and the work of Lydgate's fellow Chaucerian Thomas Hoccleve. Hoccleve's *Series*, which includes his translation of Henry Suso's *Ars moriendi* ... appears in five of the manuscripts containing the A version." See also Roger Ellis, ed., "*My Compleinte*" *and Other Poems* (Exeter, UK: University of Exeter Press, 2001). All quotations are taken from Ellis's edition in conjunction with J. A. Burrow, ed., *Thomas Hoccleve's Complaint and Dialogue*, EETS, 313 (Oxford: Oxford University Press, 1999).

[50] Mathew Boyd Goldie, "Psychosomatic Illness and Identity in London, 1416-1421: Hoccleve's Complaint and Dialogue with a Friend," *Exemplaria* 11.1 (1999): 23-52.

[51] Saunders, "'The thoghtful maladie,'" 67-87 (70).

sometimes by sleeplessness or hallucinations, or by atypical social behaviour, whether withdrawal from society or fear of being alone.[52]

There is also a further distinction to be made between melancholy and mania that illuminates the disconcerting feelings that Thomas describes in his "Complaint." According to Luke DeMaitre, melancholy and mania were considered chronic mental illnesses that overlapped yet "were also sharply differentiated":

> Mania was defined as a disorder of the imaginative faculty in the frontal cell of the brain and characterized by fury and explosive energy. It was attributed to an imbalance or inflammation of the hot and dry yellow bile that, in turn, might be due to dietary errors or such emotional triggers as anger. Mania was most likely to occur in spring and summer, and in youth. Melancholy was understood as a malfunction of the *estimativa* and *cogitativa* faculties of reason in the central cell, which was manifested by suspicion and gloom. Predictably, it was most common in fall and winter. It was blamed on superfluous or burned-out black bile, which might be caused by vapors arising from some foods or from incomplete digestion, not only in the stomach but also in the liver and other parts of the nether regions.[53]

Making a differential diagnosis between melancholy and mania not only foregrounds the distinctions between these two conditions but reveals the ways in which they could be confused one for the other or conflated entirely. Add to the challenges of diagnosis the condition called "franesie," or phrenitis, a disease often confused with melancholy and mania but distinguished by the fever and delirium that accompanied it. For medieval physicians, the accuracy of diagnosis demanded observation and questioning of the patient, an interpretation of the body as if it were a text to be read and explicated. Akin to the diagnostic procedures of narrative medicine noted earlier, Thomas discloses the nature of his illness through the telling of what the audience is led to believe is a personal story, one that acknowledges the observations of the narrator's friends on his behavior and appearance. In his recounting of the illness he claims to have suffered five years in the past but now has overcome, Thomas looks into a mirror to try to see what everyone around him is seeing. What emerges is a significant

---

[52] Saunders, "'The thoghtful maladie,'" 70.
[53] Luke Demaitre, *Medieval Medicine: The Art of Healing from Head to Toe* (Santa Barbara, CA: Praeger, 2013). The distinction made by Demaitre is also found in John of Trevisa's translation of Bartholomaeus Anglicus's *De Proprietatibus Rerum*, as noted in the *MED*: "madnes is infeccioun of the myddel celle of the heed with privacioun of resoun ... these passiouns beth divers: madnes that hatte mania & madness that hatte malencolia" (135).

disparity between his sense of himself and the way others perceive him. Like the difference in perception between a patient and her doctor, arriving at an accurate diagnosis requires a comprehensive understanding of all the issues involved. Clearly, Thomas has undergone a transformation at odds with the changes his friends have witnessed in him.

Change and "variaunce," in fact, become thematic threads throughout the "Complaint" and the *Series* as a whole, and while this suggests Boethian influence, there is more to Thomas's disclosure of his medical status than simply a downturn of Fortune's wheel. When the focus shifts from conventional tropes to details of a material environment and a body/soul in distress, there is more to be said about the psychophysiological presentation of a chronic mental illness more akin to melancholy than mania. Even the lovesickness so prevalent in the work of other authors and taken seriously as an illness in Lydgate's *Fabula mercatorum duorum* is ruled out in this case.[54] There is, for instance, an absence of the symptoms of the species of madness caused by unrequited desire, no overt malaise or physical paralysis, but rather erratic movement of eyes and legs, inarticulate speech, and indecorous demeanor. Neither is there an indication of any courtly relationship with an unattainable lover nor the seasonal setting of courtship or mating—no verdant meadows, no sun-seeking daisies, no chirping birds. Instead, there is a distinctly noncourtly change of season noted in the work's Prologue: "Aftir that hervest inned had his sheves / And that the broun sesoun of Mihelmesse / Was come, and gan the trees robbe of her leves / That grene had ben and in lusty freisshnesse, / And hem into colour of yelownesse / Had died and doun thrown undirfoote, / That chaunge sank into myn herte roote" (ll. 1-7). This is the time of the year—the "brown season of Michaelmas [late September]"—in which Thomas lies awake as he mulls over the "thoghtful maladie" that "so vexyd me." The illness he calls a "wylde infirmitee"[55] so immerses him in a shadow of darkness that he wishes to die: "the dirke shour / Hilded doun right on me and in languor / Me made swymme so that my spirite / To lyve no lust had, ne no delyte" (ll. 25-28). His friends tell him that he looks like a "wylde steer" (l. 120), his feet and eyes dart here and there; he experiences the loss of his "tonges keye" (l. 144), his ability to speak coherently; he feels "now frosty cold / how fyry hoot" (l. 154).

---

[54] See Christina von Nolcken, "'O, Why ne had I learned for to Die?': *Lerne for to Dye* and the Author's Death in Thomas Hoccleve's Series," in *Essays in Medieval Studies: Proceedings of the Illinois Medieval Association* (Chicago: Illinois Medieval Association, 1987), 25-51.

[55] The *MED* defines "infirmite" as "disease, sickness"; "an instance of a disease, a bout of sickness," and "a plague, an epidemic." Given the integral connection between the universe and the human body, it stands to reason that this species of infirmity applies both to Thomas and to the outside world. Hence, his infirmity is directly related to the pestilence he observes around him.

When he gazes at himself in the mirror, he appears unlike what others have observed, but soon wonders whether he is "blynd" to his own condition. While he talks about his illness as having occurred in the past, he recognizes that others consider him still to be mad: "As yit this day ther deemeth many oon / I am not wel" (ll. 208-09). Nonetheless, he clings to the notion that he has been cured as suddenly as he had been afflicted; both the illness and its remedy come from God, he says: "Right so thogh that my witte were a pilgrim, / And wente fer from home he cam again / God me voided of this grevous venim / That had enfectid and wildid my brain. / See howe the curtise leche moost soverain, / Unto the seke geveth medecyne / In nede and hym releveth of his pine" (ll. 232-38). As if his reason (witte) were a pilgrim who had traveled away from home, he returned again and the "leche moost soverain" provides the medicine to neutralize the venom that has infected and caused havoc in his "brain."

Thomas's affliction is not explicitly indicative of pestilence (had that been the case he most certainly would have died), but rather the psychological trauma the epidemic had the capacity to provoke. The conflicted thoughts and fragmented sense of self, no less than the physical symptoms he describes so vividly, are consistent with a premodern medical diagnosis of melancholia, or what Thomas comes to diagnose in himself as the "thoghtful dissese" (ln. 388). And while he credits his eventual recuperation in part to his reading of a book—Isidore of Seville's *Synonyma*—the remedy seems to be more in line with temporary palliative care rather than long-term, decisive "cure." When the tome is taken back rather abruptly by his friend, a full understanding of the advice given by Reason, Isidore's figure of wisdom, is rendered impossible, leaving Thomas's diagnosis unresolved. That the accusation of incomplete reading he makes of the friend who takes his book away is one reason for Thomas's lingering illness is testimony to the problematics of such reading. Had the diagnosis been accurate Thomas and his friend might have realized that melancholy is a serious malady, as potentially deadly in its own way as the actual plague. That he expresses a wish to die more than once—"To lyve / no lust hadde, ne no delyt" (l. 28) and "His tyme is me to crepe into my grave" (l. 261)—provides additional evidence for the seriousness of his condition. For Penelope Doob, "Hoccleve thus paints an accurate and convincing portrait of the melancholic man as described in medical treatises; the use of commonly recognized symptoms and cures contributes greatly to the realism and vividness of the account."[56] Whether Thomas's testimony is autobiographical

---

[56] Penelope B. R. Doob, *Nebuchadnezzar's Children* (New Haven: Yale University Press, 1974), 218.

or simply the work of a writer in tune with the medical discourses of the day seems a moot point when the narrative is believed to be so authentic by so many readers. The ailment that Thomas describes is neither imaginary nor in the category of divine madness as exhibited by preeminent prophets and saints, but rather a condition both realistic and credible, decidedly nonprophetic and unsaintly. The cadences of speech, the level of despair, the loss of the will to live, the darting eyes and feet, and the appearance of "wyldenesse" and "braynseek[ness]" add up to something other than an abstract literary madness inspired ostensibly, in this case, by the reading of a book. Even were it the case that Thomas replicated medical treatises for his listing of symptoms, the anguish he evinces is more than detached intellectual acknowledgment or mindless scribal copying. Rather, his descriptions register experience in the world not derived entirely from textual authority but from life itself. At least that is what Thomas seems to be saying. Hoccleve, on the other hand, seems to say something else.

The details that underscore the authentic-sounding persona in the "Complaint"—his disclosure of his age (fifty-three years) as well as the nature of his illness—recall the poet's earlier work, "La Male de Regle" (1402), in which he appeals to the god of Health, to whom he enumerates his youthful and subsequently regrettable pursuit of pleasure. The personal disclosures, the confessional themes, and the centrality of the sickness brought on by the speaker's admitted profligacy—too much revelry and not enough discipline—establish something of a baseline for what Thomas describes in his later works. Reason, who becomes a significant figure in the "Complaint," is notably cast aside in this early work for the sake of riotous living: "Reson me bad, and redde as for the beste, / To ete and drynke in tyme attemprely, / But wilful youthe nat abeie leste / Unto that reed, ne sette nat therby" (ll. 105-08). Thomas admits to having been engaged in worldly excess for many years, for which he has suffered the consequences in the form of illness: "[s]eeknesse, Y meene, riotoures whippe / Habundantly that paieth me my wage, / So that me neithir daunce list, ne skippe" (ll. 118-20). Like the revelers of Chaucer's "Pardoner's Tale," he frequents taverns and delights in playing games of chance. More specifically he identifies his melancholy as having been caused by gluttony: "Excesse of mete and drynke is glotonye; / Glotonye awakith malencolie; / Malencolie engendrith werre and stryf; / Stryf causith mortel hurt thrugh hir folie. / Thus may excesse reve a soule hir lyf" (ll. 300-04). While the link between body and soul underscores an important assumption of humoral theory, the connection between gluttony and melancholy is most relevant here, especially if we recall that certain foods were thought to encourage the overproduction of black bile, the humor taken to be the cause of melancholia.[57]

Also necessary to foreground for diagnostic purposes in relation to the "La Male Regle" is the analogy the speaker makes when he talks about the evils of flattery as a "lurking pestilence" (l. 260).[58] The oddness of the comparison, out of sync as it is with more typical synonyms for this insidious form of persuasion calls attention to the usage. Associated as it is with Ulysses' encounter with the Sirens and his attempt to block his own and his crew's ears for fear of the peril these "mermaids" would bring upon them seems not quite the appropriate descriptor for the experience. And perhaps that jarring misuse is what draws our attention to the line when Thomas uses the word "pestilence" to describe the deadliness of mermaid song. Like the plague recurring throughout Hoccleve's lifetime, lurking in the shadows only to emerge when least expected, flattery threatens to lure the unwary individual into its snares. At the same time there is an undeniable warning, a siren sounding off to alert the audience of an imminent threat. Yet the stunningly offbeat simile is a means by which an attentive audience might access the narrator's thoughts, perhaps even to explain the melancholic madness that Reason's advice, offered in the "Complaint," cannot remedy: "Wrastle... ageyn hevynesse / Of the worlde, troublis, suffringe, and duresse" (ll. 342-43). If the pestilence is lurking in Thomas's disclosure, prompting heaviness, suffering, and suicidal thoughts, his malady is not likely to be cured anytime soon: that the themes of this early work emerge again in the poetry written decades later seems to prove the point.

Knock, Knock, Who's There?

Beginning with an abrupt knocking on Thomas's chamber door the "Dialogue" that commences when his friend appears in the doorway expands upon the themes of melancholic despair. Unlike the casual acquaintances of the "Complaint," the friend in this part of the *Series* offers more than a simple willingness to go on

---

[57] For an interesting discussion of the connections between modern notions of trauma and premodern melancholy, see Donna Trembinski, "Comparing Premodern Melancholy/Mania and Modern Trauma: An Argument in Favor of Historical Experiences of Trauma," *History of Psychology* 14.1 (2011): 80-99.

[58] For a discussion of flattery, see Ethan Knapp, *Bureaucratic Muse*. "Hoccleve, the inveterate flatterer, warns his readers to beware flattery. The irony is heightened by Hoccleve's persistent metaphoric connection between himself and the Sirens in alluding to their 'harmony' as 'poesie'. By creating the metaphoric link Hoccleve casts himself as a Siren and acknowledges the flattering intent of his petitional verse" (41).

pilgrimage on his behalf as Thomas's other friends had. Presented as a benevolent intervention, this friend offers a diagnosis, proclaiming instead that Thomas's illness has been caused by studying too much: "Of studie was engendred thy seeknesse / And that was hard" (ll. 379-80). When Thomas tells his friend of his desire to translate Henry Suso's *Ars moriendi*, a desire that itself suggests chronic melancholy, the friend doubles down on his counsel. When Thomas discloses his intent to finish writing something fitting for Duke Humphrey of Gloucester ("For him it is that this book shal make" [l. 541]), his friend redirects the assignment, advising him instead to make amends to the women he has ostensibly disparaged in his translation of Christine de Pizan's *Epistre au Dieu d'Amours* (Hoccleve's *Letter of Cupid*).[59] And while Thomas rejects his friend's insinuation of misogyny, describing himself as a mere reporter and therefore not accountable for originating the work or manipulating its meaning, he changes his mind and accepts the assignment nonetheless.

This is a choice worth lingering on for a moment since it suggests that meaning is made not by the author of the work or even the translator/reporter but rather by the reader. In terms of narrative medicine, this paradigm would presume the reading of the body as the action that generates an understanding of that body from which emerges an accurate diagnosis and an acceptable treatment plan. Are Thomas's readers the diagnosticians in this scenario or are they collectively sick and in need of their own remedies? Certainly, Thomas's friend seems to gain something from the verbal exchange, even to the point of being understood as a figure for the reader.[60] And just as certainly as his friend receives something of benefit to him, the audience gains something from being made privy to a conversation that focuses on what it means to achieve a state of well-being if only by comparison. Whatever the answer is to the vexing question of whether misogyny is written into his translation of Christine de Pizan's *Epistre au Dieu d'Amours*, Thomas expresses remorse and apologizes directly to "the ladies" in the audience: "My ladyes all, as wisly God me blesse, / Why that yee meeved been can I nat knowe. / My gilt cam nevere yit to the ripnesse, / Althogh yee for your fo me deeme and trowe. / But I your freend be, byte me the crowe / I am al othir to yow than yee weene. / By my wrtynge hath it and shal be seene" (ll. 806-12). This is the point at which he launches an "Englishing" of the first fable from the *Gesta Romanorum*. But first a word on the useful art of dying.

---

[59] Rory G. Critten, "Imagining the Author in Late Medieval England and France: The Transmission and Reception of Christine de Pizan's 'Epistre au dieu d'Amours' and Thomas Hoccleve's *Letter of Cupid*," *Studies in Philology* 112. 4 (2015): 680-97.

[60] See Taylor Cowdery, "Hoccleve's Poetics of Matter," *Studies in the Age of Chaucer* 38 (2016): 133-64.

Learning to Die

Were it not for the inclusion of the translation of Suso's treatise as Hoccleve's *Lerne for to Dye*, perhaps faking a serious illness or creating a persona to fake a serious illness believable to readers of the text is what we would have here. Like practitioners of Rita Charon's narrative medicine, we become as aware of what is *not* said as we are of what *is* said, aware of disrupted chronologies and gaps in the story, dissonant diction, odd comparisons, text selections, and interpolations that call attention to themselves and the subject of the text in which they appear. When Thomas returns to his translation of Suso's work, his amplification of the original[61] provides evidence of a lingering melancholy animated by several figures in a macabre conversation on the art of dying. In it the poet gets as close as possible to a near-death experience as he recounts the slowing of the pulse, the difficulty breathing, the heaviness of the limbs, and the clouding of the vision and the power of sight: "Stirtemeel gooth my pows [pulse] and ells naght. / Mortel pressures sharply me manace. / My breeth begynneth faille, and eek the draght / Of it fro fer is fet and deepe caght. / No lenger Y now see this worldes light. / Myn yen lost han hir office and might" (ll. 660-65). This is Sapience's lesson as requested by a speaker (later referred to as the "disciple") wanting to gain a better understanding of universal knowledge and all that repository of information entails. In compliance and initiating a more dramatic dialogue, the figure for wisdom, as Sapience was known to be, assumes the image of a dying man to engage in conversation with the disciple in a poignant enactment of artful dying: "Beholde now the liknesse and figure / Of a man dyynge and talking with thee" (ll. 85-86). The "image" as Sapience is subsequently identified assumes the countenance of a thirty-year-old man in the prime of life, too young to die, he says to Death: "O deeth, o deeth, greet is thy crueltee. / Thyn office al to sodeynly doost thow. / Is ther no grace? Lakkist thow pitee? / Spare my youthe. Of age rype ynow / To dye am I nat yit. Spare me now" (ll. 141-45).

The treatise is literally a wake-up call to readers living in the time of the plague to think about the next stage of their soul's existence: the concern enunciated here is that people are not paying heed to the warning signs; they are blind in their thoughts, closed in their minds, and unwilling to know what will become of them when they die; in short, according to the speaker, they lack the fear of God: "And al for lak of dreede of God and awe" (l. 875) and must somehow be

---

[61] Steven Rozenski, "'Your Ensaumple and Your Mirour': Hoccleve's Amplification of the Imagery and Intimacy of Henry Suso's *Ars Moriendi*," *Parergon* 25.2 (2008): 1-16.

shocked into reality. As a reminder of what awaits the unrepentant soul, there is included a vision of Purgatory, its afflictions and "fyry flaumbes." And just to end on a more optimistic note, the speaker includes a vision of the New Jerusalem, the heavenly City of God that awaits penitents eager to atone for their sins. The dying man has delivered a new awareness of the afterlife in a display of wisdom transmitted through his dialogue with Death. At the poem's end he turns to the audience to implore them to learn from his experience, to inhabit his body, to see themselves as recipients of Death's rod: "Let me be your ensaumple and your mirour, / Lest yee slippe into my plyt miserable. / With God, despende of your youthe the flour. / If yee me folwe, into peril semblable / Yee entre shuln. To God yee yow enable" (ll. 295-99). The offer of the dying man to be the example and mirror for a reading audience is reminiscent of Thomas's epiphany as recounted in the "Complaint." In his interpolations, his word choices, and his ability to create realistic dialogue, Hoccleve infuses Suso's treatise with the breath of life even as it emanates from the image of a dying man, amplifying, as Steven Rozenski reminds us, both its imagery and intimacy.[62]

Fables from the *Gesta Romanorum*

Lerne for to Dye is the work that separates the two fables from the *Gesta Romanorum*, the first a story of the trials and tribulations of the virtuous Empress of Rome, conventionally known as "The Tale of Jereslaus's Wife," and the second, a narrative about the trials and tribulations of a first-year college student, known as "The Tale of Jonathas."[63] The first is the choice of text recommended by Thomas's friend to atone for his alleged misogyny, while the second is a request by the friend for the benefit of his unruly fifteen-year-old son, a cautionary tale for young men with a tendency to engage in riotous behavior. At first glance, these tales seem not to be related to one another but appear instead to be antithetical, taken up for different purposes and featuring protagonists who differ by gender as well as the challenges they face. Nonetheless, critics such as Karen Winstead claim that "the two tales have much in common. In fact, their plots are virtually identical. Jonathas, like Jereslaus's wife, repeatedly gets into

---

[62] Rozenski, "'Your Ensaumple and Your Mirour,'" *passim*.
[63] In Roger Ellis's edition these titles appear as follows: "*Fabula de quadam imperatrice Romana*" (The Story of a Certain Roman Empress), and "*Hic additur alia fabula ad instanciam amici mei predilecti assiduam*" ("Here is added another fable at the earnest request of my dear friend").

trouble by trusting the opposite sex."[64] While this is certainly the case, there are many more variations in the details of plot and characterization than this would imply. The following synopses clarify some of those differences.

The first fable is about the virtuous Empress of Rome, whose troubles are reminiscent of Chaucer's and Gower's tales of Custance in which the protagonist suffers exile, assault, a charge of murder, and accusations of infidelity.[65] Left in the company of her brother-in-law when her emperor husband decides to go to the Holy Land, the Empress soon becomes the target of her kinsman's indecent proposal. As in so many female saints' lives, romances, and *exempla* that incorporate the trope of the woman whose virtue is tested usually in sexual ways, the Empress is propositioned by her husband's brother, an act that she escapes. Finding herself alone outside the court, however, her tribulations begin, and she is assaulted several times—hanged by the hair, framed for murder, abducted, betrayed, sexually harassed, and nearly raped. But as this moralized narrative would have it, the rapacious and violent men whom she eludes without forfeiting her chastity acquire diseases that only she can heal. The most dramatic scene of the tale marks that transformative moment. When the Empress, having found sanctuary in an abbey, develops a reputation for healing that traverses the known world, the villains who have harmed her come to seek a cure for their illnesses.[66] In a trope that enables public disclosure of the injustices she has suffered at their hands, the Empress, now an abbess, demands their full confession before the healing can commence: "Now shul yee all have of me medecyne. / Shee died hir art and helid every wight / Of his seeknesse and voided al his pyne" (ll. 925-27). She then reveals her identity to all those in attendance, including, of course, the villainous men she has just healed. Proven to be innocent vis-à-vis the confessions of her assailants, she is reunited with her emperor husband and heralded as a model of compassion and forgiveness.

The second fable, the "Tale of Jonathas," as it has become known, concerns a young man who is given three magical objects at the death of his father: a ring, a brooch, and a cloth with the caveat to avoid dishonest, untrustworthy, and wicked women. As it turns out, the young man is instructed by his mother

---

[64] Karen Winstead, "'I am al other to yow than yee weene': Hoccleve, Women, and the *Series*," *Philological Quarterly* 72.2 (1993): 143-55 (149).

[65] See Holly A. Crocker, *The Matter of Virtue: Women's Ethical Action from Chaucer to Shakespeare* (Philadelphia: University of Pennsylvania Press, 2019).

[66] Holly A. Crocker, "Engendering Affect in Hoccleve's Series," in *Medieval Affect, Feeling, and Emotion*, ed. Glenn D. Burger and Holly A. Crocker (Cambridge, UK: Cambridge University Press, 2019), 70-89. The ailments the men contract "index the harms perpetrated against the Empress" (76).

to take care of the gifts he has been bequeathed. She gives him the ring and sets him on his way to the university where he almost immediately finds a paramour (Fellicula)[67] eager to acquire the ring that brings wealth and love to its wearer. As the astute reader will immediately anticipate, the ring is stolen by Fellicula, at which point the completely bamboozled Jonathas returns home to tell his mother his tale of woe. Instead of lecturing her son on his foolishness, however, his mother gives him the second object, the brooch, along with another caveat to take care of his gifts. As with the ring, the magical brooch provides Jonathas with everything he wants until Fellicula tricks him a second time, covering up the theft with her seductive words. Once again, Jonathas returns to his mother to tell his tale and acquire his third and final gift. This is the "cloth" that, like a magic carpet, will soon take Jonathas and his lover to an unfamiliar and frightening otherworld. As in the case of the other two objects, Fellicula steals the carpet and abandons Jonathas in this terrifying place where he burns his feet to the bone in an unknown body of water and eats the fruit of a strange tree that gives him leprosy. These two afflictions are soon reversed by antidotes—healing water and fruit—a remedy he shares with the physicians he meets on their way to a king who is also a leper whom many have tried but failed to cure. Having heard Jonathas' story of the healing water and fruit, they offer these remedies to the king, who is immediately cured. That is not the end of the tale, however. When Fellicula falls ill many years later, Jonathas, who has become a renowned physician by that time, is called into her presence for diagnostic purposes, and as any conscientious doctor would do, he checks her urine and her pulse—"He sy hir uryne and eek felte hir pous" (l. 604)—before making a determination. But because her sickness is "strange and merveillous," he says, rather than administering the water and fruit that had cured his own malady in the otherworld, he administers the water and the fruit that burned the flesh off his feet and changed him into a leper. The result of the treatment is dramatic and horrifying: "Hir wombe opned and out fil eche entraille / That in hir was" (ll. 664-65). Instead of healing his former paramour, he sees to it that she dies wretchedly for her deception and theft. Without an expression of remorse, Jonathas recuperates the purloined magical objects Fellicula had stolen, returns home to his virtuous mother, and lives in joy and prosperity for the rest of his life.

---

[67] Fellicula's name here has resonance with health and the body. According to Isidore of Seville in his account of the history of medicine "[t]he Greeks call yellow bile [such] because it is bounded by the space of one day, whence also it is called choler, that is, fellicula, for this is an effusion of bile." See Faith Wallis, ed. *Medieval Medicine: A Reader*, 7.

Reading the Fables Allegorically

Acquiescing to a prompt from his book-savvy friend, Thomas adds the moralizations typically found after each tale in the *Gesta Romanorum*, in what he calls "prose wrytynge... hoomly and pleyn" (l. 977). As all such supplements in this well-known and widely disseminated work, the *moralites* were thought to guide readers toward an orthodox interpretation of the colorful *exempla* deployed in part to humanize the dry didacticism of sermons. In these two tales, for example, Jereslaus' wife becomes a figure for the soul, while Jonathas becomes the test case for a never-ending human battle against carnality. The villains in the stories—the four rapacious men in the first tale and the deceitful paramour in the second—challenge the virtue necessary for the soul to be reformed and granted an optimum place in the afterlife. The narratives are thus allegorized for purposes of the health and welfare not of the body temporal but of the soul eternal.

Read as allegory, the narrative provides another level of meaning in the exegetical model of interpretation that ecclesiastics were expected to understand and practice in their explications of biblical narratives. Yet, as several critics have observed, the collection of moral *exempla* was not confined to the clergy but rather extended to nonclerical groups of readers, including women and children.[68] A wider nonclerical audience such as this also accounts for Thomas's decision to write in plain prose rather than an artful form of poetry that could easily be misinterpreted. Reading from the perspective of allegory does not preclude other levels of interpretation, of course, but it does change the emphasis of the narrative by removing the tale from a living environment and relocating it to the realm of the symbolic where hidden meanings need to be uncovered and interpreted.[69] If read exclusively through the perspective of allegory, the tale becomes a didactic moral lesson rather than a story designed to lift the spirits and stimulate the imagination of a lay audience mixed by gender, age, and status. This is the standard of storytelling and interpretation for the fables of the *Gesta Romanorum*.

---

[68] Lynnea Brumbaugh-Walter, "Selections from the *Gesta Romanorum*," in *Medieval Literature for Children*, ed. Daniel T. Kline (New York: Taylor & Francis, 2003), 29–44.

[69] For Angus Fletcher, *The Theory of a Symbolic Mode* (Ithaca, NY: Cornell University Press, 1966), there is a connection between allegory and the fear of contagion. According to Jeremy Tambling, "Allegory and the Madness of the Text: Hoccleve's *Complaint*," *New Medieval Literatures* 6 (2003): 223–48, "[Fletcher] refers to a relationship between contagion, sickness, and allegory; the Latin *infectio* means a dyeing, or staining, just as allegory as a form of symbolic expression is a staining of the subject" (226).

When read allegorically, the medical details embedded in a story of sex and violence evaporate into the mist of abstraction wherein the act of sacralization obfuscates maladies and treatments explicitly cited. Instead, healing of the spiritual sort overtakes the scene and brings about a swift denouement that circumvents the realities of the afflictions noted in the tale. In both fables the Empress who has become a holy woman renowned for her healing skills and Jonathas, the young man who has acquired mastery over "physik," confront challenges to their medical expertise. In the first tale, the four villains come down with illnesses known to a medieval audience from real-world experience: leprosy, palsy, blindness, deafness, gout, and "franesie" (frenzy).[70] And while one might expect the most devastating disease of Hoccleve's era to be represented on this list perhaps as earlier insinuated in "La Male Regle" as the "lurking pestilence," it does not appear overtly. Instead, these medical conditions, many of which are associated with the behaviors carried out by the male villains, are physically visible and fully identifiable. That said, the odd one on the list—franesie—seems to be in another category of illness, calling attention to itself, especially in relation to Thomas's melancholy. Frenzy, or phrenitis as it is called medically, is differentiated from both melancholy and mania not only because it is an inflammation of the brain characterized by fever and delirium but because it is an illness signaled by erratic behavior.[71] The assignment of this malady thus appears to be in accordance with the earlier rape attempt while also alluding if only by way of contrast to Thomas's melancholy.

Each of these conditions would present a challenge to a conscientious physician attuned to the scientific aspects of medical treatment, but the Empress is "a woman so holy / And therto so konnynge" that she is presumed to be capable of driving away "seeknesses alle," simply by "doing her art": "Shee died hir art and helid every wight / Of his seeknesse and voided al his pyne" (ll. 926-27), though not before her "patients" have made a public confession. And while the need for confession of the transgressor Fellicula is also present in the "Tale of Jonathas"—"Lady, yee muste openly yow confesse" (l. 617)—she recognizes that without full disclosure, regaining her former status would be impossible. Of course, her expectation for clemency is not forthcoming and she is subjected to a horrifying death.

---

[70] While Roger Ellis glosses this term in his edition as "dementia," a gloss that conjures thoughts of Alzheimer's disease, it is more likely that the term refers to phrenitis.
[71] The *Gesta Romanorum* was compiled originally in Latin in the thirteenth century before the bubonic plague hit Europe, which may account for why he does not add "pestilence" to this list of ailments.

It is also worth noting that while the virtuous Roman Empress heals the bodies of her assailants swiftly and without malice aforethought, the scenario is not the same in Jonathas' tale. Rather, the juxtaposition of antidotes and poisons, the causative with the curative, made apparent in the protagonist's earlier experience underscores the interaction of opposites central to the humoral concept of medicine. As ancient Greek philosophers and physicians as well as later medieval healers were aware, sometimes a therapeutic medication had the capacity to exacerbate the disease it was supposed to cure, to do harm as well as to heal.[72] While there are clearly symbolic implications in the efficacy of the curing water and the healing fruit, Jonathas' use of their lethal effects to punish rather than to cure illuminates both the poisonous potential of therapeutic medicine and the importance of the credibility of the medical practitioner. As noted above, the lady in question (Fellicula) offers her confession fully expecting that Jonathas in his role as professional healer will provide efficacious treatment for her illness. Her death despite her confession is shockingly graphic and no doubt staged to elicit that very response, that is, to shock an audience into paying attention to, if not feeling the pain of, what just transpired.

If we recall Thomas's translation of the *Ars Moriendi* wherein the dying man laments that people do not fear God, the graphic violence of this scene would certainly strike a chord in the hearts of its readers. Fellicula's gruesome death would surely capture the attention of Thomas's friend and his unruly fifteen-year-old son, the ostensible *raison d' être* for the tale. No doubt the women readers to whom these narratives were directed to ameliorate Thomas's alleged misogyny would also take notice. That the young and naïve Jonathas suffers at the hands of a deceitful paramour and later carries out a grotesque revenge in his capacity as a physician adds up to a memorable and cautionary tale especially for those who identify with the unvirtuous. Whether the narrative retains the antifeminist sentiment that Thomas was advised to eradicate through the telling of a more palatable, pro-feminist story seems instead deliberately abandoned. The same could be said for the fable that casts the virtuous Roman Empress in the role of serial victim, albeit resourceful one, with an ending that reunites her with the emperor husband who abandoned her for the sake of his own salvation. It is also worth noting in terms of the gendered differences between these two fables that while Fellicula dies a horrifying death in the "Tale of Jonathas," the four villains in the "Tale of Jereslaus's Wife" are healed of their afflictions. Such

---

[72] See the *Phaedrus* in *The Collected Dialogues of Plato*, ed. Edith Hamilton and Huntington Cairns (Princeton, NJ: Princeton University Press, 1961), 475-525. There is also a question of whether writing is a remedy or a poison.

gender differences encourage scholars to wonder why the poet would dedicate the *Series* to Joan Beaufort, the Countess of Westmoreland, as he does in an autographed version of the work.

Go Little Book, Go!

In an envoi reminiscent of the ending of Chaucer's *Troilus and Criseyde*, Hoccleve sends a copy of his work to one of the most influential noblewomen in England, the only daughter of John of Gaunt and Katherine Swynford, and a prominent member of the Lancastrian dynasty. As was typical for such conventional dedications, Hoccleve presents himself as humble petitioner imploring a woman of higher status to receive his work in the spirit in which it is being given, that is, to "please hir wommanhede":

> Go, smal book, to the noble excellence
> Of my lady of Westmerland, and seye
> Hir humble servant with al reverence
> Him recommandith unto hir nobleye
> And byseeche hir on my behalve and preye
> Thee to receyve for hir owne right,
> And looke thow in al manere weye
> To please hir wommanhede do thy might.
> Humble servant to your gracious noblesse,
>
> (ll. 733-41)

T. Hoccleve

This is the holograph copy bequeathed circa 1422 to the Countess of Westmoreland[73] that prompts questions as to why the poet would have thought it appropriate to dedicate a work containing negative stories about women as in the "Tale of Jonathas" to such a formidable noblewoman.[74] She does, of course, belong to the Lancastrian court to which Thomas considers himself an affiliate, however tangential, though clearly his desire to write something for Duke Humphrey of Gloucester suggests closer connections. Presumably then he would be familiar with the countess's personal history: that she was the

---

[73] Lee Patterson, "'What Is Me?': Self and Society in the Poetry of Thomas Hoccleve," *Studies in the Ages of Chaucer* 23 (2001): 437-70 (450).

[74] Ibid. As did many widows of the time, the countess joined a religious order later in life, in this case, the Sisterhood of the Abbey of St. Albans, where she lived until her death in 1440.

"legitimated" daughter of John of Gaunt and Katherine Swynford and "the niece of Chaucer";[75] that her first marriage [to Robert Ferrers] was arranged when she was fourteen years old; that she gave birth to two daughters shortly thereafter; that when Ferrers died, she married Ralph Neville and gave birth to another fourteen children, four of whom died at a young age; that after Neville's death, she accrued additional wealth and landholdings; that she, a niece of Chaucer, encouraged literary culture; and that she had in her possession a number of manuscripts, not only including Chaucer's *Troilus and Criseyde* but also the works of others, such as the *Chronicles of Jerusalem, The Voyage of Godfrey Boullion*, a French translation of William of Tyre's *Historia rerum in partibus transmarinis gestarum*, Gower's *Confessio amantis*, and a book identified as "Tristrem," thought to be Thomas of Erceldoune's *Sir Tristrem*.[76] The point to be made here is this: Joan Beaufort, Countess of Westmoreland, was neither a naïve ingenue nor an out-of-touch matron even in her sequestered widowhood. Rather, by all accounts, she was fully engaged in the interpersonal politics of the nobility and intensely involved in the literary and religious cultures of the time. Perhaps for these reasons she was an appropriate recipient and potential patron for Hoccleve's work. As Holly Crocker observes, "It would be hard... for the Countess of Westmoreland to reject Hoccleve's petition for favor, even if she objected to his characterization of women's deceptiveness, destructiveness, and greed.... Only those women who are themselves at fault will object to his representation of feminine perfidy. Virtuous women, by contrast, will prove their worth through their approval of Thomas' writing."[77]

There are, of course, virtuous women in the fables of the *Gesta Romanorum* who would certainly pique the interest of the countess and her ladies no less than the intricacies of plot and characterization, the incorporation of magical objects, harrowing escapes, and vivid transformations. The first of these virtuous women would be the Empress of Rome, who, at the end of a series of tribulations, entered a women's religious community, rose to the position of abbess, and earned a reputation for healing. The second would be, as Crocker points out, the mother of Jonathas who gives him the gifts his father had bequeathed with explicit caveats to take care of them. Jonathas' mother, despite her seemingly secondary position, functions nonetheless as the moral center of the narrative, the woman to whom Jonathas returns at the tale's end. In other words, while

---

[75] *Thomas Hoccleve: A Facsimile of the Autograph Verse Manuscripts*, with Introduction by J. A. Burrow and A. I. Doyle, EETS, s.s. 19 (Oxford: Oxford University Press, 2002), xxxi.
[76] *The Oxford Dictionary of National Biography*, npa.
[77] Crocker, "Engendering Affect in Hoccleve's Series," 70-89.

both stories depict antifeminist sentiment and violence against women, so too do they address the role of women in healing and caring for others in some way. Even Fellicula, the most destructive of the female characters in these tales, sets Jonathas' transformation from a naïve young man to an experienced practitioner of medicine into motion. Whether his actions as a physician are justified is, of course, left to the determination of an audience of savvy women readers not the least of whom was an influential noblewoman. As someone who was intimately familiar with the trauma of childbirth, and the death of several children, Joan Beaufort would be an excellent reader of this tale, perhaps even to the extent of finding Jonathas' actions to be somehow justified.

The sequence of writings that comes to be known as the *Series* makes for riveting reading not only in terms of its collective narrative vivacity but for the medical discourse in which Thomas speaks to an audience in need of a provocative reminder of the transience of life. Like the food needed to fuel the body and maintain its humoral balance, a regimen so often emphasized by medical writers, books, and the stories they contain provide food for well-being as well as a new way of thinking about physical and spiritual health. With its references to Isidore of Seville's *Synonyma*, the translated letter of Christine de Pizan, Henry Suso, and the anonymous writers of the *Gesta Romanorum*, as well as an emphasis on the therapeutic effects of writing, clearly Hoccleve's *Series* qualifies as bookish in nature or at the very least fully engaged in the making and dissemination of literature conversant in medical matters.[78] Books gave sustenance to readers whether they were affluent and influential like Joan Beaufort and her circle of friends, family, and acquaintances or when such readers considered written texts to be pertinent resources for diagnosing and treating household illnesses and understanding medical recipes as food for the soul as well as the body. For medical writers as well as medically astute poets such as Lydgate and Hoccleve, "[b]ooks were to be read digestively, through rumination, chewing over the pages in one's mind."[79] Dietetic medicine extended to the digesting of reading matter to hone memory, elevate mood, and uplift the vital spirits of the heart. Stories such as those offered in Thomas's translation of the *Gesta Romanorum* and Suso's treatise on death, as well as his intimate disclosure of madness in the "Complaint" and his cathartic dialogue with a friend, render the *Series* a

---

[78] J. A. Burrow, "Hoccleve's *Series*: Experience and Books," in *Fifteenth-Century Studies: Recent Essays*, ed. Robert F. Yeager (Hamden: Archon Books, 1984), 259-73. As Burrow noted years ago, the *Series* is "a profoundly bookish work … aware of its own existence as a book, or its derivation from other books, and of its destination in the hands of patrons and readers" (260).

[79] Stephen Katz, "Dementia, Personhood and Embodiment: What Can We Learn from the Medieval History of Memory?" *Dementia* 12.3 (2013): 303-14 (307).

work worthy of digesting. In terms of narrative medicine, Hoccleve as writer has positioned his audiences as diagnosticians whose task is to discern the meaning of these often shocking yet highly engaging texts. As were the readers of the past, we are charged with diagnosing this body of work to come to some heightened comprehension of the dis-ease it so urgently articulates; in other words, while we assume the physician's role, as friendly diagnosticians, Thomas assumes the position of patient in need of a doctor's advice. Like the friend who directs him to certain books and encourages his continued writing, we are directed to situate this work within a wider medical discourse in which other prominent authors were known to have participated.[80] As Hoccleve the writer makes clear, reading on its own can fall short of providing a way back to mental health, yet by writing, translating, and acquiring the support of ladies in high places, he can overcome his melancholy, at least in theory.

A close contemporary of Lydgate, Thomas Hoccleve died in 1426, a few years after he sent his work to the Countess of Westmoreland. The cause of death remains unknown. What we do know, however, is that the pestilence was still present in England at the time. When Lydgate died sometime between 1449 and 1451,[81] also of unknown causes, several outbreaks of the plague had occurred, leaving many more deaths in its wake, and anticipating more to come. Whether we understand Hoccleve or Lydgate to have expressed an obsessive concern about the disease lurking around them or the unconscious fear and anxiety it provoked, the works presented here demonstrate both poets' medical consciousness. These poets lived, wrote, and died in the time of the Black Death. What they tell us through their narratives contributes to our heightened awareness of the trauma caused by the pandemic and the significance of the narratives that patient-storytellers disclose even while appearing to avoid the topic.

---

[80] See Knapp's *Bureaucratic Muse* and his comment on the *Series* as "a poem marked by both a self-referential meditation on writing and a form in which the development of narrative tends to exceed the bounds of the framing device" (161).

[81] Derek Pearsall, *John Lydgate, 1371-1449: A Bio-bibliography* (Victoria, CA: ELS Editions, 1997).

4

Inscribing Medicine: Thornton Household Remedies

Who will been holle & keep hym from sekenesse
And resiste the strok of pestilence,
Lat hym be glad, & voide al hevynesse,
Flee wikkyd heires, eschew the presence
Off infect placys, causyng the violence;
Drynk good wyn, & holsum meetis take,
Smelle swote thyng[es], & for his deffence
Walk in cleene heir, eschew[e] mystis blake.

—John Lydgate,
"A Diet and Doctrine for the Pestilence"[1]

In addressing sickness and death, as noted in the previous chapter, both Lydgate and Hoccleve participate in a medical milieu in which pestilence competes for the attention of an increasingly literate and medically conscious vernacular audience. Virtual conversations between poets and medical practitioners, friends and acquaintances, whether in real time or vis-à-vis literary representation prove to be revealing for all affected parties. Writers who represent events of quotidian life provide access to material reality through historical narrative, or pathways into other worlds that offer opportunities for their readers to transcend an unpleasant and threatening environment. Concerns about one's own mental health as well as basic physiological functions, as Hoccleve and Lydgate remind us in much of their work, become enfolded into the language of medicine and manuals for governing the body and thwarting disease. As expressed in the verse epigraph cited above, the advice to distance the body "from sekenesse" by "drynk[ing] good wyn," [eating] "holsum meetis," smelling "swote thynges"

---

[1] *The Minor Poems of John Lydgate, Part III*, ed. Henry Noble MacCracken, EETS (1934): 702, lines 1–8.

and walking in air devoid of "mystis blake" is as pragmatic as it is poetic. To "resiste the strok of pestilence," it says, demands that each individual "be glad, & voide al hevynesse." This is the beginning of Lydgate's "Dietary," in the prologue known as the "Doctrine for the Pestilence," a poem especially relevant in this chapter because it was known to Robert Thornton and copied into his London manuscript, one of two compilations attributed to this fifteenth-century "gentleman, reader, and scribe."[2]

As the excerpt above suggests, what an individual consumed or experienced outside the body affected the health of that body. Self-care and habituated behaviors such as those noted in the "Dietary" and the earlier medical poem, the *Regimen sanitatis Salernitanum*, influenced medical thinking during Thornton's lifetime, raising the medical consciousness of practitioners and nonpractitioners alike. The integral relation between naturals—the humors, their qualities, complexions, and temperaments—and the non-naturals, the "air which surrounds the body… food and drink, exercise and rest, sleep and waking, fasting and fullness, and finally affections of the mind"[3] together demonstrate the centrality of the body and its place in the cosmological scheme of the things. Each internal organ, each bodily fluid, each compartment of the brain had a function predicated upon a humoral system linked inexorably to the planets, the stars, and everything thought to exist beyond the sphere of the Earth. Causes of sickness—attributed to faulty diet, too much or too little to eat or drink, too much exposure to polluted or venomous air, or too little respect for divine authority—made etiological certainty less precise and far more speculative to many practitioners. Health and well-being depended upon the governance of one's own body, to be sure, but also required genuine expressions of piety.

An understanding of the kinship between the human body and the outside world (the natural vs. the non-natural) or the medieval relation between body and soul, for that matter, is in many ways analogous to the kinship between genres of writing, medical prose, on the one hand, and narrative poetry, on the other. How do such genres often considered to be in separate categories intersect thematically in household miscellanies like Robert Thornton's, which, by their very definition, were collections of disparate items? What, if any, tropes or uses of language create a sense of thematic unity among such a wide-ranging gathering

---

[2] George Keiser, "Robert Thornton: Gentleman, Reader and Scribe," in *Robert Thornton and His Books*, ed. Susanna Fein and Michael Johnston (York: York Medieval Press, 2014), 67-108.

[3] Julie Orlemanski, "Thornton's Remedies and the Practices of Medical Reading," in *Robert Thornton and His Books*, ed. Susanna Fein and Michael Johnston (York: York Medieval Press, 2014), 235-55.

of materials or even account for differences between the two compilations themselves? Both the London and Lincoln Cathedral 91 codices contain texts that seem not to relate to one another in any substantive way but rather appear to be selected randomly and without an overall strategy for coherence. Yet if the motives driving Thornton's textual choices in each of these compilations include a desire to "address a variety of needs within a household or family context,"[4] then putting together a range of genres makes perfect sense. While both manuscripts may have been designed, compiled, and copied by Thornton himself, casting an aura of "masculine vernacularity"[5] upon his work, the variety of items in each of these collections suggests a purview and set of concerns beyond the scribe-compiler himself. The contents of these two miscellanies are likely to have appealed to other members of the Thornton clan, in other words, even friends and acquaintances beyond the household. Thornton's awareness of the diversity of his audience of familiars, whether by age, by gender, by social or political status, or by occupation and estate, speaks to his concerns for their welfare while at the same time broadens the scope of his textual repertoire.

Such an expansive vision may be inferred by the variety of selections in each codex. While the contents of the shorter London manuscript appear to feature debates between young and old, skewing toward a concern perhaps for the education of the next generation,[6] those in the Lincoln Cathedral MS 91 represent a more expansive array of genres: romances, prayers, charms, hagiography, sermons, satire, ghost stories, mystical writings, and entries on miscellaneous topics, commemorating a birth and describing thunder, for example.[7] More extensive and varied than the London collection, what differentiates the Lincoln codex from its counterpart even more distinctively is its addition of the medical recipes found in the *Liber de diversis medicinis*, a collection of items located in its final section. If the interests of an audience may be inferred by the diversity and range of a manuscript's contents, then the Lincoln Cathedral manuscript presumes an audience not only interested in listening to exhilarating

---

[4] Phillipa Hardman, "Domestic Learning and Teaching: Investigating Evidence for the Role of 'Household Miscellanies' in Late-Medieval England," in *Women and Writing c. 1340-1650*, ed. A. Lawrence-Mathers and P. Hardman (Woodbridge, UK: York Medieval Press, 2010), 15-33 (21, 23).

[5] Louise Bishop, *Words, Stones, & Herbs: The Healing Word in Medieval and Early Modern England* (Syracuse: Syracuse University Press, 2007).

[6] Such as the "Parlement of the Thre Ages," "Wynnere and Wastoure," the "Childhood of Christ," a childhood narrative of Mary, several romances, and Passion poems. For a complete list of the contents of both manuscripts, see Susanna Fein, "The Contents of Robert Thornton's Manuscripts," in *Robert Thornton and His Books*, ed. Susanna Fein and Michael Johnston (York: York Medieval Press, 2014), 13-65.

[7] *The Thornton Manuscript (Lincoln Cathedral 91)*, Introduction by D. S. Brewer and A. E. B. Owen (London: The Scolar Press, 1974).

tales of adventure, harrowing stories of legendary saints, and uncanny fables of the marvelous and the magical but also keen to have numerous remedies for everyday maladies at their fingertips. That there is considerable attention paid to quotidian life-and-death issues as well as alluring pathways into the world of the imaginary suggests a rationale for the variety of texts in Thornton's selections. As George Keiser observes, the scribe-compiler's

> reason for compiling such a book most certainly was a desire to preserve for himself and his family works that appealed to his tastes and that would improve and uplift their spirits and, in the case of the medical receipts, heal their bodies. In this desire he seems to reflect an attitude common to a society which, except for its poorest members, must have been coming to accept the book as a natural and even necessary aspect of its domestic life.[8]

When provocative stories and pragmatic medical recipes are brought together to "uplift" the spirits of a diverse household, it is not difficult to see how the poetical and the medical might intersect both linguistically and thematically.[9] While narrative poetry speaks to the capacity of literary art to stimulate the body's vital spirits to facilitate a healthy balancing of humors, medical writing addresses psychophysiological ills in a more material way. Care of the body as well as the soul brings the psyche into closer contact with the physiology it is thought to animate, not in the negative way that modern practitioners speak of psychosomatic illness but rather in the humoral understanding of the body's major organs and the animating spirits that influence their functions. The importance of having access to so many mood-altering, if not emotionally cathartic stories cannot be overlooked in view of the strategies of narrative medicine that recognize the importance of storytelling to diagnosis and treatment planning. The telling of tales becomes the means by which the emotional responses of individual audience members are affected, their afflicted bodies transported to other worlds if only for the duration of the telling. Thornton's household readers are akin to patients in need of treatment, to be sure, but they also play the role of diagnosticians who read and interpret the text as medical practitioners read and interpret the body. In a process akin to narrative medicine's urging of medical practitioners to interact more substantively with their patients, Thornton's texts encourage his audience to listen to the tales being told to them, to internalize them, to empathize with characters and situations, and put their fears aside. At

---

[8] George R. Keiser, "Lincoln Cathedral Library MS. 91: The Life and Milieu of the Scribe," *Studies in Bibliography* 32 (1979): 158-79.
[9] One such work, according to Rosalind Field and Dav Smith, is the *Awntyrs off Arthure*, which they date to 1424-5 and suggest that Joan Neville is the likely patron. See Field and Smith, "Afterword: Robert Thornton Country," in *Robert Thornton and His Books*, 257-72.

the same time such narratives remind them to mend their ways before Death comes for them all. There is a subjective dimension to the reading, in other words, that fosters a deeper understanding of what it is to be human and what it takes to stay alive during an epidemic.

The augmented level of medical literacy that may be attributed both to the scribe-compiler and the collection of texts he inscribes and assembles fits into the tenor of the time. Just as the religious milieu began to register a widespread desire among the laity to access authoritative vernacular texts on their own, so too does it appear that such a collective movement, fostered in part by the influence of Wycliff and his followers, prompted a similar desire for pragmatic medical knowledge written in English. That Thornton was active in what amounts to an information-sharing network is especially relevant in relation to the inclusion of the *Liber de diversis medicinis* in the Lincoln compilation. Some of the recipes it contains allude to nearby parishes and local families, and explicitly cite the influence of three men, one identified as the rector of Oswaldkirk, another as Magistrum William de Excestre, and the third as William Appleton (Ser Apilton), a minorite friar, once physician to John of Gaunt.[10] Several recipes are attributed to the Oswaldkirk rector, while one is attributed to Ser Apilton and another to Master William, lending an authoritative status to the collection, each acting as a witness (*probatur*) to the efficacy of the entries associated with them. These three men are not the only authorities cited in the text, but they represent local aficionados within a larger network of medical authorities alluded to in the collection. Margaret Ogden identifies parallels to recipes in Thornton's medical text in the writings of John of Gaddesden, Bernard Gordon, Lanfranc of Milan, Henri de Mondeville, Guy of Chauliac, and John of Arderne, several of whom are mentioned by Chaucer in his description of the Physician in the *Canterbury Tales*.[11] Some of the writings of these famous practitioners overlap in the concerns presented in the *Liber*, revealing an expansive network of medical knowledge that goes well beyond Thornton's home region.

The heightened interest in medical authority discernible during Thornton's lifetime, prompted in part by recurrent outbreaks of pestilence, may be one of the

---

[10] In his essay on the *Holy Boke Gratia Dei*, Keiser adds family names to this network: "Contemporary documents in which Robert Thornton's name appears indicate that his activities may have brought him into contact with such important Yorkshire families as the Rooses, the Stapiltons, and the Gascoignes, all of whom had connections with the Ingilby family and, either through that family or by other means, had connections with Mount Grace. Thus, we have the possibility that Mount Grace was the source, either directly or ultimately, for Robert Thornton's text of GD and perhaps also for other pieces found in his hefty collection of devotional writings" (310). See George R. Keiser, "The Holy Boke Gratia Dei," *Viator* 12 (1981): 289–317.

[11] Margaret Ogden, ed. *The Liber de diversis medicinis*, EETS, 207 (London: Oxford University Press, 1938; reprint 1969).

explanations for the diverse group of people practicing some form of medicine at the time. Not exclusively made up of university-trained physicians but rather, as Julie Orlemanski notes, "apothecaries, astrologers, members of barber-surgeon guilds, itinerant 'leeches' without formal education, midwives, tooth-drawers, parish priests, monastic communities, saints' shrines and members of their own household,"[12] such a widespread interest in health and healing suggests an equally widespread need for medical services. When placed within this extensive network of practitioners, Thornton's medical writings enable us to see not only "how they relate to contemporary genres of scientific and practical knowledge,"[13] but how they contribute to an emerging medical discourse, one that brings poetry into the specialized realm of medical prose. There is more thematic unity within the Lincoln codex than meets the eye, in other words, and texts—both poetical and medical—that seem otherwise unrelated evince greater kinship when examined from the multi-generic perspective of a multidimensional discourse. From structure and organization to content and subject matter, even to shared language use, many of the texts in the collection point to an intense concern about medicine and its practice.

The arrangement of the texts of the Lincoln Thornton, from the positioning of the *Prose Life of Alexander* at its beginning to the *Liber de diversis medicinis* and the fragmented herbal at its end, lends the codex a sense of order akin to that found in a medical manual. Like the *Liber* in which remedies "are arranged according to the part of the body affected, proceeding roughly from head to foot," the codex proceeds from the top down "roughly," according to Ogden, in a way that becomes less organically unified as it progresses.[14] At its beginning, however, the recipes address the head (headaches and ear ailments), the eyes (blurred and obstructed vision), the mouth (especially toothache), the nose, throat and "voice," before proceeding to the heart, the breast, including women's "pappes," the stomach, and lower extremities, at which point it gives way to ailments more specifically defined—dropsy, leprosy, epilepsy, different kinds of fever, and gout—followed by a series of wounds, broken bones, and injuries of varying severity. All these maladies are located both before and after the treatise on the pestilence near the *Liber*'s center, suggesting an awareness about the epidemic still present at the time Thornton was putting his compilation together.

Written predominantly in Middle English with Latin interpolations scattered throughout and launched by a Latin incipit—*Hic Incipit Liber De Diversis*

---

[12] Orlemanski, "Thornton's Remedies," 238.
[13] Orlemanski, "Thornton's Remedies," 235.
[14] Ogden, *Liber*, xvii.

Medicinis & Primo Pro Capite—the remedies vary from the simplest of simples to "elaborate medicaments, compound unguents, potions, and drinks"[15] listed along with the illness or injury for which they are recommended. Directions for making each preparation are also included. As the range of ailments and treatments in the *Liber* suggest, Thornton's contributions to the medical discourse of the time appear to be both extensive and pragmatic. Yet if we understand the symbolic significance of some of the recommendations, many of these prescriptions speak just as surely to the health of the soul as they do the health of the physical body. Many recipes presume a psychophysiological unity that presents itself not only in the listing of ingredients and directions for the making and application of a medication but also in the form of charms and prayers. That many of the tales embody medical tropes that conflate Christian ideology with the scientific principles of medical education is worth noting in view of this body/soul orientation toward health and well-being.

Thornton's acceptance of the Hippocratic-Galenic system no less than the model of bodily governance it incorporates forms a unifying principle for the *Liber*, though, as Ogden points out, the work includes references to Anglo-Saxon medical writers and the Persian and Arab physicians responsible for canonizing so much medical knowledge inherited from the Greeks. In this wider purview of medical history and its development over time, Ogden also acknowledges the significance of the *Antidotarium of Nicholaus* (c. 1140), a Latin compendium of recipes made from plants and minerals, as well as Constantinus Africanus' translations of works from the Middle East. Such a collection of medical texts is impressive even without references to one of the most influential early medical poems, the pre-plague *Regimen sanitatis Salernitanum*, also known as the *Flos medicinae* or *Lilium medicinae*, written in Latin hexameter attributed to the well-known medical school at Salerno. Widely disseminated throughout Europe, the lengthy poem addresses diet, medicinal herbs, humors, and bloodletting in a poetic register that facilitates the reading. Contemporary with the Pseudo-Aristotelian *Secretum Secretorum*, a manual for governing explicitly directed toward Alexander the Great and attributed to Aristotle, the versified *Regimen* is all-the-more memorable for its subject matter, to be sure, but also memorable because of its poetic form. Together, these two works suggest that preventative

---

[15] Ogden, *Liber*, xix. The *Liber* is thought to have been composed sometime between 1422 and 1453 by an anonymous compiler. There are several such recipes. One example follows: "Tak baynewort jus a sawcerfull and als mekill of a rede cowe newe mylke & flour of whete & make it in a plaster & lay it alle warm ther-on & it sal brek it [the buboe]." See Ogden, 54 (ll. 8-10).

medicine, at least for kings, was a necessity for the health of the monarch as well as for his ability to govern well. The assumption was that a king who could not rule over his own body would not be able to rule over the body politic.

John of Burgundy's *De Epidemia* and Thornton's "Medcynes for the Pestilence"

Traditional ordering and textual transmission aside, however, one of the most distinguishing features of the *Liber* is that it contains a plague treatise located near the middle of the text.[16] Introduced by the following incipit in Middle English rather than the Latin of the *Liber*'s title—"Here bygynnes medcynes for the pestilence"—the treatise is a condensed translation of John of Burgundy's widely disseminated text on the subject aptly dubbed *De epidemia*.[17] The much longer Latin original, written c. 1385, is noteworthy for many reasons, but especially because it includes statements from the physician about his familiarity with pestilence, and a first-person testimony that lends additional authority to the doctor's identification of causes, symptoms, and treatments. Much of Burgundy's personal experience as a practicing, university-trained physician has been amended in Thornton's version of the text, copied from an already condensed translation in circulation at the time. Differences in language and length aside, however, comparisons between these two works provide a framework for marking liberties taken in the Thornton text, if not by the independent-minded scribe-compiler himself,[18] then by the anonymous English translator whose exemplar he has chosen to preserve.

---

[16] If the herbal that follows only in fragments were complete, the plague treatise is likely to have fallen in the center of the text. By George Keiser's estimate, the herbal occupied folios 315–21. For information on the transmission of Burgundy's text, see Lister M. Matheson, "*Médecin sans Frontières?*: The European Dissemination of John of Burgundy's Plague Treatise," *ANQ* 18.1 (2005): 19–30.

[17] Though it is not the version signed by "John of Bordeaux," which shows several points of variation and language use. See Marta Powell Harley, "The Middle English Contents of a Fifteenth-Century Medical Handbook," *Mediaevalia* 8 (1982): 171–88. This contains the version noted above and not the version that appears in Thornton's book. See also *Sex, Aging, & Death*, vol. 2, 588–92, and Lena Mackenzie Gimbel, "Bawdy Badges and the Black Death: Late Medieval Apotropaic Devices against the Spread of the Plague," PhD diss, University of Louisville (2012). Gimbel notes that the *Liber's* plague remedies resemble those of Guy de Chauliac and Ibn Khatima, the former who contracted the disease in 1348 but survived only to contract it again in 1361 and survive once again. De Chauliac notes that he "toke therof as of triacle, and I was preserved by Goddes grace." Cited in Margaret Ogden, ed. *Cyrurgie of Guy de Chauliac*, EETS, 265 (London: Oxford University Press, 1971), 158.

[18] In his discussion of "The Holy Boke Gratia Dei," which also appears in the Lincoln manuscript, George Keiser acknowledges the pragmatic-minded Thornton as finding ways to "reduce the task [of copying a 32,000 word work] to a more easily manageable order by taking from GD [*Gratia Dei*] only what seemed of value for their private needs" (307).

Writing in the late fourteenth century, John of Burgundy begins his treatise by locating the causes of pestilence in the realm of the cosmological:

> Everything below the moon, the elements and the things compounded of the elements, is ruled by the things above, and the highest bodies are believed to give being, nature, substance, growth, and death to everything below their spheres. It was, therefore, by the influence of the heavenly bodies that the air was recently corrupted and made pestilential. I do not mean by this that the air is corrupted in its substance—because it is an uncompounded substance and that would be impossible—but it is corrupted by reason of evil vapours mixed with it. The result was a widespread epidemic, traces of which still remain in several places.[19]

Beginning in this manner, Burgundy demonstrates his erudition and his formal education in the Seven Liberal Arts, forming a foundation for subsequent training in medicine. As noted in his introduction and elsewhere in the text, physicians were expected to understand the macrocosm of the universe in order to comprehend the human body as its microcosmic center. What is especially significant in this regard is the etiological assumption that the pestilence is set into motion by the "heavenly bodies" that corrupted the air with "evil vapors." Presumably, Burgundy is referring to a conjunction of the planets Saturn and Jupiter, thought to have released the malevolent mist that corrupted the air and initiated the epidemic in the first place. Citing Galen as his medical authority, the physician goes on to explain how corruption in the air cannot enter the body unless there exists a "blemish where corruption can take hold" or, as he explains later, by taking hot baths that open the pores of the skin to enable the contagion to enter the body. This is how the humors, especially blood, become infected, thereby causing a state of imbalance that requires purgation, preferably by bloodletting or scarification, to expunge bodily poisons. The physician whose erudition is on display from the beginning of De Epidemia goes on to explain that because corrupt air can generate "different diseases in different people, depending on their different humours," it takes a doctor who knows astronomy to understand the causes likely to lead to the cures. At the same time, he advises his readers to learn the rudiments of medical practice on their own.

As noted by medical skeptics of the time, Burgundy is not a doctor seeking monetary advantage or fame in the writing of his treatise. Instead, the physician

---

[19] Rosemary Horrox, ed. and trans., *The Black Death* (Manchester, UK: Manchester University Press, 1994), 185. See also the long version in comparison with the John of Bordeaux adaptation in *Sex, Aging, & Death in a Medieval Medical Compendium*, vol. 2, ed. M. Teresa Tavormina (Tempe, AZ: Arizona Center for Medieval and Renaissance Studies, 2006). This will factor into my discussion of Margaret Paston in a later chapter.

expresses his desire to be paid in prayer: "I have composed and compiled this work not for money but for prayers."[20] Nonetheless, if we take the statement located at the end of the text to be truthful, the humility topos located at the text's beginning in what follows here appears to be genuine rather than mere convention:

> And therefore I, John of Burgundy, otherwise known as Bearded John, citizen of Liege and practitioner of the art of medicine, although the least of physicians, produced a treatise at the beginning of this epidemic on the causes and nature of corrupt air, of which many people acquired copies…. Because the epidemic is now newly returned, and will return again in future because it has not yet run its course, and because I pity the carnage among mankind and support the common good and desire the health of all, and have been moved by a wish to help, I intend, with God's help, to set out more clearly in this schedule the prevention and cures of these illnesses, so that hardly anyone should have to resort to a physician but even simple folk can be their own physician, preserver, ruler and guide.[21]

John of Burgundy, the university-trained physician, thus gives way to the amateur whose interests in medicine may be prompted by the same conditions that moved the physician to share his knowledge in writing, that is, in response to an outbreak of the plague. And this is not the only time in the treatise that he says this, nor is it the only point he makes to underscore the urgent need for everyone to pay attention to the epidemic that "will return again in future." Nor is it the only time he will call on his readers to become like physicians to be "preserver, ruler, and guide," or the only time he will claim the superiority of medical experience over the authority of academic treatises. He makes this point explicitly yet respectfully by acknowledging the medical luminaries of the past while at the same time distinguishing himself from them in terms of his own plague experience. Having treated patients suffering from the pestilence to which he is both eyewitness and an actively engaged practitioner, he says:

> As a result, I make bold to say—not in criticism of past authorities, but out of long experience in the matter—that modern masters are more experienced in treating pestilential epidemic diseases than all the doctors and medical experts from Hippocrates downward. For none of them saw an epidemic reigning in their time, apart from Hippocrates in the city of Craton and that was short-lived. Nevertheless, he drew on what he had seen in his book on epidemics. However,

---

[20] Horrox, *The Black Death*, 193.
[21] Horrox, *The Black Death*, 186.

Galen, Dioscorides, Rhazes, Damascenus, Geber, Mesue, Copho, Constantine, Serapion, Avicenna, Algazel and all their successors never saw a general or long-lasting epidemic or tested their cures by long experience, although they draw on the sayings of Hippocrates to discuss many things concerning epidemics. As a result, the masters of the present day are more practiced in these diseases than their predecessors, for it is said, and with truth, that experience makes skill. Moved by piety and by pity for the destruction of men, I have accordingly compiled this compendium and have specified and set out the veins to bleed in these epidemic diseases, so that anyone may be his own physician.[22]

Burgundy's identification of himself as a "modern" physician faced with a real-time epidemic acknowledges "past authorities" while making a crucial point about the significance of first-hand experience. Much in the way that medieval moderns saw themselves as standing on the shoulders of intellectual giants, Burgundy looks back in appreciation for the ancients, their methodologies and medical expertise as required reading in his university education. He has been a recipient of their knowledge but has gone beyond them—he learned another dimension of medical practice from which he has benefited in ways that they have not. Unlike the ancients, who "never saw a general or long-lasting epidemic or tested their cures by long experience," he along with other "masters of the present day are more practiced in these diseases." In a comparison between experience and authority reminiscent of the Wife of Bath's claims of marital expertise in Chaucer's *Canterbury Tales*, Burgundy has acknowledged the benefits that come from the actual practice of epidemiological medicine.

This section of Burgundy's prologue is absent in Thornton's version of the text. Instead, the scribe-compiler begins with the section that in Burgundy's work outlines measures taken to thwart the pestilence before it takes hold: controlling excessive intake of food and drink, avoiding corrupt air, not taking hot baths [that open the pores], and above all not engaging in sexual intercourse. Thornton follows Burgundy's recommendation about eating little or no fruit, unless sour, and choosing easy-to-digest foods, but he modifies the doctor's prescription for quenching thirst by changing it from avoiding honey-based drinks [mead] to drinking "calde water megede [mixed] with vynagre or tysayn [barley water]." Thornton's text also omits Burgundy's discussion of various herbal medications including theriac, a highly touted pharmaceutical thought

---

[22] Some of these practitioners may not be familiar. Rhazes was a Persian physician and philosopher (c. 865-925 AD); Magister Copho(n) was a physician in Salerno. Algazel was a Muslim theologian whose work served as a primer for understanding Arab philosophical tradition in relation to the Greeks. Horrox, *The Black Death*, 192.

to cure almost anything.²³ The notion that pestilence could be thwarted by adherence to a prescribed regimen of health is a prominent feature of plague treatises that emphasized healthy habits both physical and moral: "Anyone who adopts this regimen can be preserved, with God's help, from pestilence caused by corruption of the air."²⁴ This is the point that Burgundy makes before launching into some of the remedies he recommends for its treatment: "Now if anyone should contract epidemic disease for lack of a good regimen," he says, "it is necessary to look at remedies and at how he should proceed, for these epidemic diseases take hold in twenty-four hours and it is therefore vital to apply a remedy immediately."²⁵ This introduces the doctor's discussion of the three principal organs—heart, liver, brain—and the means by which the disease travels through the body unless halted in a timely fashion mainly by phlebotomy or "scarification with pitch," a procedure designed to draw out poisoned blood by raising blisters on the skin.²⁶ These treatments are to be followed by a medication Burgundy describes as the "imperial powder" that emperors used "against epidemic illness, poison and venom" made of "St. John's wort, dittany, tormentil, pimpernel, scabious, philadelphia, ammoniac [and] medicinal earth from Lemnos."²⁷ When combined, these ingredients form a compound that Burgundy deems to be most effective in protecting against "all poisons" and to be as efficacious as "emptying the veins of blood." All "gentile" physicians agree, he says, "that however this powder is used, it makes it impossible to die of poison." That the medication is composed of several expensive and rare ingredients in Burgundy's prescription (the "medicinal earth from Lemnos," for example) suggests the economic status of some of his patients. But because this physician appears not to be the self-serving, avaricious practitioner made into a negative stereotype by medical skeptics, he acknowledges that not all patients can afford such rare medicaments, and so, for them, he suggests an alternative prescription: "if you are poor, make a distilled water from dittany, pimpernel, tormentil and scabious by blending the herbs and mixing them with an equal quantity of water."²⁸ Thornton's text does not mention the method of scarification recommended by Burgundy, nor does

---

²³ Also assigned that level of efficacy is "Saue," a special drink good for just about everything.
²⁴ Horrox, *The Black Death*, 188.
²⁵ Horrox, *The Black Death*, 188.
²⁶ This is also known as cauterization, which requires the raising of blisters by various means. As Horrox notes, "The formation of liquid in the blisters was seen as a way of draining dangerous humours from the body, and medieval doctors equipped themselves with cautery charts, which showed them where blisters should be raised on the human body to treat particular diseases." See Horrox, *The Black Death*, 189.
²⁷ Horrox, *The Black Death*, 190.
²⁸ Horrox, *The Black Death*, 189.

he list the exotic ingredients necessary for making the follow-up medications. Rather, his prescription requires only four of the principal herbs identified by the doctor for use on the poor: "detony, pympernole, tormentil and scabyous," all of which were both accessible and affordable.

Given the urgency for medical intervention in halting the spread of pestilence, the physician deploys language more often used by writers of romance to describe conflicts between combatants on the battlefield rather than the pragmatic prose of medical writing:

> poisonous air, when it has been mixed with blood, immediately seeks the heart, the seat of nature, to attack it. The heart, sensing the injury, labours to defend itself, driving the poisoned blood to its emunctory. If then the venomous matter finds its way blocked, so that it cannot ascend back to the heart by some other path, it seeks another principal member, the liver, so that it can destroy that. The liver, fighting back, drives the resinous matter to its emunctory. In the same way it lays claim to the brain. By means of these events, which are signs to the physician, it is possible to tell where the poisonous matter is lurking and by what vein it ought to be drained.[29]

Thornton's text follows Burgundy's narrative in this section, even to the point of deploying metaphors of battle, but he deviates from the physician's description in some important details, not the least of which includes the identification of the buboes that differentiate *bubonic* plague from its other forms:

> The hert kyndely flyes it that is agayne it and that venemous matere puttes to his clensying place and, for it fyndis it sperred & may noghte owt, it passes to the nexte pryncypall partie, that is the lyver, for to distroy it, & he puttis it to his clensynge place &, for that also is sperred that it may not owt thare, it passes to the thirde pryncypalle partie, that is the hernes, & he puttis it to his clensyng place & for that also is sperrede that it may norwhare owte and thus lange it is movande or it riste in any place, that is to say xii hours & mare and than at the laste with in xxiiij hours, if it passe nott owte bi blode latynge, it festres in some place & castes a man in-to an agewe & makes a boche or a kille in some place bi-fore said.[30]

The heart, by its very nature, "flyes" the venomous matter that attacks it, driving it to its "clensying place," where it will be purged by bleeding. While the verb appears to connote "fleeing" or "retreating" from the offending matter, "flyes" also means to "fight against," which is its connotation in the Latin text. The heart

---

[29] Horrox, *The Black Death*, 188.
[30] Ogden, *Liber*, 52 (ll. 9–22).

fights against its aggressive attacker in its effort to redirect the invasive poison to its cleansing place, the emunctory located in the armpit. If blocked in some way or "sperred," as the text would have it, the venomous matter then travels to the next principal organ, the liver, which attempts to "destroy" the contagion in similar fashion; as in the first scenario, if blocked at this location and not eradicated by the liver, the infection then travels to the next principal organ, that is, the brain, wherein a similar defensive response takes place. The upshot is this: the longer the poison stays in the body without being neutralized, which in Thornton's treatise is twelve to twenty-four hours, the more likely it will be that the patient will succumb to an "ague" accompanied by the distinctive buboes (boches) of the bubonic plague. What is important to point out is that Thornton describes the distinguishing characteristic of the plague, while the emphasis in Burgundy's treatise is on the physician's ability to discern the progress of the disease by determining "where the poisonous matter is lurking." The doctor's framing of the epidemic in terms of cosmology and the corruption of the air also differentiates his medical assessment from the more pragmatic Thornton version, which does not include the astronomical causes that Burgundy presumes essential to the conscientious diagnostician.

With all the attention given to the order and arrangement of the Lincoln codex, we might ask why Thornton's plague treatise is placed so close to the heart of the *Liber*? Does its position heighten its significance in relation to the meaning of the work as a whole?[31] Surely, if the placement of the other genres were done strategically, then so too is it reasonable to assume that the positioning of the treatise is also purposeful. Noteworthy too is that there are no other *probaturs* [witnesses] mentioned in this section of the medical text as Thornton had included elsewhere. Rather, in several places Thornton inscribes his own name (eleven times in the Lincoln codex),[32] creating an illusion of authority that supersedes his presumed status as scribe and compiler. The deviations from the original Latin text, the selective additions and omissions of certain ingredients, methods, and medical details, suggest that Thornton has taken matters into his own hands, customized where needed for his household audience, demonstrating a familiarity with pharmaceuticals and their applications beyond the detached inscribing done by a mere copyist. The list of medicinal herbs, discernible in the fragmented herbal following the *Liber*, suggests that this Yorkshire "gentleman, reader, and scribe" may have assumed the role of amateur empiric taking up the

---

[31] Keiser estimates the compilation to have taken place c.1450. "Reconstructing Robert Thornton's Herbal," *Medium Aevum* 65.1 (1996): 35-53. This is an estimate revised to a wider range 1430-50.

[32] Fein, "Contents of Thornton's Manuscripts," 19.

mantle of health care as prescribed by Burgundy. That Thornton includes recipes collected from local personages and practitioners known to him indicates his awareness of the importance of personal experience over textbook knowledge. In his pious yet pragmatic orientation, Thornton as amateur empiric includes a variety of remedies, even several charms and prayers, to his household medical library. He has done what Burgundy has encouraged of his readers: he has become *like* a physician whose practice, in this case, is predicated upon a holistic vision of health for all members of his household that includes an uplifting of the spirits.

From Pestilence to Wounds

Located after its explanation of the symptoms of the plague and how to treat it, the *Liber* transitions to a lengthy series of wound treatments, suggesting that pestilence and wounds are somehow associated in the gentleman empiric's mind. Indeed, if we consider the etymology of *plaga*, the Latin word for "plague," as meaning "wound" or "gash" as well as "disease," then the expanded meaning encompasses the kind of acute suffering that requires an immediate medical response. At the same time, it is important to point out that physicians and empirics were aware that a "cure" for the pestilence or other serious infections and wounds might not be possible. And perhaps that is one reason the phrase "by the grace of God" is so often included in medical treatises. One item contained in this section of the *Liber* is a medication called *"Gratia Dei"* used to cleanse and generate the growth of new tissue in open wounds. The medical and the theological, the literal and the figurative converge in the very name of this medication.[33] In the enunciation of the grace of God, the medicine brings the material world into conversation with religious language, empowering its efficacy in the mind of the recipient. The suspension of disbelief or simply the willingness to believe in the effectiveness of a medical compound used to treat wounds is instantiated in the converging of abstract concept and material substance.

The *Dictionary of Medical Vocabulary* describes *Gratia Dei* as a "plaster made by boiling herbs and wine, straining the decoction, adding beeswax and gums (in some recipes also a mineral substance, rose oil or milk)."[34] In the *Liber* this

---

[33] See Bishop, *Word, Herb, Stone*.
[34] Juhani Norri, *Dictionary of Medical Vocabulary in English, 1375-1500* (Abingdon, UK: Ashgate, 2016).

medicament comes in a couple of variations, both of which require a range of ingredients and special preparations: the first is a mineral compound made of ground lead oxide (litarge), mixed with several other ingredients and boiled in olive oil until they "wax blake." The recipe is followed by an explanation of what it is used for and what it is expected to do: "This emplaster clenses wondis and sowdis them to-gedir & dose owte ded flesche & newe flesche gars grewe."[35] When applied to an open wound, the concoction cleanses the surface area while encouraging the growth of new skin underneath. The removal of the plaster and the witnessing of living tissue must have been nothing short of miraculous. One would think that such a medication would be rendered unique for producing such an excellent result. Yet there is a second recipe in the *Liber* that requires more plant-based ingredients and a different kind of preparation. This is a variation that could be used on a wider variety of wounds, sores, ulcers, cankers, and "helle fire," a disease often mistaken for the plague.[36] That the application of a medication such as this requires explicit instructions lends it another level of medical authority goes without saying. What does need to be said, however, is that a compound, literally named for a divinely sanctioned act of salvation, inspires belief in its efficacy for both practitioner and patient.

The holistic approach to medical knowledge that I am suggesting for Thornton makes sense of his decision to include a text called *The Holy Boke Gratia Dei*, which by its very title fuses the spiritual with the physical. As Keiser observes, the *GD*, as he calls it, was "[a]pparently intended to prescribe a regimen of good conduct, both for those in the world and those removed from it," thus instilling a pious if not monastic form of devotion into the codex. Influenced by the works of Richard Rolle, the well-known Yorkshire mystic, the anonymous author of the work presents an artful discussion of the meaning of grace, replete with excerpts from patristic authorities and incorporating a range of other vernacular writings as well.[37] As Keiser suggests, *The Holy Boke Gratia Dei* addresses an important topic for the religious community as well as the laity they ministered to, but even more than that, the text renders into words what the medication by the same name demonstrates on living flesh. Thus, a theological discussion on the relationship between grace and free will becomes not only a work that had the capacity to speak to a diverse household audience but whose meaning

---

[35] Ogden, *Liber*, 68 (ll. 8-10).
[36] St. Anthony's Fire is an extremely painful and intense inflammation of the skin, also known as ergotism.
[37] Those texts include *A Ladder of Foure Ronges*; *Militia Christi*; *Lives of the Fathers, Sayings of the Father*; *Vitae Patrum, Saints' Legends*; *Ancrene Riwle*; *Pater Noster*; *Abbey of the Holy Ghost*; *Mirror of St. Edmund*; *Meditation on the Passion*, *Three Arrows on Doomsday*; *Sawles Warde*.

was made literal in healing the kinds of wounds the audience could recognize. In its fusion of the literal with the figurative, rhetorical prose with poetic style, the work delivers a serious message in a palatable form. Influenced as it was by the mystical writing of Richard Rolle, perhaps this stands to reason. As M. L. Arntz describes it:

> *The Holy Boke Gratia Dei* is marked by a judicious use of the arts of composition: 1) The repetition of sounds or of words either by alliteration, rhyme, or assonance; 2) the achievement of a rhythmical word order through the arrangement of balance, antithesis, chiasmus, anaphora, and polysyndeton. Even Rolle's own distinctive characteristic of style, a series of present participles, is not missing from this treatise. Sentence length, too, is characterized by the pleasing variety to be found in Rolle's English prose style. In addition to the care taken in word-placement, dignity is lent to *The Holy Boke Gratia Dei* through the use of metaphor, simile, vivid description, dialogue, paradox, and personification.[38]

Dubbed a prose stylist, the *Gratia Dei* author combines features of rhetoric with figures of poetry. In a fusion of oral narrative and written text, the author has produced a book that speaks to a matter of heightened concern in a time of pestilence. When the author deploys homely imagery—doors, windows, gates of the heart—and says that all must be open to Grace when she comes knocking, it is imagery that strikes a chord with lived reality. With Latin excerpts from authoritative sources interspersed and translated throughout, and an expanded network of vernacular writings included in the narration, the author channels voices and words that provide another level of authority to his text. Like the medication called *Gratia Dei*, this is a work that heals festering wounds not of the body but of the soul. In this *Holy Boke* the literal takes on symbolic meaning for the discerning reader.

From the Literal to the Literary: Wounding

Medicine and its practices are clearly a central concern of the *Liber*, but also present in other texts, especially the Arthurian tales—the *Morte Arthure*, the *Awntyrs of Arthure*, and *Perceval*—the tail-rhyme romances—*Octavian*, *Sir Isumbras*, *Sir Degrevant*, the *Erl of Tolous*, *Sir Eglamour*—and the *Life of*

---

[38] M. L. Arntz, "'The Holy Boke Gratia Dei': An Edition with Commentary," PhD. diss. (Fordham University, 1961), cxxxi-cxxxii. K. Horstmann, ed. *Yorkshire Writers* 1 (London: Swan Sonnenschein & Co., 1894), 132-56 and 300-21.

St. Christopher, stories that depict physical violence and contain allusions to physicians, treatments of wounds, broken bones, antidotes to poison, and references to special remedies. So too is there a kinship between the medical texts and romance since this is the kind of story that, as Keiser observes, "perceives the relation between sickness and the sick person as equivalent to that of the foe and the hero of medieval combat narratives."[39] And since we have seen how medical writing can appropriate the language of such tales to describe the body's battle with invasive infections, tropes that resonate even in modern-day discussions of illness become even more significant. In its capacity to provide both practical advice and entertaining narrative poetry for presentation in a household setting, storytelling accrues another level of therapeutic value; adventure stories whether of Alexander the Great or King Arthur provide a means by which members of a household audience may escape the realities of the day, allowing themselves to be carried away into imaginative otherworlds, if only for the duration of the telling.[40] These are works that do not express the terminal optimism of many of the tail-rhyme romances in the collection, however, but rather focus on imperial conquest and the making and breaking of would-be empires. As indicated in their graphic depictions of combat wounds and in the ultimate death of the principal figures, these are stories of trauma and pain incurred during battle. And perhaps this is an aspect of such narratives that takes on a supernatural dimension over time. Despite their emphasis on a secularized mode of heroic action, the violence of the battle scenes and the symbolic nature of the wounding create an aura of the sacred.

In her discussion of religious violence, Mary Michele Poellinger foregrounds episodes of the near-fatal injuries done in the hand-to-hand combat depicted in the *Morte Arthure*, so evocative of the suffering of the crucified Christ.[41] Having identified Thornton's affective piety and fondness for Marian lyrics and the poetry of the Passion, both of which are designed to elicit empathy from readers, Poellinger focuses on one of the most violent scenes in the narrative, the battle between Gawain and Priamus, during which both are severely wounded and subsequently healed by an application of "holy salve." Not unlike *Gratia Dei*, at least in terms of its healing power, this is a miracle medicine made from the

---

[39] George R. Keiser, "Verse Introductions to Middle English Medical Treatises," *English Studies* 84.4 (2003): 301-17.
[40] Many of the speech markers in the romances indicate oral transmission.
[41] Mary Michele Poellinger, "'The rosselde spere to his herte rynnes': Religious Violence in the *Alliterative Morte Arthure* and the Lincoln Thornton Manuscript," in *Robert Thornton and His Books: Essays on the Lincoln Thornton Manuscript*, ed. Susanna Fein and Michael Johnston (York, UK: York Medieval Press, 2014), 157-75.

water of the well that "flowes owte of Paradice" carried in a vial by Priamus and subsequently used to cleanse and heal the wounds both of himself and his opponent. But as Poellinger suggests, the holy salve does more than debride the injured flesh and generate new growth. Instead, "the process cleanses their physical, spiritual and chivalric wounds."[42] The battle between the two, in a reading that fuses the concrete with the abstract, the physical with the spiritual, is an "example of knightly sacrifice ending in fellowship."[43] The violence in which a knight engages during war can itself be viewed as a sacrificial act, and the *Morte* poet, and Thornton by extension, seems keen for his audience to view his Arthurian heroes in this way. The knights in the alliterative narrative become as one in a blood sacrifice "when they agree to fight for Arthur to remain free of the Emperor's oppression, submitting their bodies to physical jeopardy as Christ does on the Cross."[44] The blood that results from the violence of hand-to-hand combat is made manifest in a graphic scene in which Gawain pierces Priamus so fiercely that "with the lyghte of the sonne men myghte see his lyvere" (l. 2561), while Gawain's blood "voydes... violently" after Priamus severs a vein (l. 2571). Such violations of the body, a piercing and severing so severe that blood pours out forcefully from one combatant while the liver becomes visible in the other, foreground the grievous nature of the injuries. It takes a wonder drug to heal these wounds, and that is, of course, the precious substance that Priamus carries in his vial. The violence marked by a great effusion of blood is clearly made to capture the attention of an audience aware of what it represents. Also necessary to underscore in relation to this scene is that another knight, this one unnamed, acts as a physician to facilitate the healing of his compatriots. "With [the] clere watire a knyghte clensis theire wondes" (l. 2711). Unlike an ordinary empiric, or battlefield surgeon, this knight commences healing with a substance that proves to be miraculous. So too is this unnamed knight acting in the place of the *Christus medicus* as he applies the holy balm that promises to heal these otherwise mortal wounds and at the same time forge a new fraternal bond. Soon hereafter Priamus is converted, baptized, and brought into the Arthurian brotherhood created through interpersonal violence. Descended from the Nine Worthies, one of whom is Alexander the Great, Priamus has proven himself to be a worthy addition to the Round Table.

Because the *Prose Life of Alexander* and the alliterative *Morte Arthure* are stories that glorify the conquests of two of the Nine Worthies, they foreground

---

[42] Poellinger, "Religious Violence," 169.
[43] Ibid., 168.
[44] Ibid.

many of the conflicts that arise among imperial leaders, including betrayals by some of their closest compatriots and kin. In the *Morte Arthure*, that traitor is Mordred, Arthur's illegitimate and overly ambitious son; in the Alexander romance, that figure is a doctor bearing poison instead of medicine. Both rulers meet their demise in an unexpected twist of fate: for Arthur that ending is in the turn of Fortune's Wheel, for Alexander an unrelenting desire to know when his life would end. Having achieved extraordinary success as larger-than-life imperialists, both meet their destined downfall at the hands of trusted familiars. The cautionary dimension of these narratives is made manifest in the tragic demise of what could have been, that is, world conquest and the promise of judicious rulership. Yet such tales also demonstrate strength and resilience where otherwise there would be weakness and despair; they show, among other things, how an illegitimate or disenfranchised boy could grow up to be a conquering hero. These are the tales that encourage children and the adults responsible for raising them to engage in their imaginative worlds, to be entertained and educated on the vicissitudes of life even when such difficulties confront heroic figures such as Alexander the Great and King Arthur.

Reading for Disease

If the Thornton Lincoln manuscript is read from beginning to end—from the epic tales of Alexander and Arthur to the *Liber*—in the methodical manner of a medical treatise, the compilation may be understood as a body of work concerned with the health of the body, both individual and communal. When Thornton's *Liber* is read in like manner, that is, from head to toe with the treatise on the pestilence understood to be the heart of the text, it suggests that the epidemic is of central concern to the entire collection, becoming the disease of the time, the disruptive event affecting the entire body politic. Like the *Secretum Secretorum*, wherein the head of society governs the lower classes, so too does Thornton's arrangement of the *Liber* and the manuscript as a whole make sense of his placement of the *Prose Life of Alexander* at the manuscript's head. Preceding the *Morte Arthure*, the tail-rhyme romances, and the *Life of St. Christopher*, this is the story that launches a series of tales that chart a trajectory from the fall of imperialist conquerors to the medical recipes contained in the *Liber de diversis medicinis*. Delusions of grandeur and attempts to annex and dominate the world thus give way in this sequence to a wide range of traumatic injuries and bodies in pain for which these remedies are designed.

Perhaps that is one reason Thornton juxtaposes tales of violence and death with stories that have more pleasing outcomes. Narrative poems such as the Northern *Octavian* or *Sir Isumbras*, in which class differences, misalignments, and misunderstandings elicit mirth and joy where otherwise there would be sorrow and despair, are apt examples. When infants are abducted by apes, lions, griffons, and unicorns, audiences are transported into worlds inhabited by fanciful creatures such as those often found in the margins of illuminated manuscripts. When dragons and giants fall to the unflinching courage of impervious youth, or when children riding on the backs of wild animals rescue their parents, everyday troubles dissipate. When the hero is an unknown youth, the charting of his ability to overcome great obstacles to gain recognition as a glorious knight, to win the hand of a beautiful maiden, such a tale has the capacity to produce a satisfying kind of pleasure. The story of Perceval is especially fitting for the ways in which a youth defies his mother's resistance to earn his chivalric spurs in the company of men. Perceval "offers humour and wordplay that are not so often found in those works ... the Lincoln romance collection becomes richer and more comprehensive than it had been."[45] If Thornton sought to alter the mood of the members of his household or distract them from the anxieties and fears of a lurking pestilence, what better way to do it than by providing material for them to listen to or read aloud? How better to send the vital spirits coursing more vigorously through the humoral body than by reciting the stories of marvelous creatures, invincible heroes, seductive ladies, secretive trysts, resistant fathers, go-between servants, bumbling squires, and the glamor of chivalry? What could be more effective than moments of laughter and intrigue mixed with the threat of mortal injury? Fear and joy become intermingled in these stories.

Yet there is more to be said about the emotional suffering embedded in such tales, the wounds of the heart that resist medical treatment. Three of the nine romances in the compilation—*Erl of Tolous*, *Sir Degrevant*, and *Eglamour of Artois*—"are fundamentally of the romance of adventure pattern" with an amatory element providing the primary motivation for the hero's quest.[46] Love won

---

[45] George R. Keiser, "Robert Thornton: Gentleman, Reader and Scribe," in *Robert Thornton and His Books*, ed. Susanna Fein and Michael Johnston (York: York Medieval Press, 2014), 67-108 (89).

[46] John Finlayson, "Reading Romances in Their Manuscripts: Lincoln Cathedral MS 91," *Anglia* 123.4 (2006): 632-66. These tales are available in the TEAMS Middle English Texts Series, *Erl of Tolous in The Middle English Breton Lays*, ed. Anne Laskaya and Eve Salisbury (Kalamazoo: Medieval Institute Publications 1995); Sir Degrevant in *Sentimental and Humorous Romances*, ed. Erik Kooper (Kalamazoo: Medieval Institute Publications, 2005); and *Eglamour of Artois* in *Four Middle English Romances*, ed. Harriet Hudson (Kalamazoo: Medieval Institute Publications, 1996). https://d.lib.rochester.edu/teams/text-online

through challenge and hardship is not only a salve for the heartsick lover (almost always male) but taken to be an illness with discernible physical symptoms: change of complexion, loss of appetite, frequent weeping, inertness, and lethargy. Such medical need positions the beloved in the role of healer responsible for the lover's recuperation: in what is constructed as a heteronormative paradigm, only she has the power to assuage the suffering experienced by her benighted lover. *Eglamour of Artois*, as indicated by its eponymous title, is concerned with the loss of love by a youth whose very name encompasses amorous feeling. In this narrative poem the hero expresses his desire for Christabelle and despite her father's objections aspires to marry her, a proposal to which she consents willingly. Soon a complication arises in the form of an illegitimate child born of their union and Eglamour is presented with several challenges by his lady's angry father—battles with a giant, a boar, and a dragon—before he is rendered eligible to reunite with his family. Sir Degrevant, a courtly figure "doughty in battle, expert in music and a great huntsman,"[47] falls in love with a maiden named Melidor and fights several battles to prove himself worthy of marriage to her; wounded many times, he suffers greatly before he is proven fit enough for that honor. The *Erl of Tolous* features an accusation of adultery leveled at the virtuous lady of the romance, Dame Beulybon. Not unlike the Constance stories featuring the motif of the "calumniated queen," Beulybon is exonerated of the charge and free to marry her champion at the end. When young women demonstrate agency, and their desire is consensual, there is something to be said about the ability of storytelling to address matters of concern to their socially astute audiences.

Even when love is devotional, as it is in many of Thornton's selections, the effect can be registered in a physical way. These are stories that contrast with the violence against women so often found in romance as well as the challenges presented by marriage or the absence of marriage and childbirth, whether legitimate or not. Stories of the Fair Unknown (as in the story of Perceval) contain examples of women faced with social ostracization, the loss of reputation, and the abject poverty of single parenting; they bear the brunt of social violations, while others suffer sexual assault and rape. For those in the audience who may not identify with the youthful heroes and heroines whose stories end happily, such tales may be more cautionary than not, providing an education applicable to real-life situations. Family relations, interfamilial alliances, territorial disputes, consensual versus arranged marriages, illegitimacy, and legal actions factor into

---

[47] Finlayson, "Reading Romances," 653.

romances that also accommodate the marvelous and the miraculous. Of the three narratives mentioned here two have ties to historical events (*Erl of Tolous* and *Eglamour of Artois*). Whether they reshape the consciences of their audiences or elicit an emotional response of some kind, they offer an opportunity for readers and listeners to "be glad & void al hevynesse," as recommended in Lydgate's "Dietary" and other regimens of health.

In her article "Women's Wounds in Middle English Romance,"[48] Barbara Goodman addresses the differences in depictions of violence in the *Awntyrs of Arthure*, a narrative told in two parts, the first a ghost story featuring Guenevere's dead mother and the second a chivalric tale featuring the gallantry of Gawain. In the former, the queen's mother appears from the dead to warn her daughter about the pitfalls of engaging in the kinds of activities glorified by courtly love. As she makes clear to her daughter, Guenevere's mother is being punished for her sexual transgressions, and she comes to warn the young queen of the horrifying consequences of engaging in dangerous liaisons. The ghoulish condition in which she appears, an apparent *contrapasso* for her sexual sin, describes her "as having toads biting into her skull, sunken hollow eyes that burn like coals, and serpents that encompass her body."[49] The wounds caused by the biting toads contribute to the hideousness of her otherwise fleshless body rendered even more grotesque by the serpents wrapped around her. Like a negative example of Eve, her appearance underscores the notion of original sin as disobedience to divine authority, only here with a sexualized twist. To drive that point home, the ghost is pursued by "fendes of helle" who violate her body before boiling her in a cauldron of brimstone as hot as a bonfire: "thei harme me in hight / In bras and in brymston I bren as a belle" (ll. 187-88).[50] Her grotesque appearance is rendered visible in Guenevere's response when she asks her mother to provide an explanation of her condition so that she can "make sere men [several men] to singe for thi sake / But the baleful bests that on this body bites / Al blendis my ble—thi bones arn so blake" (ll. 210-12). For Goodman, "Guenevere's mother is a warning of the poisonous effects of sexual transgression," as she explains to her daughter, "That is luf paramour, listes and delites / That has me light and laft logh [left low] in a lake" (ll. 213–14). While she is in a place that

---

[48] Barbara A. Goodman, "Women's Wounds in Middle English Romances: An Exploration of Defilement, Disfigurement, and a Society in Despair," in *Wounds & Wound Repair in Medieval Culture*, ed. Barbara A. Goodman, Larissa Tracy, and Kelly DeVries (Leiden: Brill, 2015), 544-71.

[49] Goodman, "Women's Wounds," 564–5.

[50] *The Awntyrs of Arthure* is one of the romances in *Sir Gawain: Eleven Romances and Tales*, ed. Thomas Hahn, TEAMS Middle English Texts Series (Kalamazoo: Medieval Institute Publications, 1995), 178-201.

resonates with portrayals of transgressive women such as the courtesan Thais in Dante's *Inferno*, she is also a figure for Death not unlike that in Lydgate's "Dance of Death," noted in the previous chapter. Like Death who warns those whose souls are in peril, Guenevere's mother warns her daughter about the impending demise of the Arthurian court at the hands of "the barne [who] plaes at the balle" (l. 310). In a fleeting allusion to the future endeavors of the illegitimate Mordred, she forecasts the fall of Arthur's kingdom, and in so doing urges a change of heart with charity and chastity at its center. This is maternal advice that proves to be persuasive in that it elicits a promise from Guenevere to have a "myllion of Masses" said to alleviate her mother's suffering. This is the mother's departing message: "Fede folke for my sake that failen the fode / And menge me with matens and Masse in melle. / Masses arn medecynes to us that bale bides; / Us thenke a Masse as swete / As eny spice that ever ye yete" (ll. 319–23). The emphasis on charity and the Masses she desires to be spoken on her behalf underscore the power of prayer to act as a medicine, in this case, to save a soul from eternal damnation.

In what has been described as an "interactive dialogic diptych,"[51] the second half of the text responds to the first half in its foregrounding of "male wounds obtained in hand-to-hand battle" that validate the "imperialistic dreams and rewarding male combatants with acceptance at Arthur's court."[52] The battle scene between Gawain and the knight who opposes him, Sir Galeron, in this case, is protracted and bloody. Both knights battle fiercely in an episode that lasts "for over 100 lines and includes references to blood-stained mail, injurious strokes, and numerous wounds until Galeron falls to the ground, groaning and writhing in pain."[53] Even Gawain's horse is killed in the heat of battle, decapitated by Galeron in a single stroke, to dramatize the moment when mounted combat is replaced by a hand-to-hand confrontation that bruises and bloodies the faces of both men. In an echo of the blackened bones of Guenevere's mother, the darkening of their complexions is a sign of grievous injury that requires the kind of medication that only a million Masses can provide. The combat is so severe and protracted, in fact, that both knights' ladies request Arthur's intercession, a duty he carries out in this case by bequeathing territory to each combatant, rewarding Gawain for his valiance and enfolding Galeron into the Arthurian brotherhood.

---

[51] See Hahn, ed. *Sir Gawain: Eleven Romances and Tales*, citing A. C. Spearing's categorization in "The Awntyrs off Arthure," in *The Alliterative Tradition in the Fourteenth Century*, ed. Bernard S. Levy and Paul E. Szarmach (Kent, OH: Kent State University, 1981), 183-202 (186-7).
[52] Goodman, "Women's Wounds," 564.
[53] Goodman, "Women's Wounds," 567.

Then, in another act of poetic symmetry necessitated by the diptych structure of the poem, Guenevere carries out her promise to her mother when she sends a message to the clergy "to rede and to singe; / Prestes with procession to pray were prest, / With a mylion of Masses to make the mynnynge" (ll. 704-06). Masses spoken in the authoritative voices of priests in a ritualized action function as verbal medicine for Guenevere's mother to be sure. Just as surely, however, such gestures of piety alleviate the suffering of the injured knights.

How can a secular story be infused with religious meaning, a religious story with secular meaning? How can medical narratives be embedded in works of poetic art? To the first of these questions: the healing language of religion has the capacity to transform the secular into the sacred in a single word or a well-placed trope. There is, in fact, an element of sanctification attached to the hero in his role as heroic savior and an echo of the Virgin Mary in representations of virtuous women. In fact, many of these narratives may be spoken in the language Northrop Frye has called "secular Scripture"[54] in their deployment of tropes often reserved for biblical figures and saints. As John Ivor Carlson notes, "By dividing his miscellanies evenly between religious tracts and moralistic secular content, Thornton signals to his audience that these texts should function as exemplars for good living.... Although perhaps not self-evident, a connection between Thornton's interest in presenting chivalric tales as if they were secular saints' lives and his copying habits can be made."[55] If one of Thornton's aims was to motivate members of his household to engage in pious action, to move them to prayer as a prophylactic measure for guarding against disease, how better to do it than through narratives such as these? *Sir Isumbras*, found in the romance section of Lincoln Cathedral 91, is often described as a secular saint's life, adapted from the story of Eustace, a legendary holy martyr whose stalwart adherence to Christianity leads to his execution. Like Eustace, Isumbras faces a series of personal setbacks: loss of his family, his wealth, and his status as a knight. His story is one of arrogance corrected by humility, of stature reduced, of lavish feasting reversed by pangs of hunger. As in the tropes of so many romances of the fifteenth century, those featured in *Sir Isumbras* remind an audience of the benefits of living a life based on charity and community rather than self-interest and the hoarding of personal wealth. These are some of the themes enfolded into the developing medical discourse to which Thornton contributes so significantly.

---

[54] Northrop Frye, *The Secular Scripture: A Study of the Structure of Romance* (Cambridge, MA: Harvard University Press, 1978).

[55] John Ivor Carlson, "Scribal Intention in Medieval Romance: A Case Study of Robert Thornton," *Studies in Bibliography* 58 (2007-2008): 49-71 (63).

Finding balance in terms of moral and ethical conduct is integrally related to finding balance in the humoral body.

Intersections of the secular and the sacred can also be recognized in hagiographies such as the *Life of St. Christopher*, the legend that provides another context for testing the effectiveness of a medication. In this tale the saint's original identity as a Canaanite giant named Reprobus ("Outcast") introduces him and his search for the greatest prince in the world. During his quest he meets a hermit who gives him several challenges, one of which is to go to the nearby river and help people get across. This is the scene most often recalled in iconography that depicts the giant carrying a child on his shoulders through turbulent water. As the story goes, Christopher's diminutive passenger gets heavier and heavier, until the giant nearly drowns in his attempt to provide transport. When he asks the child why he has gotten so heavy the boy replies: "because I am the Creator of the universe, and I carry a great burden."[56] To prove his identity, the child then gives the saint a staff and tells him to plant it in the earth with the promise that it will bear leaves and fruit the next day. It does, and now renamed Christopher, the saint sets out to convert the Saracens to his newly acquired religion. Eventually captured and tortured, the holy man refuses to renounce his faith; the Saracen king in an act of utter exasperation orders his archers to shoot him. While most of the arrows stop in mid-air before reaching their target, one rebounds and hits the king in the eye, blinding him instantly. Enraged and in great pain, the king then orders Christopher to be executed by beheading this time. Before he dies, however, the saint implores his oppressor to apply the blood of his sanctified corpse to the damaged eye. When he does, a miracle ensues, and the Saracen monarch regains his eyesight.

The Healing Power of Blood

Blood is, of course, a significant bodily fluid in the humoral system and one that physicians could regulate through phlebotomy and cauterization. The blood of a saint, as the *Life of St. Christopher* suggests, could also be understood as a sacred substance that when used as an eye medication was so powerful that it could restore even the sight of a Saracen king, a traditional enemy of Christianity. The application of a liquid made holy by the spoken word and given credence by the

---

[56] Jacobus de Voragine, *The Golden Legend: Readings on the Saints*, trans. Willliam Granger Ryan, (Princeton: Princeton University Press, 1993), vol. II, 10-14 (12).

saint's *imitatio Christi* invests his blood with transformative power enough to provide a compassionate resolution to a narrative filled with brutality and torture. St. Christopher's death is not to be understood as tragic, however, but rather indicative of a moment of transition both for him and for the tyrannical king healed by the saint's blood. Just as crossing the turbulent river marks the divide between Christopher's status as an outcast and his conversion to Christianity, his gruesome death signifies a passing from one ontological state to another. That this is the saint who is literally the bearer of Christ as well as the patron saint of travel and the traveler is significant in this regard: his journey through troubled waters signals the transition from social and religious exclusion to belonging to a community of saints. Recognized in the later Middle Ages as one of the Fourteen Holy Helpers, saints assigned as patrons of a range of illnesses, including pestilence, Christopher accrues additional signification and intercessory potency.[57] Perhaps it is not a coincidence that a wall painting of the saintly giant carrying the Child Jesus is to be found at a local parish church.[58] Commissioned around 1450, during the time Thornton was putting his compilation together, raises the question of whether there is some link between the inclusion of the narrative in the codex and the visual image.[59]

The story of St. Christopher and the use of his own blood as a healing salve finds resonance in the many recipes that focus on treating eye problems such as blurriness of vision, visual obstructions, and eye infections in the *Liber*. While not of the miraculous potency of a saint's blood, Thornton's medical book is filled with treatments both pragmatic and marvelous, so marvelous in fact, that many of them work like a charm. There is one treatment that uses blood for healing in this wondrous way, not for eyes, in this case, but rather for nosebleed. In what is indicated in the margin as a "charm" for the ailment is offered as follows: "Tak the blode of hym that bledis & wryte in his front + a + g + l + a." This is no ordinary directive but rather a ritualized procedure that requires the presiding authority to write these letters in the patient's blood on the patient's forehead. The result is not stated, but the assumption is that this is a procedure proven to be efficacious.

---

[57] Other saints on this list include Agathius, Barbara, Blaise, Catherine of Alexandria, Cyriacus, Denis, Erasmus, Eustace, George, Giles, Margaret of Antioch, Antaleon, and Vitus.

[58] See also Julie Nelson Couch, "Apocryphal Romance," in *Robert Thornton and His Books*, ed. Susanna Fein and Michael Johnston (York: York Medieval Press, 2014), 203-34, for a discussion of a Child Jesus narrative found in the London Thornton manuscript.

[59] The Pickering Parish Church is not far from the Thornton estate and still viable. https://www.pickeringchurch.com/gallery.html

For Francisco Alonso-Almeida, charms such as the one above should be understood as speech acts, in this instance, a single utterance consisting of two distinct parts, "the first one, i.e. 'Tak the blode of hym that bledis,' is a prerequisite for the second action to be done,"[60] which requires the presider to write on the patient's forehead with the patient's own blood. Spoken as commands, the verbal directive accrues additional illocutionary authority by conveying an urgency in its delivery that makes the magical four letters—+A +G +L +A—especially attention getting. Thought to signify "the name of the deity,"[61] according to Ogden, these four letters call upon the transformative power of ancient divinity much in the way that the utterance of certain Latin words—*hoc est corpus meum*—signaled the transubstantiation of wine and wafer into the blood and body of Christ. The medical remedy for the staunching of a bloody nose as described above calls for a ritualized gesture which, like the sign of the cross on a communicant's forehead, was believed to facilitate the patient's recuperation.

Considered by some practitioners to be superstitious remedies of last resort, charms such as these are nonetheless included in the *Liber* in a list of medications identified explicitly in the margin of the text.[62] Along with other prescriptions in the book such ritualized remedies are especially prevalent among those cited for nosebleed, fever, toothache, and childbirth. As noted by scholars such as Lea Olsan, these prescriptions were taken seriously not only by medical practitioners such as Gilbertus Anglicus, John of Gaddesden, and Thomas Fayreford (among others) but also by the religious community in Thornton's "neighborhood."[63] The charms and prayers found in the *Liber* differ from the other medications in that they require vocalization by a presider and sometimes by the patient as well. As a form of verbal healing or speech act, charms and prayers come from a longstanding oral tradition that reaches back to the Anglo-Saxon and classical Latin past. The word that becomes associated with "charm," in fact, has its roots in the Latin lexicon. As Olsan notes, "*Carmen* is the word that in classical Latin meant, among other things, 'a solemn ritual utterance, usually sung or chanted in a metrical form' .... The word denoted, on the one hand, a religious hymn,

---

[60] Francisco Alonso-Almeida, "Oral Traces and Speech Acts in a Corpus of Medieval English Healing Charms," *ANQ*: 23.1 (2010): 6-14 (7).
[61] Ogden, *Liber*, 103.
[62] Katharine Park, "Medicine and Society in Medieval Europe, 500–1500," in *Medicine in Society*, ed. Andrew Wear (Cambridge, UK: Cambridge University Press, 1992), 59–90, points out that medical practice "did not exclude the use of occult and magical remedies, which fell within the natural realm and were often used by learned physicians" (82).
[63] Lea T. Olsan, "Charms and Prayers in Medieval Medical Theory and Practice," *Social History of Medicine* 16.1 (2003): 343–66.

or on the other, a magical chant, spell, or incantation."[64] Verbal charms in Latin embodied a sonorous metricality and rhythm that mimicked the cadences of poetry akin to that found in the alliterative and tail-rhyme romances, forms often vocalized. In a similar way, the code-switching between Middle English and Latin found in Thornton's *Liber de diversis medicinis* blends the language of the Church into the vernacular idiom, conveying meaning even to those who were not Latin literate. Many of the Latin phrases embedded in the charms would have been familiar to the churchgoing laity and memorable from recitations of the liturgy. At the same time there were many charms, especially those that incorporated Greek words, that must have sounded completely alien and mystical.[65] Holy words were powerful, in any case, but especially when enunciated by a credible authority to a sick parishioner. Such words spoken by authoritative practitioners had the capacity to convey the presence of a transcendent being at a time when comfort and healing were most needed. Everyone in the Thornton household would likely have recognized and responded to the "magic" words of charms and prayers and would have been just as likely to have anticipated efficacious results.

Medical Charms: Fever

There are many remedies for fever in the *Liber* but only a couple marked as charms by a *nota bene* device in the margin of the manuscript. Both require writing specific words on each of three wafers, accompanied by instructions to the presider to dampen each with holy water and administer them one at a time over a three-day period.[66] This is an act of inscription that adds significance to an already symbolic object in a ritual that would have been familiar and meaningful to the recipient. The three-day wafer regimen echoes Communion in its assurance that the body of Christ had literally been ingested. The writing on the wafers provides yet another aspect of the treatment that required the patient to believe in its healing potential. In another speech act in which words constitute action, this is the gesture that signifies the potency of the medication, especially if its recipient has faith in its efficacy.

---

[64] Lea T. Olsan, "Latin Charms of Medieval England: Verbal Healing in a Christian Oral Tradition," *Oral Tradition* 7.1 (1992): 116-42 (116).

[65] Julie Orlemanski, "Jargon and the Matter of Medicine in Middle English," *Journal of Medieval and Early Modern Studies* 42.2 (2012): 395-420.

[66] On the first + 1 + elie + Sabaoth +, on the second, + adonay + alpha + 0 + Messias + and on the third, + pastor + agnus + fons +

The second of the fever charms features Greek and Latin words that together lend an additional aura of divine mystery to the healing process. In a tradition that reaches back into the ancient past this combination of languages taps into early religious culture, recalling its roots in the gospels, especially the Gospel of Luke, known traditionally to have been written by a Greek physician. This second recipe requires taking three wafers and writing these words and signs on them—+ *Pater est Alpha* + & *O* +*Filius* + *vita* + *Spiritus sanctus remedium*— thereby invoking the Trinity in addition to the Alpha and Omega of Revelation. The second part of the instruction requires the presider to write the following ancient Greek words—*Agios, Otheos, Atanatos, yskiros, ymas, eleson*—"without regard to their meaning,"[67] on a piece of parchment to be followed by a series of Latin words: *Ego sum Alpha + & O + Christus vincit + Christus regnat + Christus imperat +*. These are the sanctified verbal signs that would have been recognizable even to those who did not understand the languages being spoken. Yet that is not only what imbues the words with magical potency. Rather, as Marianne Elsakkers notes, "writing—whatever the language—was considered magical,"[68] and in that sense potentially dangerous. Katharine Park tells the tale of a man named Roger Clerk, who was "prosecuted for malpractice after attempting to cure an old woman with a charm on parchment… convicted as illiterate and an 'infidel', he was sentenced to be paraded through London with the offending parchment, two urinals, and a whetstone around his neck."[69] That written words such as those deployed by Roger Clerk and presiders such as the one who administers the charm in the *Liber* as noted above were never to be used again suggests signification so powerful that once the patient was healed the charm was to be cast into the fire ("when he [the patient] es hale [healed], caste the charme in the fire").[70] The holy words along with the holy signs inscribed in the parchment are to be enacted once and only once.

Medical Charms: Toothache

There are several recipes for toothache but only one that requires the recitation of a prayer to St. Apollonia, the holy martyr who becomes the patron saint of dentistry over time. Executed by having her teeth extracted or smashed,

---

[67] Ogden, *Liber*, 109.
[68] Marianne Elsakkers, "'In Pain You Shall Bear Children' (Gen.3:16): Medieval Prayers for a Safe Delivery," in *Women and Miracle Stories: A Multidisciplinary Exploration*, ed. Anna-Marie Korte (Leiden: Brill, 2003) 195.
[69] Katharine Park, "Medieval and Society in Medieval Europe," 82.
[70] Ogden, *Liber*, 63 (ll. 20-21).

depending on which version of the story is read, the saint is often depicted in the iconography as holding a forceps in which there is an extracted tooth.[71] Designated "a charme for the tethe" in Thornton's text, the prescription urges the recitation of a Latin prayer that begins with the traditional Invocation before turning to St. Apollonia for her intercession on behalf of the patient. That the prayer is to be spoken aloud in Latin is indicated in the speech markers located in the text while the ritual that accompanies it underscores the authenticity of the procedure.[72] As made apparent in the other charms used for toothache listed in the *Liber*, Latin prayers and incantations were often indistinguishable in their purpose; both were aimed at assuaging fears and instilling a sense of calm in the patient and faith in the procedures to be undertaken. What differed among them was whether Latin or Greek predominated over the vernacular included in the recipe, both of which imbued the words with additional significance when spoken by an authoritative person. Either way, as "performative rituals" such charms enabled those in pain to negotiate the challenges that even commonplace maladies such as toothache could present.[73] In this case, they acted as analgesics both in reducing the perception of pain and by putting the patient into a receptive state of mind.

Medical Charms: Childbirth

There are three charms in the Thornton manuscript that resonate with themes of narrative medicine and its techniques. In engaging with the patient as a living text, ritual performances as recounted in the *Liber* enable a twenty-first-century audience to get closer to the experience of illness and trauma in the fifteenth century whether commonplace or life-threatening or, in this case, childbirth, which could be both. The first of these and perhaps the most compelling indicated by the *nota bene* in the margin—"here bygynnes a charme for travellyng of childe"—consists of a Latin invocation followed by a prayer, also in Latin, to the Virgin Mary. The directions for saying the prayer are not in Latin but rather in the vernacular and directed toward the speaker who then repeats the words to the travailing woman: "Say this charme thris & scho sal [shall] sone bere childe,

---

[71] See Gheorghe Gh. Bălan, et al. "Saint Apollonia: Between Paganism and Christianity in Medicine," *International Journal of Medical Dentistry* 5.19 (2015): 3-83. See also "The Martyrdom of St. Apollonia," a painting by Jean Fouquet available online.

[72] Lea T. Olsan, "Charms and Prayers," 343-66.

[73] Peter Murray Jones and Lea T. Olsan, "Performative Rituals for Conception and Childbirth in England, 900-1500," *Bulletin of the History of Medicine* 89.3 (2015): 406-33.

if it be hir tyme."[74] The magical number three recalls the Trinitarian invocation as well as the trope of resurrection so firmly embedded in the numerology of the time. So too does the charm recall the story of Lazarus, the brother of Martha and Mary, who, dead and entombed for four days, is called back to life by Jesus. Traditionally read as a prefiguration of Christ's resurrection, the gospel story underscores the kinship between life and death, whether understood literally or in symbolic terms. When a charm begins with the invocation as noted above, such words, as Lea Olsan observes, "position the earthly event of giving birth within a Christian cosmology that will protect the mother and bring the infant safely into the world."[75] In a typological analogy and like Lazarus or Christ himself, the infant is called out from a place of darkness into a world of light. To speak the charm three times is to facilitate that process.[76]

Such tropes, accompanied by symbolic gestures and words as they are, recall scriptural texts in a provocative way, to be sure, but what is especially intriguing in the directions for saying this charm is the caveat at the end. Speaking the sacred words three times replicates liturgical rituals that would certainly signal the sanctity of the occasion, yet at the end of the direction for saying the charm, there is a condition that claims the words will have their effect only "if it be hir tyme." Perhaps this hypothetical "if" clause offers a way to explain the possibility of the charm's inefficacy, suggesting instead that Nature will take its course no matter what words are said. Such a shift to Nature's role in parturition would account for the listing of additional remedies for childbirth designed to bring about a successful outcome, presumably if the holy charm failed. Two more charms in the sequence require writing a Latin phrase on parchment or a piece of cheese or butter to be ingested by the patient. Should these household edibles not be available, an alternative treatment was to have the woman drink butter and honey mixed with hot wine and "womans mylke with oile of olive," a remedy that recognizes the therapeutic value of breast milk and its implicit symbolic meaning. In the use of a lactating woman's milk, Olsan sees "a fully developed mimesis of the Eucharist that employs a mother's milk in place of wine."[77] A third prescription requires an invocation to the Virgin Mary to be written on velum and wrapped around the woman's stomach, literally encircling her with the name of the Mother of God. As the icon of human compassion and nurturing

---

[74] Ogden, *Liber*, 56 (ll. 37-38).
[75] Lea T. Olsan, "The Language of Charms," 34.
[76] Ibid. "The sacred words echo Christ calling Lazarus out of the tomb in the Gospel according to John 11:42 and are directed to the unborn child: '+ In the name of the Father + Lazarus, and of the Son + Come forth + and of the Holy Spirit + Christ calls you.'"
[77] Olsan, "The Language of Charms," 34.

maternity, there is great confidence in her efficacy in this regard. Yet there is also an intriguing disparity between the maternal power of a lactating saint and a more ordinary form of "womans mylke" used in childbirth remedies to be acknowledged here.[78]

Arguably one of the most traditional recipes in the childbirth series requires writing a charm not only directed to the Virgin but to her mother as well. Aptly dubbed the "holy mothers" charm but also referred to as *peperit* charms, these invocations were designed to harness the puissance of maternal sanctity by invoking not only the most powerful of the maternal saints, Anna and the Virgin Mary, but also Elizabeth, the mother of John the Baptist. In Thornton's version the charm deviates from the more typical *peperit* birth formula by omitting the reference to Elizabeth and ending with a nod to all the apostles, martyrs, confessors, and holy virgins, thus expanding the exclusive network of maternal saints to a wider range of sanctified support, including confessors. One thinks immediately of Margery Kempe's narration of the not-at-all-reassuring words of a priest during her birthing experience and the possibility of his inducing additional trauma. But what is especially important here, as Peter Murray Jones and Olsan point out, is that the verbal healing performance "focuses on the spoken ritual that could be voiced by any Christian comfortable with speaking Latin words, including the parturient woman, who is named as the recipient of the intercessions of Mary."[79] That there are no explicit instructions for recitation by the presider suggests that the words were likely to have been known to all those present in the birthing chamber. What is especially intriguing about this vocal performance is that the laboring woman is encouraged to replicate the cadences of the spoken charm and to speak it herself. Such a recitation, in effect, becomes "a work song," understood as a way that a woman in labor could regulate her breathing and assert some control over the birth of her child.[80] Not unlike the rhythms of poetry, parturition involves a pattern of rising and falling, an ebb and flow of the pangs of labor and the breaking of water, to be sure, but also the determination to bring the event to a successful conclusion. It is not surprising in view of this rhythmic sequence that the waters of the ocean and the anticipation of new life are associated with the spoken words of charms such as this.

---

[78] A woman's milk is an ingredient in recipes other than childbirth.
[79] Peter Murray Jones, Lea T. Olsan, "Performative Rituals," 419.
[80] Elsakkers, "In Pain You Shall Bear Children (Gen.3:16)." 179-209. "Labor, after all, is work, hard work, and labor is also in essence rhythmic: contractions and periods of relaxation alternate.... As the birthing process progresses, the speed of the birthing rhythm is gradually accelerated, progressing from initial labor, through advanced labor to active labor, when the contractions are close together and intense, finally culminating in the birth of the child" (203).

In the written charm bound to the woman's body mentioned above are Latin words that recall the surging of the sea. It is a charm in which some scholars have heard an echo of one of Virgil's poetic lines: "*Oceanum interea surgens Aurora reliquit*" ("Meanwhile, Aurora rising left the ocean"). The allusion to a Virgilian work lends another dimension of meaning to the incantation, signaling the presence of classical poetry in what many would consider to be a nonliterary form of writing. As it turns out, this line points to a pivotal episode in Book IV of the *Aeneid* that marks the moment that brings Dido and Aeneas together. While hunting in the woods the two nobles are driven to find shelter in a cave when Venus conjures up a thunderstorm for the purpose of advancing their intimate liaison. Given the implications of the scene, soon-to-be lovers in a secluded place in the woods leading to an alliance Dido would later call marriage, it is difficult to see why such an episode would be invoked in a birthing ritual centuries later. Yet the echo of Virgilian poetry in a late medieval charm for childbirth in Thornton's *Liber* offers us another way to think about the meaning of charms as a generative form of poetry. As is well known, Virgil was understood by many medieval writers to be the *vates* who prophesied the birth of Christ and extolled the virtue of the Virgin in his fourth eclogue. So too the *Aeneid* is an epic poem that charts the birth of Rome, out of which evolved the fictional genealogy of the British people reaching back centuries to Aeneas himself. When the allusion to Virgil in this charm is acknowledged, in other words, it not only illuminates the presence of poetry in texts not often considered to be literary, or memorable for that matter, but infuses the words of a revered poet and a glorious Roman past into a text literally wrapped around a laboring woman's body. As Elsakkers notes, this was poetry worth remembering, "hexameters from Vergil seem to indicate that these texts were considered to be poetry, i.e. they were felt to be rhythmic, and could therefore easily function as a mnemonic device."[81] Not only could such charms be used to regulate the breathing of a laboring mother, to encourage her efforts, but they could be used as verbal healing rituals that crystalized memories of the event itself. That Thornton included a commemoration of a birth in his compendious collection may factor into his compilation strategies in this regard.

Given the integral kinship between life and death implicit in every birth likely to have taken place in the Thornton household during the plague years, it is not surprising that the childbirth series in the *Liber* ends with how to deliver a stillborn: for this there are two recipes. In the first, the woman is to have her navel and stomach covered in the leaves of leeks scalded in fire. In the second,

---

[81] Elsakkers, "In Pain You Shall Bear Children (Gen 3:16)," 193.

the woman is to be given a drink made of mugwort and rue or, lacking these ingredients, the juice of vervain. Neither of these recipes is accompanied by a prayer or a charm or even an allusion to Virgilian poetry but rather presented as a straightforward prescription without ritual performance. Instead, the procedure seems to remind its audience of the precariousness of childbirth and the possibility of death whether for child or mother or both. From texts such as these we begin to hear the voices of those in the throes of labor; we begin to understand the extent of their everyday illnesses as well, perhaps more viscerally and with greater empathy. The patients who are recipients of these prescriptions and treatments repeated, ingested, and literally embodied these texts. Such practices tell us what we otherwise would not be able to hear or see or feel.

Narrating Medicine in Thornton Household Recipes

Reading the *Liber de diversis medicinis* as a collection of medical recipes designed to provide remedies that factor into the life rhythms of those residing in Thornton's household enables us to internalize and empathize with their experience. Pain and trauma incurred by a child or an adult as well as those who have undergone childbirth or endured any number of illnesses speak their stories even through the silence of written texts. As in the diagnostic procedures outlined in narrative medicine, they provide us, as readers of their bodies and words, stories that speak of their sickness and injury, their aspirations and desires, their doubts and beliefs. Whether imperialist in their goals and tragic in their outcome, organized around a family household and marriage, or extolling the adventures of knights and ladies, whether pious in their principles or cautionary in their views, the tales collected in this manuscript run the gamut of possibilities for enhancing the lives of Thornton's family and friends as well as Thornton himself. Medical reading exposes some of the health-care challenges facing fifteenth-century gentry households: all are aware of the possibility of sudden death at the "strok of pestilence." And perhaps that accounts for the number of charms and prayers dedicated to childbirth and the continuation of the Thornton family. Women and children, even when not addressed directly or by name, are present in their absence, indicated by the selections made for the compilation, the fleeting reference to the birth of a child, and the extended attention paid to parturition and the efficacy of a woman's milk. In Thornton's compilation there is an implicit and keen medical consciousness brought to fruition in the *Liber de diversis medicinis* in its wide range of recipes, in the cadences of its poetry, in the centrality of its treatise on pestilence.

If we return to John of Burgundy's advice to his readers to become their own physicians, and we accept Thornton not only as an accomplished scribe-compiler and "gentleman reader" but also as an arbiter of health and well-being, we may begin to appreciate his work anew. If we accept Thornton's participation in an emerging medical discourse, then to read the manuscript from a medical point of view becomes not only plausible but necessary. To make those in the middle of a recurring epidemic aware of how that disease could overtake the body, what to do should it strike, and how to prevent it from occurring is to care for the self as well as others. By combining medical recipes with narrative poetry and ritual performances, Thornton infuses his codices with a heartbeat that lives on in his work.

5

Women Healers, Life Writing, and Therapeutic Reading

Ipocras this bok sende to the Emperor Sesar.
Wite thou wel that this bok ys leche
To alle thing that hit doyth teche;
Do also this bok hym bit,
Hit techeth lechys al here wyt,
Of ech maner evyl what-so-evere it be,
So here aftur thou myght se
Man or womman that havth nature,
How thou schalt him take in cure.
Now thou man tak good yeme [heed]
How thou schalt thi body yeme.

—Anonymous, MS Douce 84[1]

Here begynnys A tretis fyne
Made in ynglys owt of latyne
Hyt techis the helpe and the defens
Agaynes the seknes of the pestilens

—Attributed to John of Bordeaux, 1390[2]

… the pestylens ys so fervent in Norwych that thay ther [dare] no lenger abyde ther….

—Margaret Paston (to her husband),
18 August 1465[3]

---

[1] Rossell Hope Robbins, ed. *Secular Lyrics of the XIVth and XVth Centuries*, 2nd edition (Oxford: Clarendon Press, 1954), 95. See also M. Teresa Tavormina, "The Middle English Letter of Ipocras," *English Studies* 88.6 (2007): 632-52. See also, George R. Keiser, "Verse Introductions to Middle English Medical Treatise," *English Studies* 84.4 (2003): 301-17.

[2] Rossell Hope Robbins, "Medical Manuscripts in Middle English," *Speculum* 45 (1970): 282-98 (407). The manuscript in which this quotation appears is Egerton 1624, f.216r.

[3] *Paston Letters*, vol. 4, Project Gutenberg. https://www.gutenberg.org

When read within the context of late medieval household miscellanies like Thornton's Lincoln Cathedral MS 91 manuscript, the answer to what kinds of writing contribute to a medical discourse takes on greater clarity. Whether written in alliterative or in tail-rhyme verse, narrative poetry offers scenes of medical treatment and imaginative escape, prayers convey medical efficacy in verbal performance, saints' lives tell stories of intercessory healing and fortitude, and charms show how matter and metaphor could combine to relieve pain, staunch bleeding, and aid in childbirth. In like manner, objects could become healing instruments, rituals could increase confidence in therapeutics, and adventure stories could have a mood-altering effect. Not only are words necessary for medical treatment but they register in the sick body, the social context surrounding that body, and the shared experience of illness that all humans have at one time or another in their lives. As Louise Bishop observes, there is "an inescapable physicality embedded in words," enabling stones and herbs as well as words spoken or written to become vibrant purveyors of health and well-being.[4] Thus *Gratia Dei*, or "virtue given by God," could be understood both as liturgical expressions and as medicinal compounds, pearls and other stones could become healing objects, and herbs such as rosemary could be understood as the Rose of Mary.[5] When surgeon-physicians such as Guy de Chauliac, John of Arderne, and Gilbertus Anglicus concur that "to thre things God gaveth vertu: to worde, to herbis, and to stonis," they signaled the recognition of healing by practitioners as both psychological and physiological, the "vertu" ascribed to words, herbs, and stones understood as a natural force of regeneration, growth, and healing or what Holly Crocker considers to be an "embodied excellence" attributed to women.[6]

As noted in the first epigraph above, medical treatises, or "bokes of phsik" as they were also known, could be made into speaking objects, talking practitioners whose task was to encourage their readers to heed the medical advice found within. The conceit that Hippocrates sends a book of advice to the emperor suggests that medical authority could supersede political authority when it came to the health of the body. Originally written in Anglo-Norman by an anonymous

---

[4] Louise Bishop, *Words, Stones, Herbs: The Healing Word in Medieval and Early Modern England* (Syracuse: Syracuse University Press, 2007), 12.
[5] According to the *Dictionary of Medical Vocabulary in English*, 1373–1550, both John of Arderne and Guy de Chauliac knew of this compound, conveyed in texts that came to light in 1425 (1195). But what is especially intriguing about the expression "virtue given by God" is that it is the name of a medication, an "ointment" proven to be effective on "ocular lacerations."
[6] Holly A. Crocker, *The Matter of Virtue: Women's Ethical Action from Chaucer to Shakespeare* (Philadelphia: University of Pennsylvania Press, 2019), esp. chapter 3.

author in the mid-thirteenth century, the poem's translation into Middle English in several manuscripts of the fifteenth century affords another dimension of medical puissance. As in John of Burgundy's urging of his readers to become their own physicians, this book ostensibly by Hippocrates encourages those in need of health care to become their own doctors. Like Thornton's copy of the *Liber de diversis medicinis*, texts such as these are invaluable in the dissemination of medical information both credible and authoritative to a vernacular audience. As "speaking" texts, they convey advice and pragmatic remedies sorely needed in a time of pestilence or, as the treatise by John of Bordeaux in the second epigraph above suggests, "hyt techis the [you] helpe and the defens / Agaynes the seknes of the pestilens."

The shift from the pseudo-Hippocratic voice to a book that speaks on behalf of medical practice recalls the self-doctoring advice carried on in translations attributed to John of Bordeaux (as in the epigraph above) that applies not to an emperor but rather to those who read the work as a guide for carrying out prescribed treatments on their own. There are limitations to the book's reach, however, in its implicit presumption that its audience is made up of aspiring *male* practitioners, a perception clarified in another verse circulating at the time: "Man that wole of lechecrafte here / Rede over this booke & he may lere / Manye medycenys ben goode & trewe, / To leche sore both olde & newe" (1-4).[7] That this verse does not include women in its immediate audience but rather presumes the practice of medicine to be the exclusive province of men captures the prevailing attitudes toward women practitioners or anyone presuming to practice medicine without validation from male authorities. As Katharine Park observes, there were efforts at the time "to limit the number and variety of healers by excluding certain groups from legitimate medical practice," a move in which women got "caught in the crossfire," according to Monica Green.[8] That such a process of exclusion did not happen overnight but rather grew in urgency over time is prefigured in the *Regimen sanitatis Salernitantum*, the long poem associated with the medical knowledge of Salerno, the home of the renowned Trotula. In a section of the text marked "Medicaster" the text's author critiques those considered to be "false doctors," a category in which he includes the "unlettered, the empiric, the Jew, the monk, the actor, the barber, the old woman,

---

[7] Robbins, *Secular Lyrics*, 95.
[8] Katharine Park, "Medicine and Society in Medieval Europe, 500-1500," in *Medicine in Society*, ed. Andrew Wear (Cambridge, UK: Cambridge University Press, 2010), 59-90 (78). See also Monica Green, "Women's Medical Practice and Health Care in Medieval Europe," *Signs* 14.2 (1989): 434-73 (447).

each pretend[ing] to be a doctor, as does the alchemist, the maker of cosmetics, the bathkeeper, the forger, the oculist"—all of whom he claims were profiting in and denigrating "the power of medicine."[9]

Indeed, the gradual exclusion of women from professional medical practice in the early fifteenth century is a narrative often recounted in histories of medicine that reach back to the School of Salerno and the well-known female physician-author associated with it (Trotula).[10] While that history includes women who practiced openly as did Jacoba Felicie in France, England's Statute of 1421 indicated that female practitioners were to be prohibited from engaging in their craft. As Green explains it,

> it was not until 1421 that a petition was put before Parliament requesting, among other measures to ensure the physicians' hegemony, "that no Woman use the practyse of Fisyk undre the same payne" of "long emprisonement" and a fine of forty pounds. That this measure was ultimately ineffectual does not diminish the fact that the desire to prohibit women's medical practice was obviously real.[11]

Such regulatory statutes did not dissuade women from delivering medical services in a multitude of ways to a wide variety of patients, however, as empirics, midwives, wetnurses, hospital sisters, "nurses," herbalists, and householders.[12] Nor were they deterred from deploying what Laura Kalas identifies as "spiritual medicine" in their written work.[13] In other words, women healers were quietly engaged in medical treatment, both spiritual and physical, practicing a mode of caregiving that male practitioners would or could not do; they served the sick, the disabled, the poor, the disenfranchised with neither legal recognition nor financial compensation but rather to serve others or accrue what one scholar calls "social capital."[14] Some were part of a network of women healers, while some were not; some acquired their healing skills from family members or informal mentors; some simply acquired their knowledge from experience and necessity.

---

[9] Park, "Medicine and Society," 76. The category of particular interest in this list is the "old woman," a character type who will become associated with witchcraft over time.

[10] That controversy appears to have been settled as has the debate over whether female practitioners exclusively treated women or whether they crossed gender boundaries. See Celeste Chamberland, "Female Healers and the Boundaries of Medical Practice," Concordia University, MA thesis, 1997.

[11] Green, "Women's Medical Practice," 449.

[12] I agree with Laura Kalas's inclusion of nursemaids, governesses, and foster parents in the category of "nurses." See *Margery Kempe's Spiritual Medicine: Suffering, Transformation and the Life Course* (Cambridge, UK: D. S. Brewer, 2020), 130.

[13] Kalas, *Margery Kempe's Spiritual Medicine*, passim.

[14] Ashlee Barwell, "The Healing Arts and Social Capital: The Paston Women of Fifteenth-Century England," *Canadian Bulletin of Medical History* 35 (2018): 137-59.

The women healers addressed at the outset of this chapter are writers not often thought of as having contributed to medical discourse or engaged in the healing of actual patients. Nonetheless, Margaret Paston, Julian of Norwich, and Margery Kempe enable us to hear their narratives from a broader purview and range of experiences than other writers of the time. Each of these women deploys healing in ways that differentiate one from the other, ranging from the pragmatic to the theoretical, from an embodied mode of expression to religious abstraction. When we consider them to be healers as well as mystics and/or mothers, their writing accrues medical meanings beneficial to readers in need of medical care as well as to women interested in healing. Like John of Burgundy, whose medical writing incorporates his knowledge of medicine and its applications, these women writers lend an authentic subjectivity to their written work. Considered within the context of an evolving medical discourse and understood in terms of narrative medicine, the Paston letters, *The Book of Margery Kempe*, and the Short and Long Texts of Julian of Norwich enable us to see how women who were not recognized formally for their healing practices could contribute to the medical knowledge of the time. Their stories let us hear narratives of illness from a woman's point of view, enabling us to acknowledge the range of women's engagement with health care, filling in some of the silences left in the history of medicine in that regard.

So too do the narratives of fictional women have something to say. The translation and adaptation of Latin medical texts that become such a notable feature of late medieval book production finds correspondence in the translation and adaptation of Anglo-Norman romances and Breton lays many of which feature women healers in prominent roles or doing health-care work silently in the background. Heroines of romance enable their vernacular audiences to witness their active engagement in medical practices beyond those so often ascribed to them. Literary women of medicine such as Morgan le Fay, Josian of *Bevis of Hampton, Le Bone Florence of Rome*, Chaucer's Trotula and Pertelote, Dame Emme of *Piers Plowman*, Gower's Medea, and even the Pearl-maiden demonstrate how medicine administered by women alleviates the ills of society as well as the ailments of individual bodies. These are some of the characters who heal the wounds of knights injured from battle, who cure lovers debilitated by lovesickness, who reverse the incapacities of old age, and provide therapeutic reading for audiences in need.[15] Whether historically verifiable or

---

[15] "Therapeutic reading" is a term used by Daniel McCann in his book on "Soul-Health," deployed here to describe a different sort of reading, especially appealing to women and their allies.

verifiably ahistorical, the women healers addressed in this chapter contribute to the health of all those around them whether through their writing or through their experiences in the world. That the medical recipes often administered by women—ointments, salves, plasters, medicinal drinks, and so on—find correspondence in recipe books as well as in other genres brings the material environment into conversation with innovative modes of healing. As Louise Bishop observes, some recipes, in fact, were so strongly associated with women that they were presumed to be their "devisers."[16] While Bishop is referring explicitly to the recipe for *Gratia Dei* attributed to Margaret Beauchamp, the maternal grandmother of Henry VII, there are remedies made with ingredients associated with female saints; the medicinal herb known to practitioners as rosemary, for instance, is made virtually miraculous by the story of its origin. When the Virgin Mary spread her azure cloak over a flowering bush one day, the gesture turned its blossoms from white to blue, indicating not only that a transformation had taken place but that the object of that transformation had accrued a wondrous power. Hence the blossoming bush came to be known as the Rose of Mary.[17]

Women Healers and Communal Medicine

Not often thought of as healers, the three women writers addressed at the outset of this chapter provide evidence of a holistic approach to health care in the 100+ years under investigation in this study. But rather than identifying their writing within traditionally ascribed genres—Margaret Paston's as epistolary, Margery Kempe's as autobiographical or semi-autobiographical, and Julian of Norwich's Short and Long texts as visionary revelation—here I consider their work to be a form of "life writing." Just as Linda Erhsam Voigts observes that "it is artificial to separate prose from verse in considering Middle English medical writings,"[18] the life writings of these women should not be separated from the poetry of the male authors noted in previous chapters—Chaucer, Gower, Langland, Lydgate, and

---

[16] Bishop, *Words, Stones, and Herbs*. One such example is found in Additional 33996, wherein the recipe for *Gratia Dei* is attributed to "the lady bechampe, the erles wyf of Warwyk," presumed to be Margaret Beauchamp (144).

[17] See English Heritage. https://blog.english-heritage.org.uk/ See also Ian Hemphill and Lynne Cobiac, "The Historical and Cultural Use of Herbs and Spices," *MJA Supplement: The Medical Journal of Australia* 185.4 (August 21, 2006): S1-S24.

[18] Linda Ehrsam Voigts, "Medical Prose," in *Middle English Prose: A Critical Guide to Major Authors and Genres*, ed. A. S. G. Edwards, et al. (New Brunswick, NJ: Rutgers University, 1984), 315-35 (317).

Hoccleve—or deemed a lesser form of textual production. Rather, by considering their writing to have emerged from experience rather than *auctorité*, we get a better sense of how to register their suffering and listen attentively to their stories. Treating their writings in a way that acknowledges the materiality of the female body and the status of women in society enables us to see how their work factors into the evolving medical discourse of the time. While all of these women speak through a less formalized textual network than their male counterparts, often through verbal exchanges, scribal associations, and ecclesiastical contacts, they nonetheless open up "'pathways to wellbeing' without resorting to professional medicine."[19] In their writings, Margaret Paston, Julian of Norwich, and Margery Kempe forge a "pathway to wellbeing" indispensable to a more fulsome perception of late medieval health care and medical practices that include women. Their writings provide a more comprehensive view of the experience of pestilence while marking an important shift to women's roles in ministering to the spiritual and physical health of others.

Pestilence and Household Healing

It is perhaps a commonplace to note that women were the center of the household and largely responsible for the everyday health of its occupants. Margaret Paston is exemplary in this regard, and her letters reveal a level of medical consciousness that exceeds that of the correspondence of the women of other households in the region. According to Hannah Ingram, of the three contemporary gentry families—the Pastons, the Stonors, and the Plumptons—Margaret is the most prolific writer, and arguably the woman who acquires the greatest authority in pharmaceuticals and their use.[20] In view of Margaret's skepticism about university-trained physicians, an opinion shaped by her witness of the failure of medical treatment for her sick uncle Philip, perhaps this heightened medical consciousness stands to reason. As Ingram explains,

> [a] particularly illustrative example of when the Paston letters record the use of a medical professional occurred in 1452, when Margaret reported upon her Uncle Philip's sickness, noting that his health had deteriorated to such an extent that he was unlikely to survive without "redy help" and so he was travelling to Suffolk as there was "a good fesician" (a good physician) there … the subsequent death

---

[19] Faye Getz, *Medicine in the English Middle Ages* (Princeton, NJ: Princeton University Press, 1998), 85.
[20] Hannah Ingram, "'Pottes of Tryacle' and 'Bokes of Phisyke': The Fifteenth-Century Disease Practices of Three Gentry Families," *Social History of Medicine* 32.4 (2018): 751-72 (753).

of her Uncle Philip from his sickness, and presumably the failure of his hired physicians, had a profound effect upon Margaret, effectively justifying her, and by extension, her family's negative opinion of professional medicine.[21]

That skepticism played out several years later in Margaret's letter to her husband to warn him not to be tempted by the "medesynys" of the physicians of London, explaining that she would never trust them after what happened to her uncle. With this level of doubt, it appears that Margaret turned to home remedies much more frequently than did the women of the other families noted above. Compared to the Stonor and Plumpton women, Margaret demonstrates a notable knowledge of a range of medical preparations; she knows, for example, the medicinal value of the most expensive imported pharmaceuticals available. On the 1st of July 1451 she asks her husband to send along a "potte with treacle in hast; for I have ben rygth evyll att ese, and your dowghter bothe, syth that ye yeden hence, and on [one] of the talles yownge men of this parysch lyth syke and hath a grete myrr."[22] The therapeutic preparation known as treacle or theriac is a compound thought to be especially effective in treating pestilence as well as other ailments. Margaret requests that it be delivered quickly to assuage the fear she shares with her daughter about the disease that has afflicted a young man so close to home. While the *MED* defines "myrr" as a nose infection, Margaret's reference to it as a "grete myrr" suggests that this may be a more fearsome condition than initially reported.[23] Described as one of the handsomest young men in the parish, and presumably the vision of strength ordinarily, he has been incapacitated by this infection, stricken down and relegated to a sickbed. Were this description offered in another medical milieu at a different moment in history, the possibility that this illness is less than it seems would be taken at face value. But because Margaret Paston's writings reference pestilence frequently enough to create the impression that outbreaks in Norwich and surrounding regions remain a cause for concern, it is probable that the young man has contracted the illness. Several of Margaret's family members were known to have died of the plague, including her son William.

In another reference made on the 18th of August 1465, Margaret writes to tell her husband that her cousin, Elizabeth Clere, will host his mother at Elizabeth's

---

[21] Ingram, "The Fifteenth-Century Disease," 761.
[22] *Paston Letters*, vol. 2, July 1, 1451. Project Gutenberg. https://www.gutenberg.org See Ingram, "The Fifteenth-Century Disease," 751-72. The *MED* defines "myrr" as a nose infection, while in her book on the Pastons, Diane Watt translates the term to "pestilence." See *The Paston Women: Selected Letters* (Cambridge, UK: D. S. Brewer, 2004), 59.
[23] Park, "Medicine and Society," 61.

house in Caistor "for the pestylens ys so fervent in Norwych that thay ther [dare] no lenger abyde ther,"[24] and on November 5th, 1471 she asks for money to repay a debt to the same cousin with an update on the spread of the epidemic: "we levyn in fer, but we wut [know] not qweder [whether] to fle, for to bet better than we ben here."[25] Margaret's anxiety about not knowing where family members could flee to escape the epidemic is a chilling reminder of the plague's ubiquitous presence. In one of his letters to his father (November 6, 1479), Margaret's son John III also remarks upon the perilous circumstances surrounding them: "The pepyll dyeth sore in Norwyche, and specially abought my house, but my wyff and my women come not ought, and fle ferther we cannot; for at Sweynsthorpe, sythe my departyng thens, they have dyed, and ben syke nye in every house of the towne."[26] There was a notable need for medical remedies made all the more urgent by recurrent outbreaks of pestilence in Norwich throughout most of the fifteenth century. The fear of contagion and exposure to corrupt air as noted by John of Burgundy and other plague doctors translate into a concern that Margaret and other members of her family register in several of their correspondences. Thus, it is not surprising to learn that this medically savvy woman requests a "recipe book to tackle pestilential illness in 1452" or that her son commissioned a version of Burgundy's treatise for family use.[27] There is, in fact, evidence that "John Paston II received a letter in 1468 from William Ebesham, a scribe he had recently employed. Included in this otherwise innocuous looking letter was a bill for Ebesham's work, a section of which cited a price of twenty pennies for the 'wrytyng of the litilll boke of phisyke' which John had evidently commissioned."[28] That this appears to be a version of the plague treatise that Robert Thornton had in his possession and included in the Lincoln Cathedral manuscript suggests the dissemination of variants of the tract among Northern gentry families. The version in the Pastons' possession, identified as the treatise found in Ballard Catalogue No. 19 (fols.43r-49v), is closely related, according to Marta Powell

[24] *Paston Letters*, vol. 4, August 18, 1465. Project Gutenberg. https://www.gutenberg.org
[25] *Paston Letters*, vol. 5, November 5, 1471. Project Gutenberg. https://www.gutenberg.org
[26] *Paston Letters*, vol. 6, Project Gutenberg. https://www.gutenberg.org Written by John III on St. Leonard's Day, 1479 to Sir John Paston.
[27] Elaine Whitaker, "Reading the Paston Letters Medically," *English Language Notes* (1993): 19-27. "Sir John Paston, too, appears to prefer controlling his health care-in-house when he commissions 'a litill booke of pheesyk' from William Ebesham. A. I. Doyle has identified the handwriting of Ebesham in Boston Medical Library MS Ballard Catalogue No. 19, a medical manuscript in both Latin and Middle English dating from ca. 1450-1475" (22). Linda Ehrsam Voigts, in "Medical Prose," describes the medical book the scribe copied for John Paston as follows: "In this manuscript, the Middle English treatise on urine is followed by the Latin 'Expositione Urinarum in Ordine.' The English 'John of Burdeux' plague tract is a paraphrase or summary of the Latin 'Tractatus contra Morbum Epidemialem' which precedes it" (316).
[28] Ingram, "The Fifteenth-Century Disease Management Practices," 765.

Harley, "to the Latin plague tracts that precede and follow it. The first Latin treatise (fols. 33r-43r), which bears the name John of Burgundy, is the apparent source of the Middle English piece, a shorter tract in four chapters ascribed to John of Bordeaux."[29] This implies that the pestilence was more than a minor presence in the medical milieu of the time and threatening enough to prompt the Pastons to take matters into their own hands.

Like the translated John of Burgundy treatise, this plague treatise identifies itself in a similar way, its author claiming to be "Bearded John also known as John of Burgundy" (*Iohannis de Barba alias dicti Iohannis de Burdegalia*), who has written "in the English language against the deadly pestilence or epidemic" (*in lingua Anglicana contra morbum pestilencialem sive epidemialem*). As in the version of the pestilence treatise in Thornton's manuscript, the author identifies himself more explicitly in English as the "gode phisician Iohn of Burdeux" before launching into a synopsis of the chapters that will tell of "hou a man shall kepe hym in tyme of pestilence that he fall nat into that evill"; "hou this sekenes coomyth," what "medicyn [to use] ayen this evill"; and "hou he shall be kepte in hit."[30] The text then elaborates on each of these topics, explaining what a man should eat and drink to prevent the plague from taking hold, what procedures should be followed to address the illness if contracted, followed by variations on the medicinal regimens to treat the illness should the patient survive its initial onslaught. As in the treatise in the Thornton *Liber*, the author uses the language of combat to describe how the disease attacks the body's principal organs— the heart, the brain, and the liver—before explaining how to track the poison's progress once it has entered the body. He describes how to go about doing a phlebotomy, concentrating on where to do the incisions: the cardiac vein for the heart, the cephalic vein for the head, "between thee thies [thighs] and the body" (l. 72) for the liver. Should the patient live through the treatment, the dietary follow-up includes a "potage of almandis" and "tysan" [barley water] (l. 101) as well as a light meal of chicken soaked in water or fish roasted and eaten with vinegar. Four herbs—ditane, pimpernel, turmentill, and scabious (l. 90-91)—make for an effective therapeutic drink, while two other ingredients available only through the "spicers" (apothecaries) are recommended should the patient be able to afford them; called "bolle armoniak (Armenian bole) and *terra sigillata*" (l. 107), the former is red clay thought to be from Armenia, while the latter is "sealed earth" presumed to be from the isle of Lemnos. The treatise

---

[29] Marta Powell Harley, "The Middle English Contents of a Fifteenth-Century Medical Handbook," *Mediaevalia* 8 (1982): 171-88.
[30] See Harley, "The Middle English Contents," 182-5.

ends by stating that if these treatments are followed, the patient shall "from this sekenesse be kepid & delivered" (l. 115), by the grace of God.

To say that Margaret Paston acquired a pharmaceutical arsenal along with the skills needed to deploy her medical weapons in a battle against the pestilence is substantiated by her written observations and her awareness of the epidemic's lethality. Recall her reference to the "gret myrr" of the young man in 1451, her report of the spread of pestilence to her husband in 1465, and her son's acquisition of a plague treatise in 1468; all of these citations are rendered more meaningful in view of Margaret's skepticism about the medical skills of London physicians, her increasing concern about the spread of the pestilence, and her taking medical matters into her own hands.

Chronicling the Pestilence

Margaret Paston's vantage point on the ubiquitous nature of the epidemic in the mid-fifteenth century in Norwich provides a useful perspective for looking back to the writings of Julian of Norwich and Margery Kempe. While neither of these mystics speaks as overtly of the plague as Margaret Paston does, there are allusions in their writings that signal their awareness of its presence. One might even argue that their work constitutes a response to an epidemic they are likely to have understood not scientifically but rather as divine punishment for human sin. The historical context and medical milieu are significant in this regard, and the chroniclers' statements that follow here serve as a reminder of how devastating and protracted the epidemic was during the lifetime of these two women.

Between the beginning of the epidemic in England in 1348 and the time of Julian's first vision and Margery's birth in 1373, there had been several outbreaks described in strikingly similar language. Henry Knighton writes: "In 1361 a general mortality oppressed the people. It was called the second pestilence and both rich and poor died, but especially young people and children." In the *Anonimalle Chronicle* the entry appears likewise: "In 1361 there was a second pestilence within England, which was called the mortality of children. Several people of high birth and a great number of children died." This second outbreak was followed by a third in 1369 that, according to the anonymous chronicler, "was great beyond measure, lasted a long time, and was particularly fatal to children." To that year's description Thomas Walsingham adds that there was "a great pestilence, which also affected larger animals. It was followed by floods and a great blight of corn, so that in the following year a measure of grain sold for 3s." The fourth outbreak occurred in 1374 and continued to 1379. Beginning "in several towns in the south of the country," it moved to London, where it killed "a large number of Londoners, from among the wealthier and more eminent citizens," even "well-placed clerks of the Chancery, Common Pleas and Exchequer." In 1375 the plague arrived in "the north country," and the following year in York, where it was "particularly fatal to children." The fifth outbreak occurred in the early 1390s:

> In 1390 a great plague ravaged the country. It especially attacked adolescents and boys, who died in incredible numbers in towns and villages everywhere.... In 1391 such a great mortality arose in Norfolk and in many other counties that it was thought as bad as the great pestilence. To take only one example, in a short space of time 11,000 bodies were buried at York. In September 1393 many died in Essex from an outbreak of the plague.[31]

Thought to have been born shortly before the plague arrived in England (1342-3 according to Nicholas Watson and Jacqueline Jenkins), Julian of Norwich is likely to have witnessed the deaths of many of the region's inhabitants, though little is known about her childhood.[32] Whether she lived as a Benedictine nun before her enclosure or as a laywoman, possibly a wife and mother who accepted enclosure at her widowhood,[33] it is highly probable that she was aware of the medical crisis unfolding around her. Whether she was an anchoress or part of a monastic order or a householder in her own right, Julian was, no doubt, familiar with medicinal herbs and palliative care if not more serious forms of medical treatment. By taking the name of Julian the Hospitaller, the saint for whom St. Julian's Church, the site of her enclosure, was named, she signals a virtual embodiment of sanctity associated with healing, hospitality, and hospitals. Commemorated in the *Legenda Aurea* this is the saint who inspired the "Knights Hospitaller, the male religious and chivalric order that has its origins in caring for sick pilgrims in the Holy Lands."[34] By assuming the name of Julian the Hospitaller, the anchoress obliterates traditional gender boundaries,

---

[31] All quotations are from *The Black Death*, ed. and trans. Rosemary Horrox (Manchester: Manchester University Press, 1994), 85-92.

[32] *The Writings of Julian of Norwich: A Vision Showed to a Devout Woman and a Revelation of Love*, ed. Nicholas Watson and Jacqueline Jenkins (University Park, PA: The Pennsylvania State University Press, 2006), 4.

[33] Liz Herbert McAvoy, *Authority and the Female Body in the Writings of Julian of Norwich and Margery Kempe* (Rochester, NY: Boydell & Brewer, 2004), 22.

[34] Diane Watt, "Mary the Physician: Women, Religion and Medicine in the Middle Ages," in *Medicine, Religion and Gender in Medieval Culture*, ed. Naoë Kukita Yoshikawa (Cambridge, UK: D. S. Brewer, 2015), 31.

enabling the development of one of the signature themes of her work—the motherhood of God. Julian's description of her own debilitating illness, one that affects her from the waist down, enables her, moreover, to assume a dual position both as patient in need of care and as arbiter of well-being for others.[35] Wielding the medicalized language of Christian theology with an emphasis on compassion and offering a more expansive understanding of gender, Julian provides therapeutic reading for a vernacular audience in need of consolation in the face of a recurring epidemic. Her frequent iteration of "alle shalle be welle" provides a calm, assuring voice in a troubled time.

The parallels between Julian of Norwich and Margery Kempe are striking enough to remark upon here. Born in the year that Julian received her visions (1373), Margery appears to have some cosmic affinity with the well-known anchoress; both share a distinctive brand of mysticism; both dedicate themselves to their chosen religious vocations; both write out of their illness experiences while at the same time, appearing to be virtual opposites. While Julian emotes in the stillness of enclosure, Margery engages in nonstop e-motion; her tears, her vocalizations, her gestures, and her pilgrimages contrast sharply with Julian's anchoritic immobility and measured utterances. Nonetheless, they come together over the course of several days, according to Margery's *Book*, in a meeting that affirms intersecting perspectives despite the differences in writing styles and approaches to devotional expression. Much in the way that a senior empiric mentors a medical student in her chosen profession, the meeting of the two women enables the sharing of spiritual knowledge in a meaningful dialogic exchange.

The historical milieu into which Julian of Norwich and Margery Kempe were born, as described so graphically by the chroniclers, was rife with pestilence, yet in Julian's writings reference to the epidemic is nearly absent except for an allusion that occurs during a conversation with Jhesu about sin. When the mystic asks whether all could be well without it, Jhesu replies that sin enables purgation, self-knowledge, and mercy: "For it purges us and makes us to knawe oureselfe and aske mercy."[36] This is the point at which Julian asks how all can be well in the face of "the grete harme that is comon by synne to thy creatures?"[37] While Watson and Jenkins read "grete harme" as original sin, here I think it is just as likely a reference to the plague and equivalent to terms like the "grete mortalite,"

---

[35] Daniel McCann, *Soul-Health: Therapeutic Reading in Later Medieval England* (Cardiff: University of Wales Press, 2018).
[36] Watson and Jenkins, *Writings*, 93. Section 13, ll. 57–8.
[37] Ibid. Section 14, ll. 3.

the "grete moreyne," the "grete pestilens," or the "grete myrr," as indicated by Margaret Paston. Given the many outbreaks both prior to and following Julian's enclosure, it stands to reason that she would not only have been aware of its presence by the stench in the air but also by witnessing its devastating effects. The "grete harme" that is common to humans may, of course, refer to original sin, but so too could it be read as referring to the human transgressions of the historical present as a provocation for the punishment that the plague was thought to be by so many clerics. Corroboration of this reading may be found in *The Book of Margery Kempe* in a conversation between Margery and Jhesu in which she asks that he show mercy to suffering people, to which he replies, "I may no mor, dowtyr, of my rytfulnesse do for hem than I do. I send hem prechyng & techyng, pestylens & bataylys, hungyr and famynyng, losse of her goodys wyth gret sekenesse, & many other tribulacyons, & thei wyl not levyn my wordys ne thei wyl not knowe my vysitacyon."[38] In other words, pestilence (along with war, hunger, and famine) is sent by God to jolt humans to attention, to make them listen, change the error of their ways, and ask for mercy. That there can be no mercy without suffering appears to be the message and envisioning the Passion as a medication capable of healing every soul is part of that message. As Julian says, "Be this medicin behoves everilke sinfulle saule be heled, and namlye of sinnes that ere dedely in the selfe."[39]

One of the other more subtle references to pestilence in Margery's *Book* occurs when the Abbess of Denny invites her to the abbey to speak with her and her fellow nuns.[40] The request would have been considered special not only because the abbey was strictly enclosed but that its abbess recognized Margery as a credible speaker, a guest who could bring comfort to those whose lives were dedicated to comforting others. Despite the prestige of the invitation, however, Margery is reluctant to make the trip, fearful that she might not endure such a journey, thinking instead that she should wait another year before venturing out. This is the point at which she is commanded by her divine interlocutor to "go forth to the hows of Denney in the name of Jhesu, for I wole that thu comfort hem."[41] Under any other circumstances Margery would have likely obeyed immediately, but the fear is so great about the presence of the plague that she is still reluctant to take a

---

[38] Sanford Brown Meech, ed. *The Book of Margery Kempe*, EETS, o.s. 212 (London: Oxford University Press, 1940; reprint 1961), 48.
[39] Watson and Jenkins, *Writings*, 101.
[40] The abbey was six miles north of Cambridge and once a Templar house, but "re-founded as a Franciscan monastery" by the Countess of Pembroke. See Anthony Bale, ed. and trans. *The Book of Margery Kempe* (Oxford: Oxford University Press, 2015), 264.
[41] Meech, *The Book of Margery Kempe*, 202.

chance. She thought she would die for no good reason: "Sche was loth to gon, for it was pestylens-tyme, & hir thowt that sche wolde for no good a deyd ther."[42] Her doubts are finally assuaged when she is given divine assurance that she would be able to go to the abbey safely and return just as safely. Nothing more is revealed about this visit in Margery's *Book* other than that it took place during a time of pestilence (probably 1420, according to Kalas). What is significant in the elusive and fragmentary telling of the tale, however, is that a meeting of the abbess, the sisters, and Margery took place during an active outbreak of the plague, and despite Kempe's faith, she was afraid to embark upon this short journey.[43]

Perhaps it is no coincidence then that both Julian and Margery become practitioners of a mode of health care focused on the psychophysiological dimension of pain and suffering. Their own illnesses—both of which affect the lower parts of their bodies—prompt them to transpose their stunning visions into writings that will ultimately benefit others. This is an audacious endeavor given their status not only as women but as "lewed, febille, and freylle" women, as Julian describes herself, an identity that Margery appears to enact through her tears and emotive gestures. One could argue, in fact, that both women's illness narratives are a recasting of the prevailing stereotype of Woman as imperfect Man, weak, inarticulate, and incapable of action. Perhaps that explains why their writing marks a departure from their prior lives and signals a moment when each acquires a voice of her own. As Liz McAvoy notes, "For both women, illness is represented as a self-initiated and transformative experience which sets in motion the process which leads to writing."[44] Out of their individual illnesses, or urged to action precisely because of those illnesses, these two women begin to express what they experience both physically and emotionally. In so doing they develop a specialized approach to compassionate caregiving.[45]

But there is another factor motivating their writing, necessary to mention here because of the epidemic milieu in which they lived. While there are no overt statements regarding the pestilence as expressed so clearly by Margaret Paston, there are nonetheless fleeting references indicating that both Julian and Margery were aware of its presence, as the examples noted above suggest. And perhaps that medical consciousness explains, at least in part, the focus of both mystics on a style of health care associated with the nurturing "herte-blod" of Christ. Both mystics transform their devotion to the Passion into a mode of

---

[42] Ibid.
[43] Kalas estimates the date of a recorded outbreak that coincides with Margery's visit.
[44] McAvoy, *Authority and the Female Body in the Writings of Julian of Norwich and Margery Kempe*, 10.
[45] Kalas, *Margery Kempe's Spiritual Medicine*, passim.

compassionate healing that features motherhood even beyond the bounds of the female body.[46] Breast milk and blood are synonymous in this bodily paradigm: the blood of the holy side wound in its proximity to the breast accrues an identification with lactation and its medicinal attributes, sacralizing the milk of women as surely as does the Virgin Mary in her nursing of the Holy Infant. Such implicit sanctification explains in part why human breast milk is taken so seriously as an ingredient in multiple household remedies.

Passion to Compassion

Compassion, as Daniel McCann observes, is a force to be reckoned with, an intense feeling that causes pain to those who meditate intently upon the crucified body. To experience that feeling is like ingesting a medicine designed to jolt the soul into a state of high alert: "Compassion for Christ," he says, is "the emotional result of engagement with the 'blod of his hert' … best understood as a compound medicine for the soul. It is not a single emotional state, but rather a complex blend of fear, penance, pity and sorrow alongside a precise configuration of intersubjective awareness."[47] The Passion becomes enfolded into devotional practices requiring a medicine to be taken into the body much in the way that the body and blood of Christ are ingested by communicants. The very structure of the word "com-passion" presumes an active participation in suffering done with others designed to aid in the healing of the soul in its medicinal effects. From a slightly different perspective Sarah McNamer writes, "Compassion is not only an emotion but also potentially the foundation for an ethic" that has "the potential to effect ethical thinking and behavior on a wider scale."[48] She describes how Julian of Norwich's visions of the suffering Christ intensified the mystic's feelings of compassion for others. Margery Kempe too is described by McNamar as having a similar response: "the sight of a leper with bleeding wounds causes her to weep… when her aged husband becomes helpless and incontinent, she 'servyd hym & helpyd hym, as hir thowt, as sche wolde a don Crist hymself.'"[49] Each mystic in her own way transposes her visions into written

---

[46] Relevant in this regard is that the Carthusian monks of Mount Grace drew hearts and flames in the margins of Margery's manuscript as *nota bene* devices indicating their comprehension and tacit affirmation.
[47] McCann, *Soul-Health*, 83.
[48] Sarah McNamer, *Affective Meditation and the Invention of Medieval Compassion* (Philadelphia: University of Pennsylvania Press, 2010), 150.
[49] McNamer, *Affective Meditation*, 150.

form and demonstrates how an intense emotional engagement with the Passion had the capacity to translate into a broader application in the world whether through personal interaction or through the writing alone. In both cases the feeling of compassion emanates from the heart.

Heart and Soul

In *A Vision Showed to a Devout Woman* (the Short Text), Julian talks about envisioning her soul in the middle of her heart (Vision, section 22): "Bot than lefte I stille wakande, and than oure lorde openede my gastely eyen and shewed me my saule in middes of my herte. I sawe my saule swa large as it ware a kingdome, and be the conditions that I sawe therin, methought it was a wirshipfulle cite."[50] As noted in Watson and Jenkins, the "wirshipfulle" city Julian envisions is the New Jerusalem as promised in the *Book of Revelation*, a kingdom so large that having a "space for all the saved ... the city is taken to be a figure for both the individual soul and the collective souls of 'alle that shalle be safe.'"[51] As with the many figures of speech enfolded into theological language, this can be understood to stand for the human body at the center of which is the heart animated by the soul's vital force. Traditionally ascribed to Aristotle, the notion that the soul is located in the heart is subsumed into the medical discourse where it was understood as the site of intelligence, motion, sensation, and even the breath of life.[52] Given the presumption of cosmic interconnectedness locating the human body at the center of premodern cosmology, it is not surprising that Julian conjures a link between the heart-soul dyad and the New Jerusalem. What is surprising, however, is that there is resonance between this communal vision and Henri de Mondeville's treatise on surgery, in which he says, "The heart is the principal organ par excellence [*membrum principalissimum*] which gives vital blood, heat and spirit to all other members of the entire body. It is located in the very middle of the chest, as befits its role as the king in the midst of his kingdom."[53] Like the genre of "Mirrors for Princes," not the least of which includes the *Secreta Secretorum* and its close relative the *Regimen sanitatis*

---

[50] Watson and Jenkins, *Writings*, 111.
[51] Ibid., 110.
[52] Heather Webb, *The Medieval Heart* (New Haven: Yale University Press, 2010), 21. The Italian physician Pietro Torrigiani is quoted as saying, "the heart is the principle of all the faculties and the source of pneuma.... The soul is in the heart, and therefore the heart is the principle of the most important bodily functions, and therefore the soul must be located there."
[53] Quoted in Webb, *The Medieval Heart*, 44.

Salernitanum, this model of sociopolitical order is aligned with the health of the monarchal body enthroned at its pinnacle. The crucial difference between these two models of order and Henri's is that while the "Mirror for Princes" is a hierarchical construct, with governance emanating from the top down, the governing power of the heart-soul model emanates from the center out. While the surgeon-physician's notion of community is cardiocentric, the "Mirror for Princes" has a ruler at the pinnacle of the body politic. Just as medical treatises were often organized from head to toe with the most important information at the beginning of the document, so too this order locates the king closer to the head than the heart, an ordering that both de Mondeville and Julian modify in differing yet complementary ways.

The emphasis on the heart as the principal organ in these configurations is notable for its other functions, including what Heather Webb describes in her book, *The Medieval Heart*, as a womblike receptivity as well as the heart's ability to "push spirit out from the body."[54] The heart must be temperate, receptive, as well as projective, she says, since "[a] heart that is not temperate enough to be receptive or womblike is a source of spiritual and physical danger. At the same time, a heart that is not able to push spirit out from the body and into the world in the form of new life or simply spiritual participation in the circulation of things is equally in peril."[55] Even before the discovery of circulation by William Harvey in the seventeenth century, medieval practitioners recognized the heart's projective force, its ability to "push spirit out," while also contending that the heart was a receptive organ like a womb, capable of receiving seminal fluids and pushing out new life. Just as medieval practitioners understood that the heart was both receptive and projective, so too did they understand it as "double-gendered."[56] As Webb observes, the heart is never ungendered but rather considered to be both male and female largely due to functions traditionally assigned to biological sex and essentialist notions of the body. Such a concept of the heart is especially applicable to Julian's double-gendered vision of God, understood predominantly as a paternal figure but also to be acknowledged as having nurturing capacities associated with the maternal. In both the Short and the Long Texts, the mystic deploys several variations on the God-as-mother trope, effacing traditional gender boundaries and the activities assigned to them. In so doing she enables the sacred "herte-blod" of the Passion to be understood as a nurturing substance akin to a woman's milk.

---

[54] Webb, *The Medieval Heart*, 98.
[55] Ibid.
[56] Ibid.

There are many differences in the visions that these two women have of the Passion, yet their interpretations intersect when it comes to the content of the soul. While Julian sees her soul as a kingdom akin to the City of God, Kempe envisions hers as containing "the Trinity and the whole court of heaven."[57] But rather than associating the heart and soul with an abstract concept, as Julian does in her vision of the New Jerusalem, Kempe more often conflates the heart with the uterus in its capacity to give birth to a receptive spirit. As Laura Kalas explains, this is not a notion original with Margery but rather to the culture of conversion: "[t]he heart is also likened to the uterus in medieval culture since conversion to Christianity is assimilated with the conception and birth of Christ in one's heart."[58] The understanding of the heart-uterus connection in the sense of compassion for others, especially those to whom she has physical ties, renders Margery's healing of her son and elderly husband all the more significant in their implicit connection to her bodily experience. These ailing family members play an important role in Margery's transition from her intense engagement with the Passion to compassionate action in the world. Kempe engages in caregiving in imitation of a nurturing Virgin if not a *Christus medicus* in part because she has experienced their suffering and transposed passive empathy into acts of compassion in the world. Not only does she demonstrate an empathic sensitivity for the pain of others but she acts upon that emotion by providing hands-on care.

Therapeutic Reading for Women

In *Soul-Health*, Daniel McCann describes reading as an activity that enables the "treatment of the soul" through a "'medicyne of words,' through texts of passion."[59] Beginning with Richard Rolle's coinage of that phrase, McCann outlines reading practices designed to "evoke emotions intense enough to enable *salus animae*, or the health of the soul."[60] In theory as well as in practice, reading is not a passive process, he argues, but rather an active part of a regimen promoting health and well-being, especially for those who read the devotional texts of the Vernon manuscript. The therapeutic interpretation I am suggesting here draws upon McCann's model but differs in its presumption

---

[57] Watson and Jenkins, *Writings*, 110.
[58] Kalas, *Margery Kempe's Spiritual Medicine*, 69.
[59] McCann, *Soul-Health*, 2.
[60] Ibid., 5.

of women (and their allies) in the audience. Therapeutic reading of this kind engages its readers emotionally as well as intellectually with alluring subject matter, action-oriented plots, vividly drawn characterizations, and riveting depictions of optimistic outcomes. In the narratives that gained in popularity during the time of the plague, many of which were translated from French antecedents, reside female characters who demonstrate atypical agency, who harness an exemplary puissance, and act upon their healing skills. These are characters who are transformative, whose narratives depict actions that affect their audiences by lifting their spirits beyond their immediate surroundings and enabling the voiding of sorrow. The "therapeutic value in the experience of reading literature," as Glending Olson observed years ago, was intended "to moderate the 'accidents of the soul' [the passions],"[61] a statement that Naoë Yoshikawa has explained as generating "an inner harmony that promotes bodily and mental health."[62] Certainly, the humoral balance and health-care regimen advocated in medical treatises is a goal for readers of devotional texts, but also desirable for those who seek escape from their own real-world environment. Whether read silently or aloud, ingesting such material infuses life into the "medicine of words," stimulating a level of engagement that brings imagination and memory into closer contact with experience, enabling quotidian events to be enfolded into narrative poems in which the dead can speak to the living, the living to the dead.

Medicine for Disease

The alliterative *Pearl* provides an apt example of a narrative poem that can be read along these lines. The story of a dead child and a grieving father speaks to audience members likely to see something of themselves in the characters, something of themselves living through a public health crisis, something that contributes to their knowledge of both in the narration. Those who are enchanted by the child's appearance in her shifting from toddler to maiden or troubled by what she says are affected in some way. That the Pearl maiden has been read as "a seed, a courtly maiden, a dead child, a daughter, the Pure Christian soul, the Pearl of Price, the Lamb of God, the Kingdom of Heaven" speaks to the

---

[61] Glending Olson, *Literature as Recreation in the Middle Ages* (Ithaca, NY: Cornell University Press, 1982).
[62] Yoshikawa, *Medicine, Religion, and Gender*, 3.

range of reference from the literal to the figurative surely with affect.[63] In what David Coley calls "palimpsestic multiplicity,"[64] she has the capacity to become many things to many readers while never relinquishing her core identity as an innocent child transformed by her father into a more mature maiden. As Judith Bennett remarks, "The anonymous poet relates the dream vision of a man mourning his dead daughter, a toddler who had died far too young to claim a virginity tested or proven as holy…. Nevertheless, the soul of this once-wee virgin is transformed in her father's vision into a full-grown maiden, pure, perfect, and richly rewarded in heaven."[65] There has been a persistent reading of the preternatural speaking child as an actual victim of an outbreak of pestilence that had affected so many children by the time the poem was written, tying the plague to the poem more decisively by remarking on its diction, the number of plague-related words, and the intense focus on "the dark blotches on the skin" characteristic of the disease.[66] The correspondence between the description of the Pearl child and the chroniclers' reports of the susceptibility of the young to the disease noted earlier has encouraged at least one scholar to redate the poem to the 1390s.[67]

But because the *Pearl* is devoid of direct reference to an actual outbreak, such historically bound readings fall short of explaining the poem's relation to its medical milieu. For Coley, the work does not simply allude to the epidemic but rather does much more in its embodiment of the "language of the plague."[68] By drawing parallels between pestilential buboes and images of the Man of Sorrows' many wounds, Coley argues a convincing case for this reading. Both literal and figurative, the poem speaks to the pestilential event in theologically inflected language, its message delivered by the nubile but otherworldly Pearl child resurrected from the dead and brought back to life in poetic form. Her appearance in the dream of her father is as jarring as are Julian's or Margery's visions of the Passion and just as likely to have had a similar effect in the time of pestilence. Compassion and grief combine to produce an intense emotional response that registers in the poetic body.

---

[63] David K. Coley, *Death and the Pearl Maiden: Plague, Poetry, England* (Columbus, OH: The Ohio State University Press, 2019), 63.
[64] Coley, *Death and the Pearl Maiden*, 64.
[65] Judith M. Bennett, "Death and the Maiden," *Journal of Medieval and Early Modern Studies* 42.2 (2012): 269-305 (279-80).
[66] Jean-Paul Friedl and Ian J. Kirby, "The Life, Death, and Life of the Pearl-Maiden," *Neuphilologische Mitteilungen* 103.4 (2002): 395-98.
[67] Andrew Breeze, "Pearl and the Plague of 1390-1393," *Neophilologus* 98 (2014): 337-41.
[68] Coley, *Death and the Pearl Maiden*, 56-89.

In what appears to be a stark juxtaposition of both subject matter and characterization in the poems of the Pearl manuscript is the figure of Morgan le Fay.[69] In *Sir Gawain and the Green Knight*, she plays a role less benevolent than the Pearl child, more threatening and directed not at a lone paternal figure but rather at the youthful Arthurian court. The poet's version of Morgan has been read, according to Coley, as "dowager, sorceress, crone, companion to the lady of the manor" as well as "the central locus of Hautdesert's courtly power and the guiding intelligence behind the Green Knight himself."[70] And while this female mastermind is presumed to be the architect of a malicious plot to scare Guenevere to death, she may also be understood as a physician delivering a harsh medicine to a court distracted from their chivalric duties. In a form of healing considered to be "social," Morgan treats the dis-ease in Arthur's realm that goes beyond individual bodies to affect the larger body politic. With her conjuring of the Green Knight and his challenge to the court, Morgan proctors a diagnostic test that all but Gawain ultimately fail; it is he who would serve as savior for what would become an exemplary narrative for the Order of the Garter, after all.

As arbiters of life and death, both the Pearl child and Morgan le Fay play a role as ghostly shapeshifters whose appearances capture the attention of their immediate audiences. Both are young and old at the same time;[71] just as the Pearl can assume the appearances of a two-year-old and a nubile maiden, so too is Morgan able to animate the bodies of the comely Lady Bertilak and the loathly lady introduced to Gawain as her companion.[72] Like the aged crone of other Gawain romances, this version of Morgan is capable of transformation, as is Bertilak to the Green Knight, for the purpose of testing Gawain's moral resolve, making him an offer he cannot refuse. When in the guise of Lady Bertilak she tests his desire to live up to the rules of the house game Bertilak has presented by offering him her body's full embrace over the course of three days, this is a test he passes. But when she offers him a way to save his own skin in the face of a fearsome executioner, he fails to live up to the chivalric code of honor. Instead,

---

[69] The bookending of these two poems in the manuscript encourages the contrast between these two female characters. So too does the juxtaposition of their ages at opposite ends of the life cycle: the Pearl, young, Morgan le Fay, old.

[70] Coley, *Death and the Pearl Maiden*, 133.

[71] The argument that Morgan as depicted in *Sir Gawain and the Green Knight* is also Lady Bertilak is convincing, especially in relation to the shifting ages of the Pearl. See Monika Kopřivová, "Women Characters in Arthurian Literature," Thesis, Masaryk University, Brno, 2007.

[72] David Coley reads Gawain's refusal of Lady Bertilak's sexual advances as an indication of his desire to thwart the pestilence. Foregoing sexual intercourse was one of the recommendations made by medieval doctors.

he accepts her offer of the magical green girdle which, like a charm, assuages his fear of dying under the axe of the Green Knight.

As for the striking juxtaposition of the Pearl child and Morgan le Fay in these two works, both figures contribute to the health of those to whom they minister; both figures provide treatment beyond a mere medicine of words; both stand as a warning to keep the faith in troubled times. That said, there is at least one distinction between the two figures and the modes of healing they deploy in need of foregrounding here: while the Pearl child offers spiritual healing evocative of the Virgin Mary herself, Morgan's healing powers reach back to Geoffrey of Monmouth's twelfth-century *Vita Merlini*, in which she is depicted as a practiced *medicus*.[73] In this pre-plague story she is one of nine sisters who reside on the "island of apples" (Fortunate Isle), a utopian paradise where nature provides "grain, grapes, and apple trees" and "people live there a hundred years or more."[74] Chief among the nine sisters, Morgan is "more skilled in the healing art," having learned "what useful properties all the herbs contain so that she can cure sick bodies."[75] Geoffrey's tale recounts how Arthur's battle-wounded body is transported to the island expressly for her medical care where she "placed the king on a golden bed and with her own hand she uncovered his honorable wound and gazed at it for a long time. At length she said that health could be restored to him if he stayed with her for a long time and made use of her healing art."[76] Geoffrey's *Vita Merlini* provides a history for Morgan that changes over time from renowned physician into a malevolent figure whose actions are read as treacherous rather than beneficial. Such a characterization is apparent in *Sir Gawain and the Green Knight*, in which she turns into the aged crone, whose very body is thought to be poisonous,[77] rather than the virtuous woman healer, with a genuine knowledge of medicine and a thoughtful approach to treating the wounds of Arthur.

---

[73] Geoffrey of Monmouth, *The Life of Merlin (Vita Merlini)* (ReadaClassic.com). Anonymous translation.
[74] Monmouth, *Life of Merlin*, 30.
[75] Ibid.
[76] See Jill M. Hebert, *Morgan le Fay, Shapeshifter* (New York: Palgrave, 2013). As Hebert explains, Geoffrey's narrative introduces Morgan to the Arthurian tradition. And while most scholars see her as a benevolent and virtuous figure, Hebert sees the seeds of ambiguity that will emerge in later depictions as malevolent.
[77] See Shulamith Shahar, "The Old Body in Medieval Culture," in *Framing Medieval Bodies*, ed. Sarah Kay and Miri Rubin (Manchester: Manchester University Press, 1994), 160-86. "… the theory, implicit in scientific texts and explicit in some works of scientific popularization, being that the old female body was capable of producing poison" (163).

Therapeutic Reading and the *Vertu* of Women's Healing

Therapeutic reading for women as I am conceiving of it here depicts female figures of exemplary authority not always evocative of the Virgin Mary but just as powerful. Sometimes these characters are drawn from stories of mythical beings, witches, and sorceresses such as Morgan le Fay. In a juxtaposition that recalls the Eve/Ave dichotomy so firmly embedded in medieval religious culture, women healers whose medical regimens prove successful are differentiated from those whose actions appear to be demonic or derived from hidden sources. Certainly, occult magic and medicine occupy a similar semantic space, the boundary between one and the other often permeable: hence the effectiveness of certain charms and incantations. On the virginal side of the dichotomy, of course, is the Holy Mother, whose reputation for healing provides a model for young married women as well as unmarried maidens both in written form and in life. In the *Life of Christine of Markyate*, for example, she accrues enough credibility with regard to her healing powers, according to Diane Watt, that she contributes to the validation of actual women healers: "the belief in Mary as Physician, in Mary as a doctor of medicine, in late medieval England was closely linked to, and indeed validated, the role of the woman as healer."[78] Acting not only in her traditional role as intercessor but also as a physician bequeaths the sacred matriarch greater authority especially in relation to household healers like Margaret Paston. In the Virgin's nurturing capacity as well as in her abilities to enact a spiritual form of healing, she inspires pilgrims to seek her aid at shrines built in her honor; Our Lady of Walsingham in Norfolk is but one example.[79] Understood as Mary the Physician, she exudes the strength and stamina that lift the spirits of those who partake of her healing powers, even to the point of curing them. Virtue as embodied by the Virgin in her role as physician represents much more than moral character or a singular aspect of ethical conduct, however. Rather, it is an energy akin to the reception and projective force recognized as functions of the heart-uterus actions brought to light by Laura Kalas in relation to Margery Kempe's spiritual medicine and applicable to the soul's animation of feeling in Julian's mode of compassionate devotion. Understanding *vertu* as manifest in female icons such as the Virgin Mary as well as herbs, stones, and words,

---

[78] Watt, "Mary the Physician", 27-44 (27).
[79] This is a site that Margaret Paston knows well. Founded in honor of the visions of an English noblewoman, Richeldis of Faverches, the shrine was dedicated to the Virgin. In one of her letters to her ailing husband, Margaret Paston promises to visit the shrine, which she does later in life. See Diane Watt's essay, "'In the Absence of a Good Secretary': The Letters, Lives, and Loves of the Paston Women Reconsidered," in *The Paston Women*, 144.

especially those used in childbirth, enables us to see how rosemary, the Rose of Mary, comes to be regarded as a wondrous pharmaceutical ingredient; the pearl, a healing stone; *Gratia Dei* and "virtue-given-of-God," extraordinary medicinal ointments, and ordinary women capable of excellence.

Two Virtuous Women of Romance

Two women of Middle English romance notable for their *vertu* as well as their medical expertise are Josian of *Bevis of Hampton* and *Le Bone Florence of Rome*. Each of these characters demonstrates healing skills that render them exemplary role models for women's agency. Both are active characters in action-adventure romances set in exotic locales with vividly drawn landscapes, colorful villains, and extraordinary obstacles. At the same time, the geographical background of the Middle East includes realistic place names and actions that lend these tales a jarring familiarity. *Bevis of Hampton* follows its youthful protagonist from England to Armenia, the world into which the eponymous hero's mother sends him for exposing her adultery and calling her a "vile whore." This is an attention-getting beginning for a narrative that charts the evolution of the child Bevis in *Bildungsroman* fashion into a mature adult who will return to his homeland to reclaim his heritage and rectify the injustice done to him by his mother. Josian is the Armenian princess whose love for Bevis enables his survival in her father's Saracen court. She heals him when he is injured and protects him against the envious and suspicious men around him. In keeping with the realistic features of the tale's plot and setting, Josian's knowledge of medicine is striking not only because she is a woman but because she is a Saracen woman whose advanced education derives from the great masters of Italy and Spain. Given the fact that women were historically excluded from university training, this is an extraordinary narrative detail that signals a marked interest in women's healing:

> While she was in Ermonie,
> Bothe fysik and sirgirie
> She hadde lerned of meisters grete
> Of Boloyne the gras and of Tulete
> That she knew erbes mani and fale,
> To make bothe boute and bale.
>
> (ll. 3671–76)[80]

---

[80] Ronald B. Herzman, Graham N. Drake, and Eve Salisbury, eds. *Four Romances of England: King Horn, Havelok the Dane, Bevis of Hampton, Athelston*, TEAMS Middle English Texts Series (Kalamazoo: Medieval Institute Publications, 2002), 297.

The place names cited here are no mere allusions but rather significant indicators of a tradition of medicine that reaches back to the medical works of famous physicians like Avicenna. In the naming of Bologna, a center known for the study of medicine, as well as Toledo, where translations of medical texts into Latin enabled their dissemination throughout Europe, the anonymous Bevis poet effectively links England to the medical knowledge of the continent as well as the Middle East. The opening allusion to Armenia is suggestive not only because Bevis' story travels to the Saracen world from England but because Josian acquires her medical expertise there from the masters of "fysik and sirgirie" presumably brought to her father's court. That Josian's medical knowledge includes both the negative and positive effects of medicinal plants— the poisonous as well as the antidotal (erbes mani and fale, / To make bothe boute and bale)—enables her to protect her chastity and devise ointments to heal Bevis' wounds. Worth noting at this point is that Armenia is a place where certain effective medications could be found. Especially relevant in this regard is a substance known as armoniak (Armenian bole), an ingredient in *Gratia Dei*, the compound believed to heal all wounds.

That Josian has a sophisticated understanding of the medicinal properties of stones as well as herbal medication plays out in the narrative when she uses her magic ring to protect herself from sexual assault. Herbs and stones, as Corinne Saunders observes, "were thought to be instilled with nature's power and God's grace" thus the stone in Josian's ring "cannot be associated with the black, ostensibly demonic, magical arts. Rather, its 'vertu' is an extension of her own virtue, a token of her wisdom in natural, medical magic."[81] This is a significant detail in that the healing power of the ring signifies Josian's integration into the Christian community just as medicine from the non-Christian world is disseminated throughout Europe. So too are the stones invested with *vertu* that extend to Josian herself emblematic of her "embodied excellence."[82] In her ability to use her medical knowledge for preserving her chastity as well as returning others to a state of well-being, she becomes a figure for an expanded view of healing that casts female practitioners in a positive light as resourceful

---

[81] Corinne Saunders, "Gender, Virtue and Wisdom in *Bevis of Hampton*," in *Sir Bevis of Hampton in Literary Tradition*, ed. Jennifer Fellows and Ivana Djordjevic (Woodbridge: Bowdell & Brewer, 2008), 161-75. Saunders notes, "[t]he earliest medical faculty had been established at Salerno in the mid-tenth century and flourished particularly from the late eleventh to the early thirteenth century; it was especially associated with women because of the reputation of Trotula. Records survive of actual women practitioners although such women were rare, their existence offers an intriguing context for Josian. The particular places associated by the poet with medical learning are realistic."

[82] Crocker, *The Matter of Virtue*, esp. chapter 3.

and able to negotiate difficult situations such as giving birth to twins in the wilderness without medical aid. It is also worth noting that as skilled as Josian is in medicine, she is also a capable musician who uses that skill to cure the illnesses of friends. What becomes clear in Josian's actions over the course of the narrative is the *vertu* of women's healing capabilities.

The matter of *vertu* plays out to a different effect in *Le Bone Florence of Rome*, in which the eponymous heroine is subject to several violent assaults. In an action-filled narrative akin to Chaucer's "Man of Law's Tale," Gower's "Tale of Constance," the anonymous Breton lay, "Emaré," Hoccleve's version of the "Tale of Jerelaus's Wife" (discussed in Chapter 3), and other stories of accused queens or "tried heroines," as Jonathan Stavsky calls them,[83] the obstacles that Florence faces—abduction, attempted rape, being beaten, humiliated, hanged by the hair, and framed for murder—test her personal fortitude, moral resolve, and strength of character.[84] As romances are wont to do in their push toward an optimistic resolution, the oft-abused Florence inevitably finds sanctuary in an abbey where her medical skills soon become apparent. She cures a nun's ailments so effectively, in fact, that her reputation as a gifted healer travels far and wide, encouraging the sick to seek her out. Those who come to her to be healed include the villains who had done her so much harm as well as the man she had married prior to her tribulations. Compelled to confess their sins before Florence cures them with a laying on of hands, the villains provide a public recounting of the heinous actions that her husband, upon learning, reacts to vehemently. Last in line to be healed, he is described as having "venome" bursting out of his ears and eyes, his heart in a rage ("hys herte was full throo"); he is so angry about the harm done to his wife that as soon as he is healed, he sees to it that the four villains are thrown into a fire along with all their belongings. In the end, Florence and her spouse reunite and return to Rome together, where in marital harmony they conceive a child and rule in peace. At the end of the poem the poet addresses his readers/auditors to say that it is not wise to be false to others: "Forthy schulde men and women als / Them bethynke or they be false; / Hyt makyth so fowle an ende" (2176-8). In so doing he identifies his target audience, aiming a tale about a virtuous woman to potential perpetrators in the audience.

---

[83] Jonathan Stavsky, ed. *Le Bone Florence of Rome: A Critical Edition and Facing Translation of a Middle English Romance Analogous to Chaucer's Man of Law's Tale* (Cardiff: University of Wales Press, 2017). All quotations are taken from this edition. If this story sounds familiar, it is the same tale told by Hoccleve in the *Series* as the "Tale of Jereslaus's Wife," which also appears in the *Gesta Romanorum*.

[84] Crocker, *The Matter of Virtue*, esp. chapter 3.

Bad Medicine: The Vilification of Women Healers

As these narratives suggest, female characters who overcome extraordinary obstacles through the species of *vertu* found in nature and the female body not only survive but flourish. Josian and Florence are two such *exempla* whose stories provide a modicum of pleasure and excitement in the reading/listening, especially in view of the terminal optimism with which their narratives conclude. Nonetheless, the devaluation of women healers in jokes and satirical putdowns such as those in the exchange between Chauntecleer and Pertelote in the "Nun's Priest's Tale," discussed earlier, persist[85] in spreading the kind of disparagement that develops into the vilification of women healers made manifest in the Statute of 1421 and expressed so snidely by John of Arderne.[86] Women healers marked as dangerous "witches" are discernible even in the Wife of Bath's brief allusion to Trotula, Langland's reference to Dame Emme, and in Gower's retelling of the Medea story. Yet while these negatively construed characters tell us something about the effects of misogyny, so too do they tell us something about the effectiveness of women's healing.

The allusion to Trotula made by the Wife of Bath is found in the list of women included in Jankyn's *Book of Wicked Wives* in the Wife's Prologue:

> He hadde a book that gladly, nyght and day,
> For his desport he wolde rede alway;
> He cleped it Valerie and Theofraste,
> At which book he lough alwey ful faste.
> And eek ther was somtyme a clerk at Rome,
> A cardinal, that highte Seint Jerome,
> That made a book agayn Jovinian;

---

[85] Linda Voigts, "Herbs and Herbal Healing Satirized in Middle English Texts," in *Herbs and Healers from the Ancient Mediterranean through the Medieval West: Essays in Honor of John M. Riddle* (Farnham, UK: Ashgate, 2012), 21730 (228-9).

[86] Carole Rawcliffe, *Source for the History of Medicine in Late Medieval England* (Kalamazoo, MI: Medieval Institute Publications, 1995; reprint 1998), 120. When he reports the condition of a patient whose health deteriorates, he blames it on "the medycines of ladies." See also Thomas G. Benedek, "The Roles and Images of Medieval Women in the Healing Arts," in *The Roles and Images of Women in the Middle Ages and Renaissance* (Pittsburgh: University of Pittsburgh Publications, 1975), 145-59 for a synopsis of the controversy surrounding Trotula. "a) was she actually an independently practicing female professor on a par with her male peers? b) was she the wife of Johannes Platearius, the elder, a noted Salernitan physician, and derives her fame from him, herself being only a midwife? c) was she a man? Or was there no person by that name?" (146). "The early dissemination of Trotula into folklore is attested to by the fact that she was mentioned by a non-medical author of the fourteenth century, such as Geoffrey Chaucer" (147). See also Edward Tuttle, "The Trotula and Old Dame Trot: A Note on the Lady of Salerno," *Bulletin of the History of Medicine* 50 (1976): 61-72; and Susan Mosher Stuard, "Dame Trot," *Signs* 1.2 (1975): 537-42.

> In which book eek ther was Tertulan,
> Crisippus, Trotula, and Helowys,
> That was abbesse nat fer fro Parys,
> And eek the Parables of Salomon,
> Ovides Art, and books many on,
> And alle thise were bounden in o volume.
>
> (ll. 669-81)[87]

While the famed physician of Salerno is found in the company of illustrious personages, so too may we understand her position on Jankyn's booklist to be disparaging, cited as she is among "wicked wives" rather than illustrious women who have achieved something significant as in Boccaccio's *On Famous Women* or Christine de Pizan's *Book of the City of Ladies*, which exposes the misogynist tradition that so disillusioned her. In Jankyn's *Book* the accomplished Trotula's name appears next to that of Heloise, a proximity that encourages an association between the two around matters of sexuality and marriage, the former having been discredited by misogynist disbelievers, the latter for her illicit affair with the famed Abelard. Jerome's antifeminist rhetoric put into the mouth of the Wife of Bath to argue the benefits of serial monogamy is for the purpose of making a case for the beneficial effects of marital sex on nature's "sely instruments." As an outspoken proponent of female sexuality, Alisoun calls attention to her *bele chose*, not to bring shame upon what she considers to be a principal organ of pleasure (she never uses the word "pudendum") but rather to extol its aesthetic puissance.[88] In what might be regarded as a heart-uterus expression of emotion with emphasis on the positive attributes of the ins and outs of lovemaking, Alisoun tacitly underscores the receptive and projective functions of the female heart. It is in this sense that she is aligned with Trotula, whose books on gynecology and obstetrics feature a woman's genitalia as a natural instrument of sexuality and reproduction. Nonetheless, just as Trotula's medical authority is subtly ridiculed in Jankyn's *Book of Wicked Wives*, the Wife of Bath's arguments are challenged by male members of her immediate audience.

When it comes to the attempt to discredit fictional female characters, Langland's Dame Emme and Gower's Medea provide a useful contrast with the Wife of Bath as well as to one another. While Dame Emme of Shordyche takes on the semblance of historical plausibility and the suspicion of women's medicine by elite physicians, in the hands of Gower the figure of Medea resists

---

[87] *Riverside Chaucer*, gen. ed. Larry Benson, 114.
[88] Robert Bjork, "The Wife of Bath's *Bele Chose*," *The Chaucer Review* 53.3 (2018): 336-49.

that designation, retaining her mythological reputation for occult magic, but not to the extent of women healers vilified and ostracized in other contexts. In *Piers Plowman*, Dame Emme is identified as a witch whose charms cure the morally flawed Hawkin from his many ailments. Along with an anonymous Souter [shoemaker] of Southwerk, Dame Emme is taken to be a realistic representation of a folk healer whose charms work wonders for those who believe in them. Hawkin, Langland's exemplary everyman, swears by the curatives that had led to his recuperation. No clerk, not even Christ, could cure him as well as Dame Emme, he claims. But, as Roseanne Gasse observes,

> Because one hears neither Dame Emme nor the Souter of Southwerk make the claim that their charm's mystic power supersedes that of Christ's Word, one can only remain uncertain as to whether these two witches are malicious in their attitudes toward their patients. The charms they offer, after all, would have the considerable positive effect of a placebo, and Langland would know that healing charms were regular features in even the best medieval medical practice.[89]

As we have seen in the previous chapter, charms find their way into remedy books to be used wherever necessity dictated and whenever patients were willing to believe in their efficacy. Belief in any treatment becomes necessary when remedies contain words of incantation and prayer or include stones and herbs as divinely empowered non-naturals; words, stones, and herbs are effective as Guy de Chauliac, John of Arderne, and Gilbertus Anglicus assert. At the same time, however, their healing effects depend upon the patient's willingness to believe that they emit *vertu* enough to ameliorate the ailment.

The Medea story told by Genius to Amans in Gower's *Confessio Amantis* relates to the therapeutic reading I have been developing both as a counterbalance to the restrictions of 1421 and to demonstrate that women's healing exists in the medical imaginary of the time. In his retelling of Medea's story, the poet presents a more complex view of her character than others, her medical expertise, her use of magic, and the extraordinary lengths to which she goes to reverse the aging process in Jason's elderly father. In what Will Rogers calls the "poetics of rejuvenation," Gower's retelling of the tale in Book V devotes over 200 lines to rendering a detailed account of Medea's actions, her incantations and exhortations, her gathering of exotic medical ingredients, and her administering of a complex compound to the old man, using a method of delivery that can

---

[89] Roseanne Gasse, "Witchcraft and Sorcery in *Piers Plowman*," *The Chaucer Review* 55.1 (2020): 88-112.

only be described as transfusion.⁹⁰ Medea devises and carries out a treatment that exceeds the bounds of ordinary phlebotomy and acknowledges the need for removing contaminated blood to replace it with another substance entirely. The portrayal offered by Genius, which begins in a negative register, thus becomes more sympathetic to the character whose story he tells, even in the face of Medea's infanticide. This is a tale that jolts an audience to attention not only for its violence against children but for its uncommon compassion for an aged man. For Rogers, the tale is "above all, a work deeply invested in healing, both personal—of the readers outside the text and Amans, inside it—and public, as the narrator of its genesis on the Thames suggests."⁹¹ For Ellen Bakalian, the poet's extraordinary choice of narrative is an attempt to ameliorate a tradition depicting Medea as an "evil witch":

> That Gower chooses to depict this particular literary figure as a loving wife in a mutually satisfying marriage is extraordinary, for Medea is known throughout antiquity and into the Middle Ages as an evil witch, a barbarian who dabbled in black magic. Gower's rendition of the Medea tale is notable for its shift towards Medea, his portrayal of her as a selfless woman, and his emphasis upon Jason as a perjurer.⁹²

If healing is understood to be an aspect of love, as Bakalian claims, then Medea's love for Jason is proven by her willingness to accept her husband's request to save his aged father from the inevitable failings of old age. She has already proven herself to be a faithful partner in Jason's quest for the Golden Fleece; this is simply another way to prove her loyalty to her husband and her respect for his progenitor.

Medea's magical powers are underscored from the outset as Genius describes in detail how she vanishes at midnight, going forth "as an addre doth" slithering away without anyone noticing. She prays for help from Hecate, the goddess of sorcery, who sends her a dragon-drawn chariot to transport her to exotic locales to gather herbs pulled by the roots, small stones, water from the Red Sea, medicinal plants, "fieldwode and verveyne," and of "turves of the lond" out of which she constructs two altars, one to Hecate, the other to Juvente, the goddess of youth. Here she sacrifices a black sheep, whose blood she drains and mixes with milk and honey, all the while praying to Pluto and Proserpina for

---

⁹⁰ William Rogers, "Old Words Made New: Medea's Magic and Gower's Textual Healing," *South Atlantic Review* 79.3-4 (2014): 105-17. See also Natalie Grinnell, "Medea's Humanity and John Gower's Romance," *Medieval Perspectives* 14 (1999): 70-83.
⁹¹ Rogers, "Old Words Made New," 105.
⁹² Ellen Shaw Bakalian, *Aspects of Love in John Gower's Confessio Amantis* (New York: Routledge, 2004), 85-86.

aid in carrying out her plan: Eson is anesthetized by her incantatory charms and prepared for the surgery that will purportedly make him young again. The procedure calls for her to heat up a cauldron and mix more than a thousand ingredients together, including the scales and skins of venomous serpents. But before administering the rejuvenating compound to the unconscious patient, she tests it on a dry olive branch to see whether it has any effect: immediately the dry branch bursts forth with new life. Not fully satisfied with one test, however, she does another, letting a drop of the mixture fall onto the ground with the result that where once the earth was bare now it bears flowers and green grass. Medea "thanne knew and wiste / Hir medicine is for to triste" (ll. 4153-54). Now she is ready to do the surgery, for which she takes a high-quality sword and makes an incision in the old man's side to drain his depleted blood, "fieble and cold," and replace it with the compound made of "herbes al the beste jus," which she pours "into his wounde; / That made his veynes fulle and sounde" (ll. 4163-65). Just as in the two experimental trials she had conducted before using the medication on her patient, "His hed, his herte, and his visage / Lich unto twenty wynter age. / Hise hore heres were away / And lich unto the freisshe Maii / Whan passed ben the colde schoures, / Riht so recovereth he his floures" (ll. 4169-4174).

Genius is so taken with the actions of Medea in the tale he has just recounted that he iterates her virtues immediately thereafter in a way that makes her seem uncommonly compassionate. Has any woman shown more love for Jason than Medea? he asks. She helped him acquire the Golden Fleece, she sacrificed her own family for his sake, and she rejuvenated his father "which thing non other womman couthe." All of this sets up the subsequent scene of Jason's betrayal (his marriage to Creusa), which Medea discovers upon her return; it is a revelation that provokes her killing of their children in front of Jason's eyes.

Narrating Medicine for Women

In the life writings of Margaret Paston, Margery Kempe, and Julian of Norwich, we see the making of therapeutic texts that, like the talking book of Hippocrates noted at the beginning of this chapter, speak their remedies directly to their readers. These are the healing works of women that urge attention to caregiving and the ongoing acquisition of medical knowledge. The depictions of women in the illness narratives told here provide a way for readers both then and now to comprehend prevailing attitudes toward female healers as a group and as individual practitioners. Such portrayals stand in opposition to the 1421 Statute in its attempts to limit women's participation in medical practice. But what becomes difficult in life becomes possible in the medical imaginary. Narratives such as these expose the conundrum of a system of signification thoroughly infused with theological language and religious culture. On the one hand, there are the women healers who demonstrate the skills to produce positive medical results as they engage in a variety of health-care services. On the other, women healers are cast in a negative light when their treatments differ from the standard of care determined by elite male practitioners. These are the marginalized women whose poisons were thought to overpower any antidote, women who were imagined to conjure up demonic forces for their remedies. That said, if we deploy the close reading, attentive listening, and level of engagement advocated by proponents of narrative medicine, more positive readings emerge from these stories with the potential to bring the medical and the magical, the virtuous and the villainous, into a healthy balance. What we see in the middle space between categories is a kinship between the medical ingredients listed in recipe books and the medicine of words, stones, and herbs. We see innovative applications and techniques (transfusion and active modes of compassion) that go beyond the Hippocratic-Galenic view of humoral medicine or the standard procedure for phlebotomy. We see the skills and knowledge that women practitioners from Chaucer's Trotula and Pertelote, Langland's Dame Emme, Gower's Medea, and Josian of *Bevis of Hampton* to *Le Bone Florence of Rome* bring to our attention. These are the stories that enable therapeutic reading aimed at lifting the spirits and stimulating new ways of thinking. Produced in the time of pestilence, the very moment in history in which women were being restricted from medical practice and vilified as witches and charlatans, such tales reveal how women participate in delivering health care in myriad ways, nonetheless. Their life writings and the tales about them provide access to their experiences of illness to be sure, but they also provoke feelings of healing and hope.

6

Afterword: A Prognosis

Acting like a sponge, illness soaks up personal and social significance from the world of the sick person. Unlike cultural meanings of illness that carry significance to the sick person, this third, intimate type of meaning transfers vital significance from the person's life to the illness experience.[1]
—Arthur Kleinman, *Illness Narratives*, 31

Works of poetry and prose as well as the writing of medical treatises are based upon the material world in which writers and practitioners reside and practice their respective arts. The personal and the social intersect when stories of the community and of individual experience address the matter of illness from different perspectives. As many of the tales told in narrative poetry as well as in the prose writings of the authors represented in this study suggest, subjectivity and self-reflexion both substantiate and conflict with observations made outside the individual about the experience of the plague in England. While subjective narrations animate the voices of interlocutors, personas, and fictional characters, sociohistorical accounts provide descriptions of disease from an outside perspective. While the former is demonstrably emotive and personal, the latter is notably objective and impersonal, focused not on the pain and distress of individual bodies but rather in reporting the effects of illness in the social body. Recorded documentation of the bubonic plague of the fourteenth and fifteenth centuries by chroniclers who use phrases such as "great pestilence," "a great plague," a "great mortality," and "great beyond measure" describe the immensity of the devastation, citing those affected, "young people and children," "adolescents and boys," while pointing out the susceptibility of everyone to the disease, "both rich and poor," as well as regions and communities, "the north country," "London," "Essex," "York" and the number of dead in need of burial, 11,000

---

[1] Arthur Kleinman, *Illness Narratives: Suffering, Healing & the Human Condition* (New York: Basic Books, 1988), 31.

by one estimation.² Plague chroniclers engage in written responses designed to provide the grim news of local recurrences to their audiences rather than individual accounts of suffering. Nonetheless, these historical perspectives on the epidemic offer a more comprehensive context within which individual stories of illness whether of the body or as an expression of grief at the loss of friends and family cannot be separated from the disease event unfolding around them. This is but one way that personal accounts of illness intersect with the premodern public health crisis forever infused into the collective memory as the Black Death. As Kleinman suggests, illness is indeed like a "sponge soaking up personal and social significance from the world of the sick person" even in the context of centuries past.

For modern practitioners of Medical Humanities and especially for those practicing narrative medicine, Kleinman's distinctions between illness and disease underscore some of the differences between embodied experience and the culture influencing that experience. As more recently expressed, "Disease—what happens to the body—is understood through science. Illness—what the person experiences—involves an engagement with one's body that is not only physiological, but also social and experiential" is a dichotomy far more complex and interconnected than it would seem to be.³ While such distinctions emerge from a modern understanding of medicine and science, acknowledgment of the integral relation between illness and disease is necessary for fully appreciating how premodern pestilence affects individual bodies. Placed in opposition to what medical practitioners considered to be the naturals—the humors, the elements, the qualities, the complexions—were "contranaturals" operating against the norms of nature and its presumed design.⁴ The 100+ years of the Black Death engendered a culture of disease that permeated every facet of medieval life with

---

[2] Rosemary Horrox, ed. and trans. *The Black Death* (Manchester: Manchester University Press, 1994), 62-91.
[3] Thomas R. Cole, et al. *Medical Humanities: An Introduction* (Cambridge: Cambridge University Press, 2015: reprint, 2017), 247. See also *The Edinburgh Companion to the Critical Medical Humanities*, ed. Anne Whitehead and Angela Woods, et al. (Edinburgh: Edinburgh University Press, 2016). The Medical Humanities has evolved as a field since the work of early theorists such as Kleinman into a critical model that complicates the binary between science and the humanities. "If the field has so far been chiefly interested in literature's capacity to represent experiences of health and illness and thus have moral, pedagogic and therapeutic value for readers as well as writers, the literary critical Medical Humanities, as envisioned here, is concerned more with opening up new perspectives on the history of ideas (including the nature of mind, imagination and affect), and examining in detail the aesthetic and narrative strategies through which literary texts model cognitive and affective processes"(17). Of special note in this regard are the contributions made by medievalists in the field. See a special issue of *postmedieval* 8 (2017), ed. Jamie McKinstry and Corinne Saunders and their introduction, 139-46.
[4] Luke DeMaitre, *Medieval Medicine, the Art of Healing from Head to Toe*, 331.

the potential to infect everyone. As noted by the chroniclers, the rich were as susceptible to the disease as the poor, the young were as vulnerable as the old, and women and children were as likely to succumb to the illness as men; even animals were not immune.[5]

The personal and the social are spheres of human existence so integrally linked in the Middle Ages that "dis-ease" indicates disruptions of community as surely as it refers to individual plague experiences. Just as language used to describe the epidemic began to take shape, however, there was uncertainty about how to identify its etiology. Instead, a range of speculations on the causes of the disease emerged in differences of opinion between the ecclesiastical notion that the plague had been brought on by human sin and God's punishment, on the one hand, and by the conjunction of planets, thunderstorms and lightning, comets and eclipses, earthquakes, excessive winds, droughts, floods, and poisonous vapors escaping into the air, on the other. All of this was complicated by a history of narrations reaching back to the ancient past for precedents. The Black Death, in other words, is but one event in a more complicated epidemiological narrative with a much longer history.

Researchers now identify the disease that struck Europe in the fourteenth century as bubonic plague, its pathogen as *Yersinia pestis*, a bacillus that traveled in the bodies of fleas on rats transported by land and sea from Central Asia to Europe to the coastal regions of Greenland.[6] They have identified its variations, its means of transmission, and the symptoms of each variant in its human hosts.[7] Yet because there are gaps in the written records that even supplementary genomic research cannot definitively fill, there are still questions

---

[5] While the pestilence was thought to be a disease of the poor, it also affected those of other estates and social categories. Philippa of Lancaster, John of Gaunt, and Blanche's daughter and mother of the king of Portugal died of plague in 1415. Edward III's daughter Joan died of the plague, as did Margaret Paston's son and other family members. Guy de Chauliac, physician to three popes, contracted the disease in 1348, recovering briefly before his death. Gentile da Foligno, an Italian physician, died of the plague as did Jacme d' Agramont, a physician and medical professor in Spain, shortly after finishing the writing of what is considered to be the first plague tractate, *Regiment de preservacio a epidimia o pestilencia e mortaldats* (*Regimen of Protection against Epidemics or Pestilence and Mortality*, c. 1348). See Aberth, *The Black Death*, 47-55.

[6] John Kelly, *The Great Mortality: An Intimate History of the Black Death, the Most Devastating Plague of All Time* (New York: HarperCollins, 2005). For helpful chronologies see John Aberth, *From the Brink of the Apocalypse*, esp. chapter on plague, 109-77.

[7] Ann G. Carmichael, "Universal and Particular: The Language of Plague, 1348-1500," *Medical History* 52. S27 (2008): 17-52. Researchers know that in its bubonic form it was transmitted from human to human by flea bites; they know that in its pneumonic form it was transmissible by breathing exhalants of an infected person or inhaling the air around the sick and dying; they know that in its septicemic form it infected the blood. As Carmichael suggests, however, while "*Yersinia pestis* remains the most likely pathogen to account for the most common clinical appearances in plagues.... The claim that *Yersinia pestis* was the perpetrator of many late medieval plagues cannot rest solely on the language of plague. Historical epidemiological analysis and further archaeological studies are necessary" (51).

to be asked about timelines, places of origin, the number of major outbreaks and recurrences, and whether some other pathogen or strain was part of the mix of things. So too are there lingering questions about whether historical witnesses are reliable enough to cite definitive mortality rates or whether there are regional differences that additional archaeological evidence might uncover.[8]

Clearly, plague events and the "language of plague" have captured the imagination of writers and researchers alike, indicating a fascination with the subject that compels ongoing efforts to answer such questions. From the epidemics cited in Exodus to Thucydides and the Plague of Athens, the Plague of Justinian, subsequent outbreaks in Gaul, Britain, and Ireland in the sixth and seventh centuries to the Black Death, the Great Plague of London, the Third Plague of the nineteenth century to sporadic occurrences in our own time, these are narratives that provide historical frameworks for continuing exploration.[9] To the broad historical overview of the First, Second, and Third plagues are the distinctions made for the Black Death from the time of its first appearance in Europe. Typically referred to as the *Pestis Secunda*, the Second Plague as noted above, there are subdivisions within that chronology that constitute a timeline of its own; at least one such subdivision is given a name to differentiate it from others.[10] The recurrence of 1361 known as *Pestis puerorum* or the Children's Plague is that example, while the rest are most often identified by the years in which they occurred: 1369, 1374-9, 1390-3, 1400, 1405-6, 1407, 1410-11, 1413, 1420, 1423, 1426-9, 1433-5, 1438-40, 1450-4, 1463-4, 1467, 1471, 1479–80, and 1492-4.[11] Plague history writ large in this sense provides a temporal scaffolding within which to situate more specific outbreaks. But because such documentation does not often include individual illness experiences, subjective narrations are excluded from the historical record.

There is an important distinction to be made between historically driven "grand" narratives and what has come to be known as "plague narrative," in other words, in that the former is a broad, factually verifiable overview, while the latter encompasses "fiction, non-fiction, historiography, cultural philosophy," and a range of variation in presentation and medium.[12] Those narratives that have

---

[8] See J. N. Hays and J. Hays, *The Burdens of Disease: Epidemics and Human Response in Western History* (New Brunswick, NJ: Rutgers University Press, 2009). See also David M. Wagner, et al., "Yersinia Pestis and the Plague of Justinian 541–543: A Genomic Analysis," *Lancet* 14 (2014): 319-26.

[9] Monica Green, "The Four Black Deaths," *The American Historical Review*. https://doi.org/10.1093/ahr/rhaa511. See also Winston Black, *Medicine and Healing in the Premodern West* (Peterborough, ON: Broadview Press, 2019).

[10] For a helpful chronology and historical documentation, see Winston Black, ed. *Medicine and Healing in the Premodern West: A History in Documents* (Peterborough, ON: Broadview Press, 2019).

[11] Chronologies appear in Aberth, *From the Brink of the Apocalypse*, and Byrne, *Black Death*.

[12] Jorgen Riber Christensen, "The Formula of Plague Narratives," *Akademisk* 12 (2015): 12-29 (16).

inspired such excursions include the biblical plagues of Exod. 12:29, Thucydides' description of the Plague of Athens, Procopius' account of the Plague of Justinian, and Boccaccio's *Decameron*, while subsequent plague narratives reach into contemporary fiction and film.[13] While descriptions of the pestilence cited by Gregory of Tours and Bede in Gaul, Britain, and Ireland as noted earlier are routinely excluded from such listings, they offer a means of comparison between historically inflected accounts and those that capture the imagination in some way.[14] In his survey of plague writing from Boccaccio to Camus, for instance, David Steel remarks upon the fascination of writers with the drama of contagions like the bubonic plague: "the most virulent and fearsome of diseases that Europe has known."[15] He sees in plague narratives a structure and etiology "rising from an onset, through a climax to a decline and an ending."[16] These are the anxiety-provoking stories that heighten the sense of being alive, he says, instilling feelings of pleasure when measured against immense pain. In this sense plague narratives veer away from the stories of individual writers witnessing traumatic events while narrating their own illnesses.[17] There are distinctions to be made between plague narratives and illness narratives.

Illness Narratives versus Plague Narratives

There have been claims over the years about the relative silence of English authors on the epidemic unfolding around them.[18] One of the responses to such claims is, of course, that the net has not been cast wide enough to refute such inferences.

---

[13] In his survey, Christensen includes Samuel Pepys' *The Diary* (1660-1669), Daniel Defoe, *A Journal of the Plague Year* (1722), Mary Shelley, *The Last Man* (1826), J. P. Jacobsen, *The Plague at Bergamo* (1882), Michel Foucault, *Discipline and Punish: The Birth of the Prison* (1975), Mike Rohl, *Plague: The Dead Zone* (2003), Max Brooks, *World War Z: An Oral History of the Zombie War* (2006), Neil Marshall, *Doomsday* (2008), John Dryden, *Pandemic* (2012), Ndemic Creations, *Plague Inc.* (2012), Minna Sundberg, *Stand Still, Stay Silent* (2014), and the website of Médecins Sans Frontières (2015). To this list I would add Sophocles' *Oedipus Rex*, Edgar Allen Poe's "The Masque of the Red Death," Jack London's *The Scarlet Plague*, Stephen King's *The Stand*, José Saramago's *Blindness*, Kushner's *Angels in America*, and Scott Z. Burns' *Contagion*.

[14] Sally Shockro, "Apocalyptic Disease and the Seventh-Century Plague," in *Trauma in Medieval Society*, ed. Wendy Turner and Christina Lee (Leiden: Brill, 2018), 320-40.

[15] David Steel, "Plague Writing: From Boccaccio to Camus," *European Studies* XI (1981): 88-110 (88). Steel cites Defoe's *Due Preparations*, Camus' *The Plague*, John Wilson's *The City of the Plague*, Pushkin's *The Feast in the Time of the Plague*, Manzoni's *I Promessi Sposi*, and others that demonstrate the international dimension of the fascination.

[16] David Steel, "Plague Writing," 107.

[17] J. R. Maddicott, "Plague in Seventh-Century England," *Past and Present* 156 (1997-98): 7-54. Michael McCormick, "Gregory of Tours on Sixth-Century Plague and Other Epidemics," *Speculum* 96.1 (2021): 38-96.

[18] Bryon Lee Grigsby comes to mind here as does David K. Coley.

As we know from literary studies, however, the silences, fleeting allusions, and subtle uses of language speak as loudly as explicitly descriptive prose. There is evidence that several English authors recognized and talked about the severity of the Black Death. Whether they wrote from their own observations or from their experiences, their status as storytellers who themselves experienced the trauma of that disease event in some way, these are the writers who have made it possible to envision the effects of plague as well as to contemplate more fully the pain and suffering it caused.[19] Indeed, if we examine their narrations in relation to the conditions surrounding them, we begin to see the effects of that trauma represented in the stories they tell. The narratives presented in this study and the writers who have produced them expose the integral relation between the personal and the social, the world of disease and individualized responses to illness. As Esther Cohen puts it, "pain was shared, discussed, and transmitted through speech, art, and patterns of behavior. The late medieval sufferer was not alone; she was surrounded by the entire human population of sufferers, by a cosmic history of pain."[20] To remind us of the suffering of plague victims, the well-known Guy de Chauliac offers a glimpse of that experience: "I was in so grete perile that alle my felowes trowede [thought] that I schulde be dede."[21]

The principles of narrative medicine—attention, representation, affiliation—are in need of repeating here as they underscore how this approach to medical practice relates to the texts presented in this study. These three principles obtain on how we interpret what is being said, how we process the meaning of who says it and to whom, how patients are presented, in what contexts they are positioned, all of which culminate in a better understanding of what it all means. This is a collective approach spoken of in plural pronouns by Rita Charon and her collaborators:

> By attention we mean the state of heightened focus and commitment that a listener can donate to a teller—a patient, a student, a colleague, a friend. Rare, demanding, and rewarding, attention uses the listening self as a vessel to capture and reveal that which a teller has to tell. Representation, usually in writing but also in visual media, confers form on what is heard or perceived, thereby making it newly visible to both the listener and the teller. And affiliation, which results from deep attentive listening and the knowledge achieved through

---

[19] Donna Trembinski, "Trauma as a Category of Analysis," in *Trauma in Medieval Society*, ed. Wendy J. Turner and Christina Lee (Leiden: Brill, 2018), 13–32.

[20] Esther Cohen, *The Modulated Scream: Pain in Late Medieval Culture* (Chicago: University of Chicago Press, 2010), 260.

[21] Margaret Ogden, ed. *Cyrurgie of Guy de Chauliac*, EETS, 265 (London: Oxford University Press, 1971), 157.

representation, binds patients and clinicians, students and teachers, self and other into relationships that support recognition and action as one stays the course with the other through whatever is to be faced.²²

There is, in this sense, a kinship between the material language and abstract principles, concepts, and theological symbolism negotiated in many of the stories presented here. As in the "palimpsestic multiplicity" noted by David Coley in his reading of the Pearl maiden, meanings overlap and converge, indicating the integral relation of the particular and the universal. This is an interpretive challenge that demands close reading and the identification of differences between the individual and the communal as well as points of intersection.

Looking Back

As I hope this study has shown, the writers and the stories they have written contribute to the medical discourse of the 100+ years that came to be identified as the era of the Black Death. When Chaucer's Physician holds up his jurdon and explains his reading of urine, it tells us that the body is a text with something to say to those able to read it. Cast within the context of the pestilence and the presence of a physician among the pilgrims who themselves seek salvation and a return to health vis-à-vis their journey to Canterbury, stories such as the "Physician's Tale," the "Tale of Melibee," the *Book of the Duchess*, the "Nun's Priest's Tale," among others, tell us about the anxiety caused by the loss of family members. Langland and Gower offer access to the illness of individuals and their relationship to the community by creating characters who speak to the fearful events around them in both allegorical and literal terms. Each of these poets creates a persona that enables a dialogue to function as a purgative for the soul and a means by which the body's humoral balance might be restored. Their approach to storytelling is intersubjective as they talk to interlocutors and engage in conversations addressing communal crises of hunger and poverty, the malaise of lovesickness, and the negative effects of the Seven Deadly Sins. Lydgate and Hoccleve speak to other aspects of illness related to the threat of imminent death. While Lydgate's attention to the body is foregrounded in works that address the pestilence whether by displacing it to another time or by offering a strategy for preventing it, the poet renders visible his own vulnerability. The same may

---

²² Rita Charon, et al. *The Principles and Practice of Narrative Medicine* (Oxford: Oxford University Press, 2017), 3.

be said for Hoccleve, whose *Series* features a dialogue and an attempt at self-diagnosis. Hoccleve enables a deeper comprehension of the constructed nature of madness, showing how a social environment contributes to its medicalization.

The Thornton manuscript approaches the topic from another perspective not of the poets and their strategies for telling tales that speak to the trauma of contagious disease but rather as a codex put together by a scribe-compiler whose interests are implicated in its contents. Romances, devotional works, saints' lives, and a treatise on pestilence indicate Thornton's concern for household therapeutics as well as readings both entertaining and informative. In this sense the scribe-compiler's work is as significant as that of the poets whose writings are explored in previous chapters. Thornton appears to have recognized the integral relation between the well-being of the body and the soul's health by including a medical book featuring pragmatic medication as well as mystical texts. This is a collection that suggests Thornton's acknowledgment of the need for uplifting the spirits of his household audience and urging prevention against illness as prescribed by physicians such as John of Burgundy.

Household medicine and medical knowledge extend to other writers in the region such as Margaret Paston, whose correspondences reveal her concern for the spread of pestilence. That Margaret speaks in a direct and unfiltered way makes the illnesses of others, her own anxieties, and her suspicion of London physicians legible. Her commentary on the status of Norwich in the mid-fifteenth century provides a vantage point not only for looking to Thornton's contemporary collection but also to the writings of Margery Kempe and Julian of Norwich to gauge their responses to earlier outbreaks. As mystics these two women say little about the plague itself, yet express strong feelings of compassion in their writings that signal a tacit acknowledgment of the epidemic unfolding around them. Whether working in the world or in seclusion, whether singularly or in collaboration with others, each woman crafts a narrative that delivers medicine for the soul to an audience in need of a spiritual mode of healing. Their revelations about their own illnesses and the passion of their visions enable their readers to comprehend the urgency of disease in the larger community.

Stories of women healers such as Josian of *Bevis of Hampton* and the eponymous heroine of *Le Bone Florence of Rome* whose heroic healing, medical knowledge, and virtue offer therapeutic reading for those experiencing violence and hardship. Even the Pearl Maiden, whose words speak louder than her actions, offers healing to the wounded soul. So too the characters exposed to vilification and ridicule, such as the Pearl poet's Morgan le Fay, Langland's Dame Emme, Chaucer's Trotula and Pertelote, and Gower's Medea, provide a window into the challenges for women healers, especially herbalists and caregivers faced with the need to render medical treatment without professional recognition. While these stories reveal the illnesses and injuries of others, they also indicate the healing skills of women as well as their knowledge of medicinal treatments unknown or disparaged by the medical authorities of the time.

Looking Ahead

The interdisciplinary approach embraced by the Medical Humanities dedicated to bringing scholars and researchers from the sciences and the arts together in collaboration enriches the field in ways that we are just now beginning to appreciate. Journals like *Literature and Medicine*, the *Journal of Medical Humanities*, and *New Medieval Literatures* (among others) encourage the sharing of ideas, enabling the arts and the sciences to generate new ways of thinking about disease and health both for individuals and for the public. Medievalists have contributed significantly to this growing medical discourse in special issues dedicated to some aspect of the topic. Erin Labbie and her many contributors consider the problem of pain and trauma in Middle English literature and beyond while[23] Corinne Saunders and Jamie McKinstry provide a compelling rationale for explorations of premodern medical cultures that do likewise.[24] In addition, two Medical Humanities projects underway at Durham University in the UK—Hearing the Voice and the Life of Breath—promise to deepen our comprehension of the interconnectedness of bodies and the discourses they engender across temporal and disciplinary divides. Enterprises such as these as well as ongoing research by medievalists on disability, pain, trauma, memory, mind, and emotion continue to forge new ways of thinking about the complexities of psychophysiological functions and healing practices in the Middle Ages.[25] While it seems at first glance that literatures and writers of past eras may not be of use in devising fresh approaches whether to the humanistic or the scientific side of modern medical practice, we might recall that like the

---

[23] Eric Felicia Labbie, ed. "Pain, Trauma, and Philia in Middle English Literature," *Literature and Medicine* 33.2 (2015): 235-57.

[24] Corinne Saunders and Jamie McKinstry, "Medievalism and the Medical Humanities," *postmedieval* 8.2 (2017): 139-46. See also, Corinne Saunders, "Voices and Visions: Mind, Body and Affect in Medieval Writing," in *The Edinburgh Companion to the Critical Medical Humanities*, 411-27.

[25] See Richard Godden and Jonathan Hsy, "Analytical Survey: Encountering Disability in the Middle Ages," *New Medieval Literatures* 15 (2013): 313-39. See also Irina Metzler, *A Social History of Disability in the Middle Ages: Cultural Considerations of Physical Impairment* (London: Routledge, 2013).

literary arts, the healing arts depend upon keen observation and communication, interpretation, and diagnosis of body and text and body *as* text.[26] That there could be the recognition of the need for self-education, preventative strategies, as well as communal responsibility for the health of others seems to me to reveal aspects of a premodern medical consciousness worth assimilating. Listening to the stories of patients and doctors, who acknowledge the growth of household medicine and the increased demand for medical information provides us with a better understanding of the conditions that gave rise to a discourse that brought literature into conversation with science in the first place.

Narrative medicine and its focus on intersubjective dialogue, reading the body, writing empathetic narratives, listening attentively to the stories patients tell contribute to the art of modern medical practice, one that, like the art of poetry, takes a lifetime to master. Just as writers of the past have given us the language to talk about the Black Death, so too have writers of the present provided language to communicate the suffering that accompanies HIV-AIDS, cancer, and other illnesses for which there is no known cure. Our current struggles with Covid-19, documented by the storytellers and chroniclers of our own time, add up to a story of a pandemic that like the treatises of pestilence written by premodern physicians like John of Burgundy recommend self-care, avoiding contact with other people, and breathing corrupt air. Like the writers and the writings offered in this study, present-day documentation of this new "plague" promises to honor the stories of an illness that will one day be remembered within the grand scheme of medical history, to be sure, but more importantly in the histories and stories of ordinary people.

---

[26] Howard Brody, "Defining the Medical Humanities: Three Conceptions and Three Narratives," *Journal of Medical Humanities* 32 (2011): 1-7.

Bibliography

Primary Sources

Manuscripts

MS Sloane 282, f. 18. British Library
MS Ellesmere, f. 133r, Huntington Library
MS Gg.1.1., f. 490v, Cambridge University Library
MS Selden Supra 53, f.118r, Oxford Bodleian Library

Early Printed Books

De Sensu, Epitomata seu reparationes totius philosophiae naturalis Aristotelis, Gerard de Harderwyck, item 52, Wellcome Historical Medical Library of London.

Editions and Translations

Anonymous, trans. Geoffrey of Monmouth, *Life of Merlin: Vita Merlini*. ReadaClassic.com
Arntz, M. L., ed. "*The Holy Boke Gratia Dei*: An Edition with Commentary." PhD diss., Fordham University, 1961.
Bale, Anthony, trans. *The Book of Margery Kempe*. Oxford: Oxford University Press, 2015.
Batt, Catherine, trans. *The Book of Holy Medicines by Henry Lancaster*. Tempe, AZ: ACMRS, 2015.
Benson, Larry D., gen. ed. *Riverside Chaucer*. Boston: Houghton-Mifflin, 1987.
Black, Winston, ed. *Medicine and Healing in the Premodern West: A History in Documents*. Peterborough, ON: Broadview Press, 2019.
Burrow, J. A., ed. *Thomas Hoccleve's Complaint and Dialogue*. EETS, o.s. 313. London: Oxford University Press, 1999.
Burrow, J. A. and A. I. Doyle, eds. *Thomas Hoccleve: A Facsimile of the Autograph Verse Manuscripts*. EETS, s.s. 19. London: Oxford University Press, 2002.
Cook, Megan and Elizaveta Strakhov, eds. *John Lydgate's Dance of Death and Related Works*, TEAMS Middle English Texts Series. Kalamazoo, MI: Medieval Institute Publications, 2019.

Dawson, Warren R., ed. *A Leechbook or Collection of Medical Recipes of the Fifteenth Century*. London: Macmillan, 1934.

Ellis, Roger, ed. *"My Compleinte" and Other Poems*. Exeter: University of Exeter Press, 2001.

Farvolden, Pamela, ed. *John Lydgate: Fabula duorum mercatorum and Guy of Warwyk*. TEAMS Middle English Texts Series. Kalamazoo, MI: Medieval Institute Publications, 2016.

Getz, Faye Marie, ed. *Healing and Society in Medieval England: A Middle English Translation of the Pharmaceutical Writings of Gilbertus Anglicus*. Madison, WI: The University of Wisconsin Press, 1991.

Green, Monica. *The Trotula: An English Translation of the Medieval Compendium of Women's Medicine*. Philadelphia, PA: University of Pennsylvania Press, 2001; reprint, 2002.

Hahn, Thomas. *Sir Gawain: Eleven Romances and Tales*. TEAMS Middle English Texts Series. Kalamazoo, MI: Medieval Institute Publications, 1995.

Herzman, Ronald B., Graham N. Drake, and Eve Salisbury, eds. *Four Romances of England: King Horn, Havelok the Dane, Bevis of Hampton, Athelston*. TEAMS Middle English Texts Series. Kalamazoo, MI: Medieval Institute Publications, 2002.

Horrox, Rosemary, trans. and ed. *The Black Death*. Manchester: Manchester University Press, 1994.

MacCracken, Henry Noble, ed. *The Minor Poems of John Lydgate*. EETS, o.s. 192. London: Oxford University Press, 1934; reprint 1961.

MacCracken, Henry Noble, ed. *The Minor Poems of John Lydgate*. EETS, e.s. 107. London: Oxford University Press, 1911; reprint 1962.

Meech, Sanford Brown. *The Book of Margery Kempe*. EETS, o.s. 212. London: Oxford University Press, 1940; reprint 1961.

Nicholson, Peter, ed. An *Annotated Index to the Commentary of John Gower's Confessio Amantis*. Binghamton, NY: Center for Medieval and Early Renaissance Studies, 1982.

Ogden, Margaret S., ed. *Liber de Diversis Medicinis*. EETS, o.s. 207. London: Oxford University Press, 1938; reprint 1971.

Ogden, Margaret S., *Cyrurgie of Guy De Chauliac*. EETS, o.s. 265. London: Oxford University Press, 1971.

Pearsall, Derek, ed. *Piers Plowman by William Langland, an Edition of the C-Text*. Berkeley, CA: University of California Press, 1978.

Peck, Russell A., ed. Andrew Galloway, trans. *John Gower, Confessio Amantis*. TEAMS Middle English Texts Series, 2nd edition. Kalamazoo, MI: Medieval Institute Publications, 2006. 3 vols.

Pickett, J. P. "A Translation of the Canutus Plague Treatise." In *Popular and Practical Science of Medieval England*. Edited by L. M. Matheson. East Lansing, MI: Colleagues Press, 1994. Pp. 270–81.

Robbins, Rossell Hope, ed. *Secular Lyrics of the XIVth and XVth Centuries*, 2nd edition. Oxford: Clarendon Press, 1955.

Ryan, William Granger, trans. *Jacobus de Voragine: The Golden Legend*. 2 vols. Princeton, NJ: Princeton University Press, 1993.

Schmidt, A. V. C., ed. *William Langland, Piers Plowman: A Parallel-Text Edition of the A, B, C, and Z Versions*. Kalamazoo, MI: Medieval Institute Publications, 2011. 2 vols.

Seymour, M. C., ed. *John of Trevisa's Translation of Bartholomaeus Anglicus, De Proprietatibus Rerum: A Critical Text*. Oxford: Clarendon Press, 1975-88.

Stavsky, Jonathan, ed. *Le Bone Florence of Rome: A Critical Edition and Facing Translation of a Middle English Romance Analogous to Chaucer's Man of Law's Tale*. Cardiff: University of Wales Press, 2017.

Steele, Robert, ed. *Three Prose Versions of the Secreta Secretorum*. EETS, e.s. 74. London: Kegan Paul, Trench, Trübner, 1898.

Taavitsainen, Irma, Päivi Pahta, and Märtti Makinen, eds. *Middle English Medical Texts*. Helsinki: John Benjamins Publishing, 2005.

Tavormina, M. Teresa, ed. *Sex, Aging, & Death in a Medieval Medical Compendium*. 2 vols. Tempe, AZ: Arizona Center for Medieval and Renaissance Studies, 2006.

Thorndike, Lynn and Pearl Kibre, eds. *A Catalogue of Incipits of Mediaeval Scientific Writings in Latin*. Cambridge, MA: Mediaeval Academy of America, 1963.

Voigts, Linda Ehrsam, and Patricia Deery Kurtz, *Scientific and Medical Writings in Old and Middle English: An Electronic Reference*. Ann Arbor: University of Michigan, 2001. https://cctr1.umkc.edu/search

Wallis, Faith, ed. *Medieval Medicine: A Reader*. Toronto: University of Toronto Press, 2010.

Walsh, P. G., trans. *Boethius: The Consolation of Philosophy*. Oxford: Oxford University Press, 1999.

Watson, Nicholas and Jacqueline Jenkins, eds. *The Writings of Julian of Norwich: A Vision Showed to a Devout Woman and a Revelation of Love*. University Park, PA: The Pennsylvania State University Press, 2006.

Whitehead, Anne and Angela Woods, eds. *The Edinburgh Companion to the Critical Medical Humanities*. Edinburgh, UK: Edinburgh University Press, 2016.

Wilson, William Burton, trans. *John Gower: Mirour de l'Omme*. East Lansing, MI: Colleagues Press, 1992.

Wogan-Browne, Jocelyn, Nicholas Watson, Andrew Taylor, and Ruth Evans, eds. *The Idea of the Vernacular: An Anthology of Middle English Literary Theory, 1280-1520*. University Park: Pennsylvania State University Press, 1999.

Secondary Sources

Aberth, John. *From the Brink of the Apocalypse: Confronting Famine, War, Plague, and Death in the Later Middle Ages*. New York: Routledge, 2001.

Aberth, John. *The Black Death: The Great Mortality of 1348-1350, a Brief History with Documents*. New York: Bedford/St. Martin's, 2005.

Alcaro, Mary M. "High (Plague) Anxiety: Reading the Specter of Pestilence in Late 14th Century British Literature." MA thesis, New York University, 2017.

Alford, John. "Medicine in the Middle Ages." *The Centennial Review* 23.4 (1979): 377–96.

Alonso-Almeida, Francisco. "Oral Traces and Speech Acts in a Corpus of Medieval English Healing Charms." *ANQ: A Quarterly Journal of Short Articles, Notes, and Reviews* 23.1 (2010): 6–14.

Amundsen, Darrel W. *Medicine, Society, and Faith in the Ancient and Medieval Worlds*. Baltimore: Johns Hopkins Press, 1996.

Archibald, Elizabeth. *Apollonius of Tyre: Medieval and Renaissance Themes and Variations*. Cambridge, UK: D. S. Brewer, 1991.

Atkinson, Laurie. "Why that yee meeved been / can I nat knowe: Autobiography, Convention, and Discerning Doublenesse in Thomas Hoccleve's *The Series*." *Neophilologus* 101.3 (2017): 479–94.

Bakalian, Ellen Shaw. *Aspects of Love in John Gower's Confessio Amantis*. New York: Routledge, 2004.

Baker, Patricia A., Han Nijdam, and Karine van't Land, eds. *Medicine and Space: Body, Surroundings and Borders in Antiquity and the Middle Ages*. Leiden: Brill, 2012.

Bălan, Gheorghe, et al. "Saint Apollonia: Between Paganism and Christianity in Medicine." *International Journal of Medical Dentistry* 19.1 (2015): 7–15.

Barwell, Ashlee. "The Healing Arts and Social Capital: The Paston Women of Fifteenth-Century England." *Canadian Bulletin of Medical History* 35 (2018): 137–59.

Batkie, Stephanie L. "'Of the parfite medicine': *Merita Perpetuata* in Gower's Vernacular Alchemy." In *John Gower, Trilingual Poet: Language, Tradition, and Translation*. Edited by Elisabeth Dutton, John Hines, and R. F. Yeager. Woodbridge, UK: Boydell & Brewer, 2010. Pp. 157–67.

Batt, Catherine. "Henry, Duke of Lancaster's *Book of Holy Medicines*: The Rhetoric of Knowledge and Devotion." *Leeds Studies in English* n.s. 4 (2006): 407–14.

Benedek, Thomas G. "The Roles and Images of Medieval Women in the Healing Arts." In *The Role and Images of Women in the Middle Ages and Renaissance*. Pittsburgh: University of Pittsburgh Publications, 1975. Pp. 145–59.

Beidler, Peter G. "The Plague and Chaucer's Pardoner." *The Chaucer Review* 16.3 (1982): 257–69.

Bennett, Judith M. "Death and the Maiden." *Journal of Medieval and Early Modern Studies* 42.2 (2012): 269–305.

Bishop, Louise. *Words, Stones, Herbs: The Healing Word in Medieval and Early Modern England*. Syracuse, NY: Syracuse University Press, 2007.

Bjork, Robert. "The Wife of Bath's *Bele Chose*." *The Chaucer Review* 53.3 (2018): 336–49.

Bonfield, Christopher. "The First Instrument of Medicine: Diet and Regimens of Health in Late Medieval England." In *"A Verray Parfit Praktisour": Essays Presented to Carole Rawcliffe*. Edited by Linda Clark and Elizabeth Danbury. Cambridge, UK: Boydell & Brewer, 2017. Pp. 99–119.

Bowers, Barbara S., ed. *The Medieval Hospital and Medical Practice*. Aldershot: Ashgate, 2007.

Bowers, Barbara S. and Linda Migl Keyser, eds. *The Sacred and the Secular in Medieval Healing: Sites, Objects, and Texts*. New York: Routledge, 2016.

Breeze, Andrew. "Pearl and the Plague of 1390–1393." *Neuphilologus* 98 (2014): 337-41.

Brody, Howard. "Defining the Medical Humanities: Three Conceptions and Three Narratives." *Journal of Medical Humanities* 32 (2011): 1-7.

Brumbaugh-Walter, Lynnea. "Selections from the *Gesta Romanorum*." In *Medieval Literature for Children*. Edited by Daniel T. Kline. New York: Taylor & Francis, 2003. Pp. 29-44.

Bullough, Vern L. *Universities, Medicine and Science in the Medieval West*. Aldershot: Ashgate, 2004.

Burrow, J. A. "Hoccleve's *Series*: Experience and Books." In *Fifteenth-Century Studies: Recent Essays*. Edited by Robert F. Yeager. Hamden: Archon Books, 1984. Pp. 259-73.

Burrow, J. A. "Autobiographical Poetry in the Middle Ages: The Case of Thomas Hoccleve." *Proceedings of the British Academy* 82.3 (1987): 389-412.

Bychowski, M. W. "Unconfessing Transgender Dysphoic Youths and the Medicalization of Madness in John Gower's 'Tale of Iphis and Ianthe.'" *Accessus: A Journal of Premodern Literature and New Media* 3.1 (2016): 1-38. https://scholarworks.wmich.ed/accessus/vol3/iss1/

Byrne, Joseph P. *The Black Death*. Westport, CT: Greenwood Press, 2004.

Campbell, Sheila, Bert Hall, and David Klausner, eds. *Health, Disease and Healing in Medieval Culture*. New York: St. Martin's Press, 1992.

Carlin, Martha. "The Medieval Hospital of St. Thomas the Martyr in Southwark." *Society for the Social History of Medicine Bulletin* 37 (1985): 19-23.

Carlson, John Ivor. "Scribal Intention in Medieval Romance: A Case Study of Robert Thornton." *Studies in Bibliography* 58 (2007–08): 49-71.

Carmichael, Ann G. "Universal and Particular: The Language of Plague, 1348–1500." *Medical History* 52.S27 (2008): 17-52.

Chamberland, Celeste. "Female Healers and the Boundaries of Medical Practice." MA thesis, Concordia University, 1997.

Charon, Rita. "Narrative Medicine: Attention, Representation, Affiliation." *Narrative* 13.3 (2005): 261-70.

Charon, Rita. *Narrative Medicine: Honoring the Stories of Illness*. Oxford: Oxford University Press, 2006.

Charon, Rita. "The Self-Telling Body." *Narrative Inquiry* 16.1 (2006): 191-200.

Charon, Rita. "Narrative Medicine as Witness for the Self-Telling Body." *Journal of Applied Communication Research* 37.2 (2009): 118-31.

Charon, Rita. et al. *The Principles and Practice of Narrative Medicine*. Oxford: Oxford University Press, 2017.

Chaganti, Seeta. *Strange Footing: Poetic Form and Dance in the Late Middle Ages*. Chicago: University of Chicago Press, 2018.

Citrome, Jeremy U. *The Surgeon in Medieval English Literature*. New York: Palgrave Macmillan, 2006.

Clarke, Edwin and Kenneth Dewhurst. *An Illustrated History of Brain Function*. Oxford: Sandford Publications, 1972.

Cohn, Esther. *The Modulated Scream: Pain in Late Medieval Culture*. Chicago: University of Chicago Press, 2010.

Cohn, Samuel. *The Black Death Transformed: Disease and Culture in Early Renaissance Europe*. Oxford: Oxford University Press, 2002.

Cohn, Samuel. "Epidemiology of the Black Death and Successive Waves of Plague." *Medical History* 52.S27 (2008): 74-100.

Cole, Thomas R. et al. *Medical Humanities: An Introduction*. Cambridge, UK: Cambridge University Press, 2015; reprint, 2017.

Coley, David K. *Death and the Pearl Maiden: Plague, Poetry, England*. Columbus, OH: The Ohio State University Press, 2019.

Cooper, Lisa H. "'His guttys wer out shake': Illness and Indigence in Lydgate's *Letter to Gloucester* and *Fabula Duorum Mercatorum*." *Studies in the Age of Chaucer* 30 (2008): 303-34.

Couch, Julie Nelson. "Apocryphal Romance." In *Robert Thornton and His Books*. Edited by Susanna Fein and Michael Johnston. York: York Medieval Press, 2014. Pp. 203-34.

Cowdery, Taylor. "Hoccleve's Poetics of Matter." *Studies in the Age of Chaucer* 38 (2016): 133-64.

Christensen, Jorgen Riber. "The Formula of Plague Narratives." *Akademisk* 12 (2015): 12-29.

Critten, Rory G. "Imagining the Author in Late Medieval England and France: The Transmission and Reception of Christine de Pizan's 'Epistre au dieu d'Amours' and Thomas Hoccleve's Letter of Cupid." *Studies in Philology* 112.4 (2015): 680-97.

Crocker, Holly A. "Engendering Affect in Hoccleve's *Series*." In *Medieval Affect, Feeling, and Emotion*. Edited by Glen D. Burger and Holly A. Crocker. Cambridge, UK: Cambridge University Press, 2019. Pp. 70-89.

Crocker, Holly A. *The Matter of Virtue: Women's Ethical Action from Chaucer to Shakespeare*. Philadelphia: University of Pennsylvania Press, 2019.

DasGupta, Sayantani and Rita Charon, "Personal Illness Narratives: Using Reflective Writing to Teach Empathy." *Academic Medicine* 79.4 (2004): 351-6.

Davidson, Clifford and Sophie Oosterwijk. *John Lydgate: The Dance of Death, and Its Model, the French Danse Macabre*. Leiden: Brill, 2021.

Dawson, Warren R. *A Leechbook or Collection of Medical Recipes of the Fifteenth Century*. London: Macmillan and Co., 1934.

Demaitre, Luke. *Medieval Medicine: The Art of Healing, from Head to Toe*. Santa Barbara, CA: Praeger, 2013.

Dendlle, Peter and Alain Touwaide, eds. *Health and Healing from the Medieval Garden*. Woodbridge, UK: Boydell & Brewer, 2008.

Doob, Penelope B. R. *Nebuchadnezzar's Children*. New Haven: Yale University Press, 1974.

Ellis, Roger. "Chaucer, Christine de Pizan, and Hoccleve: The Letter of Cupid." *Essays on Thomas Hoccleve*. Edited by Catherine Batt. Cambridge, MA: Mediaeval Academy of America, 1996. Pp. 19-54.

Elsakkers, Marianne. "'In Pain You Shall Bear Children' (Gen 3:16): Medieval Prayers for a Safe Delivery." In *Women and Miracles Stories: A Multidisciplinary Exploration*. Edited by Anna-Marie Korte. Leiden: Brill, 2003. Pp. 179-209.

English Heritage. https://blog.english-heritage.org.uk/

Fabbri, Christiane Nockels. "Treating Medieval Plague: The Wonderful Virtues of Theriac." *Early Science and Medicine* 12.3 (2007): 247-83.

Falk, Seb. "Gower and the Natural Sciences." In *Historians on John Gower*. Edited by Stephen Rigby with Siân Echard. Cambridge, UK: D. S. Brewer, 2019. Pp. 491-525.

Fletcher, Angus. *The Theory of a Symbolic Mode*. Ithaca, NY: Cornell University Press, 1966.

Fox, George G. *The Mediaeval Sciences in the Works of John Gower*. New York: Haskell House, 1966.

Fein, Susanna. "The Contents of Robert Thornton's Manuscripts." In *Robert Thornton and His Books*. Edited by Susanna Fein and Michael Johnston. York: York Medieval Press, 2014. Pp. 13-65.

Fein, Susanna and Michael Johnson. *Robert Thornton and His Books: Essays on the Lincoln and London Thornton Manuscripts*. York: York Medieval Press, 2014.

Field, Rosalind and Dav Smith. "Afterword: Robert Thornton Country." In *Robert Thornton and His Books*. Edited by Susanna Fein and Michael Johnston. York: York Medieval Press, 2014. Pp. 257-72.

Finlayson, John. "Reading Romances in Their Manuscripts: Lincoln Cathedral MS 91." *Anglia* 123.4 (2006): 632-66.

Frank, Arthur W. *The Wounded Storyteller: Body, Illness, and Ethics*. Chicago: University of Chicago Press, 1995.

Friedl, Jean Paul and Ian J. Kirby. "The Life, Death, and Life of the Pearl-Maiden." *Neuphilologische Mitteilungen* 103.4 (2002): 395-98.

Frye, Northrop. *The Secular Scripture: A Study of the Structure of Romance*. Cambridge, MA: Harvard University Press, 1978.

Furst, Lillian, ed. *Women Healers and Physicians: Climbing a Long Hill*. Lexington, KY: University of Kentucky Press, 1997.

Galloway, James. "The Hospital and Chapel of Saint Mary Ronceval at Charing Cross." *Proceedings of the Royal Society of Medicine* 6, Sect. Hist. Med. (1913): 191-232.

Gasse, Roseanne. "The Practice of Medicine in Piers Plowman." *The Chaucer Review* 39.2 (2004): 177-97.

Gasse, Roseanne. "Witchcraft and Sorcery in Piers Plowman." *The Chaucer Review* 55.1 (2020): 88-112.

Getz, Faye Marie. "Black Death and the Silver Lining: Meaning, Continuity, and Revolutionary Change in Histories of Medieval Plague." *Journal of the History of Biology* 24.2 (1991): 265-89.

Getz, Faye Marie. *Medicine and the English Middle Ages*. Princeton, NJ: Princeton University Press, 1998.

Gimbel, Lena Mackenzie. "Bawdy Badges and the Black Death: Late Medieval Apotropaic Devices Against the Spread of the Plague." PhD diss., University of Louisville, 2012.

Glaze, Florence Eliza and Brian K. Nance. *Between Text and Patient: The Medical Enterprise in Medieval & Early Modern Europe*. Firenze: Sismel, 2011.

Godden, Richard and Jonathan Hsy. "Analytical Survey: Encountering Disability in the Middle Ages." *New Medieval Literatures* 15 (2013): 313-39.

Goldie, Matthew. "Psychosomatic Illness and Identity in London, 1416–1421: Hoccleve's Complaint and Dialogue with a Friend." *Exemplaria* 11.1 (1999): 23-52.

Goodman, Anthony. *John of Gaunt: The Exercise of Princely Power in Fourteenth-Century Europe*. New York: Routledge, 1992.

Goodman, Barbara A. "Women's Wounds in Middle English Romances: An Exploration of Defilement, Disfigurement, and a Society in Despair." In *Wounds & Wound Repair in Medieval Culture*. Edited by Barbara A. Goodman, Larissa Tracy, and Kelly DeVries. Leiden: Brill, 2015. Pp. 544-71.

Gottfried, Robert S. *Doctors and Medicine in Medieval England, 1340–1530*. Princeton, NJ: Princeton University Press, 1986.

Gottfried, Robert S. *Epidemic Disease in Fifteenth Century England: The Medical Response and the Demographic Consequences*. New Brunswick: Rutgers University Press, 1978.

Gottfried, Robert S. *The Black Death: Natural and Human Disaster in Medieval Europe*. New York: Free Press, 1983.

Green, Monica H. "Women's Medical Practice and Health Care in Medieval Europe." *Signs* 14.2 (1989): 434-73.

Green, Monica H. ed. *Pandemic Disease in the Medieval World: Rethinking the Black Death*. Kalamazoo and Bradford: Arc Medieval Press, 2015.

Green, Monica H. "Taking 'Pandemic' Seriously: Making the Black Death Global." In *Pandemic Disease in the Medieval World: Rethinking the Black Death*. Kalamazoo and Bradford: Arc Medieval Press, 2015. Pp. 27-61.

Green, Monica H. "The Four Black Deaths." *The American Historical Review* 125.5 (2020): 1601–31.

Greetham, D. C. "Self-Referential Artifacts: Hoccleve's Persona as a Literary Device." *Modern Philology* 86.3 (1989): 242-51.

Grigsby, Bryon Lee. *Pestilence in Medieval and Early Modern English Literature*. London: Routledge, 2004.

Grinnell, Natalie. "Medea's Humanity and John Gower's Romance." *Medieval Perspectives* 14 (1999): 70-83.

Hardman, Phillipa. "Domestic Learning and Teaching: Investigating Evidence for the Role of 'Household Miscellanies' in Late-Medieval England." In *Women and Writing*

c. 1340-1650: The Domestication of Print Culture. Edited by Anne Lawrence-Mathers and Phillipa Hardman. York: York Medieval Press, 2010. Pp. 15-33.

Harley, Marta Powell. "The Middle English Contents of a Fifteenth-Century Medical Handbook." *Mediaevalia* 8 (1982): 171-88.

Hays, J. N. *The Burdens of Disease: Epidemics and Human Response in Western History*. New Brunswick, NJ: Rutgers University Press, 2009.

Hebert, Jill M. *Morgan le Fay, Shapeshifter*. New York: Palgrave Macmillan, 2013.

Hemphill, Ian and Lynne Cobiac. "The Historical and Cultural Use of Herbs and Spices." *MJA Supplement: The Medical Journal of Australia* 185.4 (2006): S1-S24.

Hickey, Helen. "Legal Personhood and the Inquisitions of Insanity in Thomas Hoccleve's Series." In *Theorizing Legal Personhood in Late Medical England*. Edited by Andreea D. Boboc. Leiden: Brill, 2015. Pp. 192-217.

Hill, Derek Ingram. *The Ancient Hospitals and Almshouses of Canterbury*. Canterbury, UK: Canterbury Archaeological Society, 1969.

Hollywood, Amy. "Acute Melancholia." *Harvard Theological Review* 99.4 (2006): 381-406.

Horobin, Simon. "Thomas Hoccleve: Chaucer's First Editor?" *The Chaucer Review* 50.3-4 (2015): 228-50.

Horstmann, Karl. *Yorkshire Writers 1*. London: Swan Sonneschein & Co., 1895.

Hunter, Kathryn M. *Doctors' Stories: The Narrative Structure of Medical Knowledge*. Princeton: Princeton University Press, 1991.

Ingram, Hannah. "'Pottes of Tryacle' and 'Bokes of Phisyke': The Fifteenth-Century Disease Management Practices of Three Gentry Families." *Social History of Medicine* 32.4 (2018): 751-72.

Jefferson, Laura, Karen Bloor, and Alan Maynard. "Women in Medicine: Historical Perspectives and Recent Trends." *British Medical Bulletin* 14.1 (2015): 5-15.

Jones, Ida A. "Popular Medical Knowledge in Fourteenth-Century Literature." *Bulletin of the History of Medicine* 5 (1937): 405-51.

Jones, Lori. *Exploring Concepts of Contagion and the Authority of Medical Treatises in 14th-16th Century England*. MA thesis, University of Ottawa, CA.

Jones, Peter Murray. *Medieval Medical Miniatures*. Austin: University of Texas Press, 1984.

Jones, Peter Murray. "Four Middle English Translations of John of Arderne." In *Latin and Vernacular: Studies in Late-Medieval Texts and Manuscripts*. Edited by A. J. Minnis. Woodbridge, UK: Boydell & Brewer, 1989.

Jones, Peter Murray. "The Surgeon as Story-teller." *Poetica* 72 (2009): 77-91.

Jones, Peter Murray. "The Survival of the Frater Medicus? English Friars and Alchemy, ca. 1370-ca.1425." *Ambix* 65.3 (2018): 232-49.

Jones, Peter Murray and Lea T. Olsan. "Performative Rituals for Conception and Childbirth in England, 900-1500." *Bulletin of the History of Medicine* 89.3 (2015): 406-33.

Kalas, Laura. *Margery Kempe's Spiritual Medicine: Suffering, Transformation and the Life-Course*. Woodbridge, UK: D. S. Brewer, 2020.

Kealey, Edward J. *Medieval Medicus: A Social History of Anglo-Norman Medicine*. Baltimore: Johns Hopkins University Press, 1981.

Keiser, George R. "Lincoln Cathedral Library MS. 91: The Life and Milieu of the Scribe." *Studies in Bibliography* 32 (1979): 158-79.

Keiser, George R. "The Holy Boke Gratia Dei." *Viator* 12 (1981): 289-317.

Keiser, George R. "Reconstructing Robert Thornton's Herbal." *Medium Aevum* 65.1 (1996): 35-53.

Keiser, George R. *A Manual of the Writings in Middle English 1050–1500*. Vol. 10. New Haven: Yale University Press, 1998.

Keiser, George R. "Two Medieval Plague Treatises and Their Afterlife in Early Modern England." *Journal of the History of Medicine* 58 (2003): 292-324.

Keiser, George R. "Verse Introductions to Middle English Medical Treatises." *English Studies* 84.4 (2003): 301-17.

Keiser, George R. "Robert Thornton: Gentleman, Reader, and Scribe." In *Robert Thornton and His Books*. Edited by Susanna Fein and Michael Johnston. Woodbridge, UK: York Medieval Press, 2014. Pp. 67-108.

Kelly, John. *The Great Mortality: An Intimate History of the Black Death, the Most Devastating Plague of All Time*. New York: HarperCollins, 2005.

Kempf, Elisabeth. *Performing Manuscript Culture: Poetry, Materiality, and Authorship in Thomas Hoccleve's Regement of Princes*. Berlin: Walter de Gruyter, 2016.

Kempton, Daniel. "The 'Physician's Tale': The Doctor of Physic's Diplomatic Cure." *The Chaucer Review* 19.1 (1984): 24-38.

Kibre, Pearl and Nancy G. Siriasi. "Matheolus of Perugia's Commentary on the Preface to the Aphorism of Hippocrates." *Bulletin of the History of Medicine* 49.3 (1975): 405-28.

Kleinman, Arthur. *Illness Narratives: Suffering, Healing & the Human Condition*. New York: Basic Books, 1988.

Knapp, Ethan. *The Bureaucratic Muse: Thomas Hoccleve and the Literature of Late Medieval England*. University Park: Pennsylvania State University Press, 2001.

Knapp, Ethan. "Towards a Material Allegory: Allegory and Urban Space in Hoccleve, Langland, and Gower." *Exemplaria* 27.1–2 (2015): 93-109.

Kopřivová, Monika. "Women Characters in Arthurian Literature." Thesis, Masaryk University, Brno, 2007.

Krug, Rebecca. *Reading Families: Women's Literate Practice in Late Medieval England*. Ithaca: Cornell University, 2002.

Krug, Rebecca. "Piers Plowman and the Secrets of Health." *The Chaucer Review* 46.1–2 (2011): 166-81.

Labbie, Erin Felicia, ed. "Pain, Trauma, and Philia in Middle English Literature." *Literature and Medicine* 33.2 (2015): 235-57.

Langum, Virginia. "'The Wounded Surgeon': Devotion, Compassion and Metaphor in Medieval England." In *Wounds and Wound Repair in Medieval Culture*. Edited by Larissa Tracy and Kelly DeVries. Leiden: Brill, 2015. Pp. 269-90.

Langum, Virginia. *Medicine and the Seven Deadly Sins in Late Medieval Literature and Culture*. New York: Palgrave Macmillan, 2016.

Larsen, Vickie and John Pendell, "Thomas Hoccleve's *Series* and English Verse in Early Fifteenth-Century London." *Philological Quarterly* 97.4 (2018): 499-514.

Laskaya, Anne. "The Feminized World and Divine Violence: Texts and Images of the Apocalypse." In *Domestic Violence in Medieval Texts*. Edited by Eve Salisbury, Georgiana Donavin, and Merrall L. Price. Gainesville, FL: University Press of Florida, 2002. Pp. 299-341.

Lawrence, Tom. "Infectious Fear: The Rhetoric of Pestilence in Middle English Didactic Texts on Death." *English Studies* 98.8 (2017): 866-80.

Leahy, Michael. "'To speke of phisik': Medical Discourse in Late Medieval English Culture." PhD diss. Birkbeck, University of London, 2015.

Lewis, Celia. "Framing Fiction with Death: Chaucer's *Canterbury Tales* and the Plague." In *New Readings of Chaucer's Poetry*. Edited by Robert G. Bensen and Susan J. Ridyard. Cambridge, UK: D. S. Brewer, 2003.

Lewis, Suzanne. *Reading Images: Narrative Discourse and Reception in the Thirteenth-Century Illuminated Apocalypse*. Cambridge, UK: Cambridge University Press, 1995.

Little, Katherine C. *Confession and Resistance: Defining the Self in Late Medieval England*. Notre Dame, IN: University of Notre Dame Press, 2006.

Maddicott, J. R. "Plague in Seventh-Century England." *Past and Present* 156 (1997-98): 7-54.

Magnani, Roberta. "Chaucer's Physicians: Raising Questions of Authority." In *Medicine, Religion and Gender in Medieval Culture*. Edited by Naoë Kukita Yoshikawa. Cambridge, UK: D. S. Brewer, 2015. Pp. 45-64.

Matheson, Lister M. "Médecin sans Frontières?: The European Dissemination of John of Burgundy's Plague Treatise." *ANQ* 18.1 (2005): 19-30.

Matheson, Lister M. "John of Burgundy: Treatises on Plague." In *Sex, Aging, & Death in a Medieval Medical Compendium: Trinity College Cambridge MS R. 14.52, Its Texts, Language, and Scribe*. Vol. 2. Edited by M. Teresa Tavormina. Tempe, AZ: Arizona Center for Medieval and Renaissance Studies, 2006. 2 Vols.

McAvoy, Liz Herbert. *Authority and the Female Body in the Writings of Julian of Norwich and Margery Kempe*. Rochester, NY: Boydell & Brewer, 2004.

McCann, Daniel. *Soul-Health: Therapeutic Reading in Later Medieval England*. Cardiff: University of Wales Press, 2018.

McCormick, Michael. "Gregory of Tours on Sixth-Century Plague and Other Epidemics." *Speculum* 96.1 (2021): 38-96.

McKinstry, Jamie and Corinne Saunders. "Medievalism and Medical Humanities." *postmedieval: a journal of medieval cultural studies* 8.2 (2017): 139-46.

McNamer, Sarah. *Affective Meditation and the Invention of Medieval Compassion*. Philadelphia, PA: University of Pennsylvania Press, 2010.

McShane, Kara. "Social Healing in Gower's *Visio Angliae*." *South Atlantic Review* 79.3-4 (2014): 76-88.

McVaugh, Michael. "Bedside Manners in the Middle Ages." *Bulletin of the History of Medicine* 71.2 (1997): 201-23.

Metzler, Irina. *A Social History of Disability in the Middle Ages: Cultural Considerations of Physical Impairment*. London: Routledge, 2013.

Mitchell, Piers D. *Medicine in the Crusades: Warfare, Wounds and the Medieval Surgeon*. Cambridge, UK: Cambridge University Press, 2004.

Montford, Angela. *Health, Sickness, Medicine and the Friars in the Thirteenth and Fourteenth Centuries*. Aldershot, UK: Ashgate, 2004.

Morrissey, Jake Walsh. "Anxious Love and Disordered Urine: The Englishing of Amor Hereos in Henry Daniel's *Liber uricrisiarum*." *The Chaucer Review* 49.2 (2014): 161-83.

Morrissey, Jake Walsh. "'To al Indifferent': The Virtues of Lydgate's 'Dietary'." *Medium Aevum* 84.2 (2015): 258-78.

Mullett, Charles F. "John Lydgate: A Mirror of Medieval Medicine." *Bulletin of the History of Medicine* 22.4 (1948): 403-15.

Nohl, Johannes. *The Black Death: A Chronicle of the Plague*, trans. C. H. Clarke. New York: Harper & Rowe, 1969.

Norri, Juhani. *Names of Sicknesses in English, 1400-1550: An Exploration of the Lexical Field*. Helsinki: Suomalainen Tiedeakatemia, 1992.

Norri, Juhani, ed. *Dictionary of Medical Vocabulary in English, 1375-1500*. Abingdon, UK: Ashgate, 2016.

O'Callaghan, Tamara. "The Fifteen Stars, Stones, and Herbs: Book VII of the *Confessio Amantis* and Its Afterlife." In *John Gower, Trilingual Poet: Language, Tradition, and Translation*. Edited by Elisabeth Dutton, John Hines, and R. F. Yeager. Woodbridge, UK: Boydell & Brewer, 2010. Pp. 139-56.

Olsan, Lea T. "Latin Charms of Medieval England: Verbal Healing in a Christian Oral Tradition." *Oral Tradition* 7.1 (1992): 116-42.

Olsan, Lea T. "Charms and Prayers in Medieval Medical Theory and Practice." *Social History of Medicine* 16.1 (2003): 343-66.

Olsan, Lea T. "The Language of Charms in a Middle English Recipe Collection." *ANQ* 18.3 (2005): 31-7.

Olson, Glending. *Literature as Recreation in the Middle Ages*. Ithaca, NY: Cornell University Press, 1982.

Oosterwijk, Sophia. "Lessons in 'Hopping': The Dance of Death and the Chester Mystery Cycle." *Comparative Drama* 36.3/4 (2002): 249-87.

Orlemanski, Julie. "Jargon and the Matter of Medicine in Middle English." *Journal of Medieval and Early Modern Studies* 42.2 (2012): 395-420.

Orlemanski, Julie. *Symptomatic Subjects: Bodies, Medicine, and Causation in the Literature of Late Medieval England*. Philadelphia: University of Pennsylvania Press, 2019.

Orlemanski, Julie. "Thornton's Remedies and the Practices of Medical Reading." In *Robert Thornton and His Books*. Edited by Susanna Fein and Michael Johnston. York: York Medieval Press, 2014. Pp. 235-55.

Page, Christopher. "Music and Medicine in the Thirteenth Century." In *Music as Medicine: The History of Music Therapy since Antiquity*. Edited by Peregrine Horden. New York: Routledge, 2000. Pp. 109-16.

Palmer, James M. "Bodily and Spiritual Healing through Conversation and Storytelling: Genius as Physician and Confessor in the *Confessio Amantis*." In *Approaches to Teaching the Poetry of John Gower*. Edited by R. F. Yeager and Brian Gastle. New York: Modern Language Association, 2011. Pp. 53-8.

Park, Katharine. "Medicine and Society in Medieval Europe, 500–1500." In *Medicine in Society*. Edited by Andrew Wear. Cambridge, UK: Cambridge University Press, 1992. Pp. 59-90.

Paston Letters. Project Gutenberg. https://www.gutenberg.org

Patterson, Lee. "'What Is Me?': Self and Society in the Poetry of Thomas Hoccleve." *Studies in the Age of Chaucer* 23 (2001): 437-70.

Pearn, John. "Bernard Gordon (fl. 1270-1330): Medieval Physician and Teacher." *Journal of Medical Biography* 21 (2013): 8-11.

Pearn, John. "Two Medieval Doctors: Gilbertus Anglicus (c.1180–c.1250) and John of Gaddesden (1280-1361)." *Journal of Medical Biography* 21 (2013): 3-7.

Pearsall, Derek. *John Lydgate, 1371–1449: A Bio-bibliography*. British Columbia, CA: ELS Editions, 1997.

Peck, Russell A. "The Materiality of Cognition in Reading, Staging, and Regulation of Brain and Heart Activities in Gower's *Confessio Amantis*." In *John Gower: Others and the Self*. Edited by Russell A. Peck and R. F. Yeager. Woodbridge, UK: D. S. Brewer, 2017). Pp. 7-31.

Perry, R. D. "Lydgate's Danse Macabre and the Trauma of the Hundred Years War." *Literature and Medicine* 33.2 (2015): 326-47.

Pochop, Irena. "Disease: Medical Terminology in Middle English." http://homes.chass.utoronto.ca/~cpercy/courses/6361pochop.htm

Poellinger, Mary Michele. "'The rosselde spere to his herte rynnes': Religious Violence in the *Alliterative Morte Arthure* and the Lincoln Thornton Manuscript." In *Robert Thornton and His Books*. Edited by Susanna Fein and Michael Johnston. York: York Medieval Press, 2014. Pp. 157-75.

Power, D'Arcy. *Treatises of Fistula in Ano, Haemorrhoids, and Clysters*. EETS, o.s. 139. London: Kegan Paul, Trench, Trübner, 1910.

Rawcliffe, Carole. "The Hospitals of Later London." *Medical History* 28 (1984): 1-21.

Rawcliffe, Carole. *Medicine & Society in Later Medieval England*. Stroud, UK: Sutton, 1995.

Rawcliffe, Carole. *Sources for the History of Medicine in Late Medieval England*. TEAMS Documents of Practice Series. Kalamazoo, MI: Medieval Institute Publications, 1995.

Rawcliffe, Carole. *Urban Bodies: Communal Health in Late Medieval English Towns and Cities*. Woodbridge, UK: Boydell & Brewer Press, 2013.

Rawcliffe, Carole. "The Doctor of Physic." In *Historians on Chaucer: The "General Prologue" to the Canterbury Tales*. Edited by Stephen H. Rigby and Alastair Minnis. Oxford: Oxford University Press, 2015. Pp. 297–318.

Rigby, Stephen and Sian Echard. *Historians on John Gower*. Cambridge, UK: D. S. Brewer, 2019.

Robbins, Rossell Hope. "The Physician's Authorities." In *Studies in Language and Literature in Honour of Margaret Schlauch*. Warszawa: Polish Scientific Publishers, 1966. Pp. 335–41.

Robbins, Rossell Hope. *Secular Lyrics of the XIVth and XVth Centuries*. Oxford: Clarendon Press, 1968.

Robbins, Rossell Hope. "Medical Manuscripts in Middle English." *Speculum* 45 (1970): 393-415.

Robbins, Rossell Hope. "Signs of Death in Middle English." *Medieval Studies* 32 (1970): 282-98.

Rogers, William. "Old Words Made New: Medea's Magic and Gower's Textual Healing." *South Atlantic Review* 79.3-4 (2014): 105-17.

Rosenfeld, Jessica. "Compassionate Conversions: Gower's *Confessio Amantis* and the Problem of Envy." *Journal of Medieval and Early Modern Studies* 42.1 (2012): 83-105.

Rozenski, Steven. "'Your Ensaumple and Your Mirour': Hoccleve's Amplification of the Imagery and Intimacy of Henry Suso's *Ars Moriendi*." *Parergon* 25.2 (2008): 1-16.

Rubin, Stanley. *Medieval English Medicine*. New York: Barnes & Noble, 1974.

St. Jacques, Raymond. "Langland's Christus Medicus Image and the Structure of *Piers Plowman*." *Yearbook of Langland Studies* 5 (1991): 111-27.

Saunders, Corinne. "'The thoghtful maladie': Madness and Vision in Medieval Writing." In *Madness and Creativity in Literature and Culture*. Edited by Corinne Saunders and Jane Macnaughton. New York: Palgrave Macmillan, 2005. Pp. 67-87.

Saunders, Corinne. "Bodily Narrative: Illness, Medicine and Healing in Middle English Romance." In *Boundaries in Medieval Romance*. Edited by Neil Cartlidge. Woodbridge, UK: Boydell & Brewer, 2008. Pp. 175-90.

Saunders, Corinne. "Gender, Virtue and Wisdom in *Bevis of Hampton*." In *Sir Bevis of Hampton in Literary Tradition*. Edited by Jennifer Fellows and Ivana Djordjevic. Woodbridge, UK: Boydell & Brewer, 2008. Pp. 161-75.

Saunders, Corinne. "Voices and Visions: Mind, Body and Affect in Medieval Writing." In *The Edinburgh Companion to the Critical Medical Humanities*. Edited by Anne Whitehead and Angela Woods. Edinburgh: Edinburgh University Press, 2016. Pp. 411–27.

Schiffman, Richard. "Learning to Listen to Patients' Stories." *The New York Times*, February 25, 2021.

Schleissner, Margaret R., et al., eds. *Manuscript Sources of Medieval Medicine: A Book of Essays*. New York: Routledge, 2013.

Shockro, Sally. "Apocalyptic Disease and the Seventh-Century Plague." In *Trauma in Medieval Society*. Edited by Wendy Turner and Christina Lee. Leiden: Brill, 2018. Pp. 320-40.

Shahar, Shulamith. "The Old Body in Medieval Culture." In *Framing Medieval Bodies*. Edited by Sarah Kay and Miri Rubin. Manchester: Manchester University Press, 1994. Pp. 160-86.

Simpson, James. "Madness and Texts: Hoccleve's *Series*." In *Chaucer and Fifteenth-century Poetry*. Edited by J. Boffey and J. Cowan. London: King's College, 1991. Pp. 15-29.

Singer, Dorothea Waley. "Some Plague Tractates (Fourteen and Fifteenth Centuries)." *Section of the History of Medicine*, 1916.

Siriasi, Nancy G. *Medieval & Early Renaissance Medicine: An Introduction to Knowledge and Practice*. Chicago: University of Chicago Press, 1990.

Smith, Kirk L. "False Care and the Canterbury Cure: Chaucer Treats the New Galen." *Literature and Medicine* 27.1 (2008): 61-81.

Smyth, Karen. "Pestilence and Poetry: John Lydgate's *Danse Macabre*." In *The Fifteenth Century XII: Society in the Age of Plague*. Edited by Linda Clark and Carole Rawcliffe. Woodbridge, UK: Boydell & Brewer, 2013. Pp. 39-56.

Snell, William. "Lydgate's *Dietary and Doctrine for Pestilence* Re-examined." *Hiyoshi Review of English Studies* 22 (1994): 121-34.

Solomon, Michael. *Fictions of Well-Being: Sickly Readers and Vernacular Writing in Late Medieval and Early Modern Spain*. Philadelphia: University of Pennsylvania Press, 2010.

Sotres, Pedro Gil. "The Regimens of Health." In *Western Medical Thought from Antiquity to the Middle Ages*. Edited by Mirko Grmek. London: Wellcome Trust Centre for the History of Medicine, 1998. Pp. 291-318.

Spearing, A. C. "The Awntyrs off Arthure." In *The Alliterative Tradition in the Fourteenth Century*. Edited by Bernard S. Levy and Paul E. Szarmach. Kent, OH: Kent State University, 1981. Pp. 183-202.

Steel, David. "Plague Writing: From Boccaccio to Camus." *European Studies XI* (1981): 88-110.

Stretter, Robert. "Rewriting Perfect Friendship in Chaucer's Knight's Tale and Lydgate's Fabula Durorum Mercatorum." *The Chaucer Review* 37.3 (2007): 234-52.

Strohm, Paul. "Hoccleve, Lydgate and the Lancastrian Court." In *The Cambridge History of Medieval English Literature*. Edited by David Wallace. Cambridge, UK: Cambridge University Press, 1999. Pp. 640-61.

Stuard, Susan Mosher. "Dame Trot." *Signs* 1.2 (1975): 537-42.

Sugito, Hisashi. "Rereading Hoccleve's Series: The Limits of Language and Experience." *Journal of Medieval Religious Cultures* 39.1 (2013): 43-59.

Sylwanowicz, Marta. *Middle English Names of Medical Preparations: Towards a Standard Medical Terminology*. New York: Peter Lang, 2018.

Talbot, C. H. "A Mediaeval Physician's Vade Mecum." *Journal of the History of Medicine and Allied Sciences* 3 (1961): 213-33.

Tambling, Jeremy. "Allegory and the Madness of the Text: Hoccleve's Complaint." *New Medieval Literatures* 6 (2003): 223-48.

Tavormina, M. Teresa. "The Middle English Letter of Ipocras." *English Studies* 88.6 (2007): 632-52.

Trembinski, Donna. "Comparing Premodern Melancholy/Mania and Modern Trauma: An Argument in Favor of Historical Experiences of Trauma." *History of Psychology* 14.1 (2011): 80-99.

Trembinski, Donna. "Trauma as a Category of Analysis." In *Trauma in Medieval Society*. Edited by Wendy Turner and Christina Lee. Leiden: Brill, 2018. Pp. 13-32.

Turner, Mario. *Chaucerian Conflict: Languages of Antagonism in Late Fourteenth-Century London*. Oxford: Oxford University Press, 2007.

Turner, Marion. "Illness Narratives in the Later Middle Ages: Arderne, Chaucer, and Hoccleve." *Journal of Medieval and Early Modern Studies* 46.1 (2016): 61–87.

Turner, Marion. *Chaucer: A European Life*. Princeton, NJ: Princeton University Press, 2019.

Tuttle, Edward. "The Trotula and Old Dame Trot: A Note on the Lady of Salerno." *Bulletin of the History of Medicine* 50 (1976): 61-72.

Van Arsdall, Anne and Timothy Graham, eds. *Herbs and Healers from the Ancient Mediterranean through the Medieval West: Essays in Honor of John M. Riddle*. New York: Routledge, 2017.

Voigts, Linda Ehrsam. "Medical Prose." In *Middle English Prose: ACritical Guide to Major Authors and Genres*. Edited by A. S. G. Edwards, et al. New Brunswick, NJ: Rutgers University, 1984. Pp. 3115–35.

Voigts, Linda Ehrsam. "Herbs and Herbal Healing Satirized in Middle English Texts." In *Herbs and Healers from the Ancient Mediterranean through the Medieval West: Essays in Honor of John M. Riddle*. Farnham, UK: Ashgate, 2012. Pp. 217-30.

von Nolcken, Christina. "'O, Why ne had I learned for to Die?': *Lerne for to Dye* and the Author's Death in Thomas Hoccleve's Series." In *Essays in Medieval Studies: Proceedings of the Illinois Medieval Association*. Chicago: Illinois Medieval Association, 1987. Pp. 25-51.

Wack, Mary Frances. *Lovesickness in the Middle Ages: The "Viaticum" and Its Commentaries*. Philadelphia: University of Pennsylvania Press, 1990.

Wagner, David M., et al. "Yersinia Pestis and the Plague of Justinian 541-543: A Genomic Analysis." *Lancet* 14 (2014): 319-26.

Watt, David. *The Making of Thomas Hoccleve's Series*. Liverpool, UK: Liverpool University Press, 2013.

Watt, David. "Thomas Hoccleve's Particular Appeal." *Pedagogy* 13 (2013): 337–55.

Watt, Diane. *The Paston Women: Selected Letters*. Woodbridge, UK: D. S. Brewer, 2004.

Watt, Diane. *Medieval Women's Writing: Works by and for Women in England, 1100–1500*. Malden, MA: Polity Press, 2007.

Watt, Diane. "Mary the Physician: Women, Religion and Medicine in the Middle Ages." In *Medicine, Religion and Gender in Medieval Culture*. Edited by Naoë Kukita Yoshikawa. Cambridge, UK: D. S. Brewer, 2015. Pp. 27-44.

Webb, Heather. "Cardiosensory Impulses in Late Medieval Spirituality." In *Rethinking the Medieval Senses: Heritage, Fascinations, Frames*. Edited by Stephen G. Nichols, Andreas Kablitz, and Alison Calhoun. Baltimore: Johns Hopkins University Press, 2008. Pp. 265–85.

Webb, Heather. *The Medieval Heart*. New Haven, CT: Yale University Press, 2010.

Wenzel, Siegfried. "Pestilence and Middle English Literature: Friar Grimstone's Poems on Death." In *The Black Death: The Impact of the Fourteenth-Century Plague*. Edited by Daniel Williman. New York: Center for Medieval and Renaissance Studies, 1982. Pp. 131–59.

Whitaker, Elaine. "Reading the Paston Letters Medically." *English Language Notes* 31.1 (1993): 19-27.

Williman, Daniel, ed. *The Black Death: The Impact of the Fourteenth-Century Plague*. Binghamton, NY: Center for Medieval and Early Renaissance Studies, 1982.

Wilson, William Burton, trans. *John Gower, Mirour de l'Omme (The Mirror of Mankind)*. East Lansing, MI: Colleagues Press, 1992.

Winstead, Karen. "'I am al other to yow than yee weene': Hoccleve, Women, and the *Series*." *Philological Quarterly* 72.2 (1993): 143-55.

Yee, Pamela M. "'So schalt thou double hele finde': Narrative Medicine in the 'Tale of Constantine and Sylvester.'" *South Atlantic Review* 79.3-4 (2014): 89-104.

York, William H. *Health and Wellness in Antiquity through the Middle Ages*. Santa Barbara, CA: Greenwood, 2012.

Yoshikawa, Nasoë Kukita. "Holy Medicine and Diseases of the Soul: Henry of Lancaster and *Le Livre de Seyntz Medicines*." *Medical History* 53.3 (2009): 397-414.

Yoshikawa, Nasoë Kukita. "Mysticism and Medicine: Holy Communion in the Vita of Marie d'Oignies and the Book of Margery Kempe." *Poetica* 72 (2009): 109-22.

Zink, Michel and Katherine Lydon. "The Time of the Plague and the Order of Writing: Jean le Bel, Froissart, Machaut." *Yale French Studies* (1991): 269-80.

Zweers, Thari. "Godfrey of Viterbo's *Pantheon* and John Gower's *Confessio Amantis*: The Story of Apollonius Retold." *Accessus: A Journal of Premodern Literature and New Media* 5.1 (2018). https://scholarworks.wmich.edu/accessus/vol5/iss1/3

Index

Adams, Robert 79
Aesculapius (Greco-Roman god of healing) 92 n.32
alchemy 77, 90 n.27
Alexander the Great 77–8, 125, 136–8
Alford, John A. 21 n.8
Algazel 129 n.20
allegory 14, 17, 42, 45, 50 n.5, 55, 99, 111–14, 111 n.69, 195
alliterative narrative 137, 147, 156, 174
Alonso-Almeida, Francisco 146
Alphonsi, Petrus 91
analgesics 149
anger 52 n.13
Anglicus, Bartholomaeus 57 n.26, 101 n.53
Anglicus, Gilbertus 9, 146, 156, 184
antidotes 65, 71, 74, 110, 113, 180, 187
aphorism 13, 17–18, 18–19 n.4, 20, 32, 47, 50, 61 n.33
Apollo (ancient god of medicine) 26
apothecaries 24–5, 36, 42, 62, 164
Appleton, William 123
Aquinas, Thomas 60
Aristotle 22 n.12, 56–7, 60, 72, 77–8, 125, 171
Arntz, M. L. 135
astrology/astrological medicine 11, 13, 86
astronomy 11, 24, 127, 132
Augustine 57, 71 n.52
authentic/authenticity 26, 38, 104, 149, 159
Avicenna 56, 59, 180

Bakalian, Ellen 185
baptism (purification ceremony) 70
Batkie, Stephanie L. 77
Beauchamp, Margaret 160, 160 n.16
Becket, Thomas 21, 22 n.9
Beidler, Peter 37–8
Benedictines
   gardens of 45
   monk 45, 83, 91

Bennett, Judith 175
biblical narratives 11, 31–2, 54, 74, 91, 111
Bishop, Louise 156, 160, 160 n.16
   masculine vernacularity 121
Black Death 1 n.1, 2, 2 n.3, 7–9, 12, 14, 16, 20, 37, 49, 89 n.26, 117, 190–2, 194–5, 198. *See also* great mortality; plague
blood 22 n.12, 52, 71, 127, 130, 170–1, 185–6, 191 n.7
   bloodletting 10, 14, 125, 127
   coagulated 73 n.56, 74
   healing power of 144–7
   and urine 27 n.21
   and violence 137
Boccaccio, Giovanni 3, 13, 20–1, 37, 49, 82 n.4, 183, 193
body and soul 4, 13, 21, 52, 56–7, 60, 74–5, 87, 108, 111, 115, 120, 122, 125
Boethius 19–20, 22, 46, 93, 102
Boston Medical Library MS Ballard Catalogue No. 19 manuscript 163, 163 n.27
brain 57, 130, 132, 164. *See also* Cell Doctrine theory; heart
   cells/ventricles of 57–8, 57 n.26
   cogitativa (thought) 59
   connections between heart and other senses 59–60
   estimativa (judgment) 57, 60
   imaginativa (image formation) 57, 60
   memorativa (memory) 57, 59–60
   phantasia (image formation) 59–60
   sensus communis (common sense) 57, 59–60
   worm 57–8
breast milk 71, 71 n.52, 150, 170, 172
bubonic plague 1 n.1, 2, 5, 36, 36 n.43, 61, 80, 112 n.71, 131–2, 189, 191, 191 n.7
Burrow, J. A. 116 n.78

Bychowski, M. W. 81
Byrne, Joseph P. 28 n.24, 84, 84 n.10, 91

Canutus 81–2, 87
Capellanus, Andreas 17, 56
cardiocentrism/cardiocentric body 60, 74, 172
   Gower on 67–72
   Langland on 63–7
Caritas 53, 60
Carlin, Martha 22 n.9
Carlson, John Ivor 143
Carmichael, Ann G. 191 n.7
cauterization 130 n.24, 144
Caxton, William 85
Cell Doctrine theory 57–8. *See also* brain
Chaganti, Seeta 95, 95 n.42
charity 31, 71, 87–8, 142–3
charms, medical 12, 14, 66, 125, 133, 145–6, 156, 177–8, 184, 186
   childbirth 149–53
   fever 147–8
   peperit/holy mothers 151
   toothache 148–9
   verbal 147
Charon, Rita 2, 5–7, 21, 46, 72 n.54, 82, 107, 194
   narrative features of medicine 6
Chaucer, Geoffrey 4, 13, 17–23, 28 n.23, 29, 29 n.26, 29 n.28, 32–4, 36–46, 50, 69, 81, 83–5, 92–3, 92 n.32, 98, 103, 109, 114–15, 123, 129, 160, 181, 182 n.86, 187, 195
   craft 13, 17–18, 19 n.4
   Ellesmere manuscript 26, 98
   healing philosophy 45–7
   pilgrims/pilgrimage 13, 20–3, 28, 37 n.46, 50, 78, 81, 195
Christian/Christianity 60, 69–71, 91, 94, 125, 143–5, 150–1, 167, 173, 180
Christus medicus 12, 46, 61, 63–5, 68, 74–6, 137, 173
chronic mental illness 101–2
Clarke, Edwin 57
Clerk, Roger 148
code-switching 147
Cohen, Esther 11, 194
Coley, David 175–6, 176 n.72, 195
   palimpsestic multiplicity 175, 195

compassion 53, 60, 64, 66, 69, 74, 87, 109, 145, 150, 167, 170–1, 173, 175, 185–7, 196. *See also* passion
confession 13, 38, 42, 50–1, 54, 61, 66, 68, 80–1, 103, 109, 112–13
   and Seven Deadly Sins 55–6
Conscience 66, 141
consilia (plague treatises) 82 n.2, 86–7
Constantine 69–71
Constantinus Africanus 56, 125
contagion 36 n.43, 37, 52, 71, 111 n.69, 127, 132, 163, 193, 196
Cook, Megan 94, 100 n.49
Cooper, Lisa H. 92–3
Cophon 129 n.20
cosmology 10, 120, 127, 132
   Christian 150
   cosmological knowledge 76
   premodern 171
cosmos 10–11
Covid-19 pandemic 2, 2 n.3, 198. *See also* pandemic
Crocker, Holly 115, 156

Daniel, Henry 93, 93 n.34
Dante Alighieri 22
da Rupescissa, Giovanni 28 n.24
Davidson, Clifford 95 n.42
death (death poetry) 4, 13–14, 21, 63, 74, 94–9, 112, 116–17, 119, 122, 136, 139, 142, 145, 150, 152–3, 166, 176, 195
   death rate among children 30–1
   learning to die 107–8
   and the physician 98–9
de Chauliac, Guy 3, 17–18, 28 n.23, 90 n.27, 126 n.15, 156 n.5, 184, 191 n.5, 194
de Corbeil, Giles 92
de Excestre, William 123
de Grosmont, Henry 66 n.44, 71 n.52
Demaitre, Luke 18, 19 n.4, 101, 101 n.53
de Mondeville, Henri 29–30, 171–2
de Pizan, Christine 100, 106, 116, 183
de Voragine, Jacobus 70, 91
Dewhurst, Kenneth 57
de Worde, Wynkyn 85
diagnosticians 51, 82, 106, 117, 122, 132
dialogic exchange 7, 14, 51, 70, 81, 167

Diana (virgin goddess) 40, 73–4
diapenidion 65, 65 n.43
Dictionary of Medical Vocabulary in English, 1375–1500 12 n.29, 133, 156 n.5
dietetic medicine 25, 87, 116
dis-ease 29, 50, 52, 80, 84, 117, 191
    medicine for 174–7
    reading for 138–44
disese 84 n.13
dissemination of medicine 50, 83, 116, 157, 163, 180
diversity 121–2, 124, 134
divine/divinity 31, 45, 53, 71, 91, 146, 168–9
    divine authority 120, 141
    divine madness 104
    divine punishment 61, 69, 165
Doob, Penelope 103
double-gendered 172
Doyle, A. I. 163 n.27
drinkable gold, medicine 90 n.27
drink of Antioch 12, 65, 74
Duke Humphrey of Gloucester 106, 114

Ebesham, William 163, 163 n.27
Ellis, Roger 108 n.63, 112 n.70
Elsakkers, Marianne 148, 151 n.78, 152
embodied excellence 156, 180
emotional trauma (etyk) 19, 92
emotive cognition 60
England 1, 3, 9, 37–9, 46, 54, 83–4, 89, 93 n.34, 114, 117, 165–6, 178, 180, 189
    Statute of 1421 158, 182
envy 52, 52 n.13, 65–6, 69, 71
    physical symptoms of 66–7
ephemeral (effymora) 92
epidemic disease. *See* pestilence; plague
epilepsy 100, 124
epiphany 71, 80, 108
ergotism 134 n.34
etiology 2, 81, 92, 120, 127, 191, 193
etymology 133
Europe 16, 112 n.71, 125, 180, 191–3

fables 40, 42, 122
    from *Gesta Romanorum* 14, 84, 100, 106, 108–14
faith 2, 50, 61, 66–7, 71, 98, 147, 149, 169, 177

Falk, Seb 76
Felicie, Jacoba 158
female practitioners. *See* women
Field, Rosalind 122 n.9
Finlayson, John 139 n.44
fisik 53 n.14
flattery 105, 105 n.58
Fletcher, Angus 111 n.69
flyes (fight against) 131–2
food/diet 25, 44, 75, 77, 92, 104–5, 116, 129
    and doctrine for pestilence 85–9
Fourth Lateran Council 62
franesie/frenzy 101, 112
Frank, Arthur 46
Frye, Northrop, secular Scripture 143

Galen 3, 13, 17, 19 n.4, 22 n.12, 56–7, 59–60, 92 n.32
Gasse, Roseanne 53 n.15, 63, 184
genres 1, 34 n.40, 43, 53, 70, 82 n.2, 83 n.8, 86, 120–1, 124, 132, 160, 171
Gentile da Foligno 28 n.24, 191 n.5
Geoffrey of Monmouth 15, 177, 177 n.76
Gesta Romanorum 112 n.71, 115–16
    fables from 14, 84, 100, 106, 108–14
Gimbel, Lena Mackenzie 126 n.15
gluttony 104
God 31, 33, 87, 90, 92 n.32, 98, 103, 107–8, 113, 130, 156, 168, 172–3
    Aesculapius (Greco-Roman god of healing) 92 n.32
    Apollo (ancient god of medicine) 26
    grace of 133, 165, 180
    punishment of 69, 71, 191
    Virtue given of God 12, 12 n.29, 156, 156 n.5, 179
Goodman, Barbara 141
Gospel of Luke 148
gospels 11 n.24, 61, 148, 150, 150 n.74
Gottfried, Robert S. 8, 83 n.5
Gower, John 4, 13, 49–51, 50 n.5, 52 n.13, 54–6, 54 n.18, 59–60, 62, 65, 78, 80–1, 83–5, 83 n.8, 91, 109, 115, 160, 181–4, 187, 195
    on cardiocentric body 67–72
    on health in unhealthy world 76–8
    physique and parfit practisour 72–5, 73 n.56

Gratia Dei (GD) 12, 126 n.16, 133–5, 156, 160, 160 n.16, 179. *See also* Virtue given of God
great mortality 1, 8, 13, 189. *See also* Black Death; plague
Green, Monica 157–8
grete harme 167–8
Grigsby, Bryon Lee 52, 84, 87 n.22

hagiography 15, 70, 144
Harley, Marta Powell 163–4
Harvey, William 172
healing (art of healing) 1, 8–9, 13, 15, 18–19, 22, 24–5, 51, 61, 64–5, 70–2, 74, 80, 112, 115–16, 124, 135–7, 143, 148, 156, 170, 177–8, 181, 185–6, 196, 198
    healing philosophy 45–7
    healing power of blood 144–7
    household healing 161–5
    spiritual 65, 177
    verbal healing/speech act 146–7, 151–2
    women healers (*see* women, women healers)
health and well-being 14, 19, 21, 27, 29, 44, 51, 55, 67, 106, 116, 120, 125, 154, 156, 167, 173, 180, 196
health care 5, 7, 15, 22, 31, 50, 80, 133, 157, 159–61, 169, 174, 187
    role of health-care provider 23
heart 40, 56, 59–61, 68, 70, 72, 77–8, 97, 130–2, 135, 164. *See also* brain
    Four Servants of 72
    heart disease 52 n.13
    heart-uterus 173, 178, 183
    and soul 57, 171–3
Hebert, Jill M. 177 n.76
herbal medication 40–1, 124, 126 n.14, 129, 131–2, 160, 164, 166, 177, 180
Hippocrates 3, 13, 17, 22 n.12, 56–7, 72, 156–7, 186
    Aphorisms/Hippocratic aphorism 17–18, 47, 50
    Hippocratic Oath 24, 33
Hippocratic-Galenic medical tradition 9, 24, 34, 125, 187
Hoccleve, Thomas 4, 14, 82–5, 83 nn.8–9, 105 n.58, 107–8, 112, 114–17, 119, 161, 195–6
    death of 117
    and Lydgate 99–105
    holograph 85, 114
Holy Church, mesure is medicine 53, 64
holy medicine 4, 66, 70. *See also* spiritual medicine
Horrox, Rosemary 30, 130 n.24
hortus conclusus 44–5
hospital 21, 22 n.9, 37, 37 n.48, 38 n.51, 166
household medicine 12, 14–15, 150, 161–5, 196, 198
How the Plague Was Ceased in Rome (Poem) 89–91
humanity 16, 90, 190 n.3
humility 83, 128, 143
humoral body 9, 22, 25, 40–2, 44, 50, 144, 195
Hundred Years' War 84
Hunter, Kathryn 68

Ibn Khatima 126 n.15
illness narratives 7–8, 169, 186, 193
    vs. plague narratives 193–5
infectio 111 n.69
infirmity/infirmite 89, 102, 102 n.55
Ingram, Hannah 161–2
interactive dialogic diptych 142–3
interdisciplinary approach 8, 197
internal medicine 4, 9, 26 n.21
interpretation 1, 6, 16, 22–3, 51, 70, 101, 111, 173, 198
intersubjective medicine 51, 64
intra-subjective medicine 80
Isidore of Seville 103, 110 n.67, 116

Jacobi, Johannes 49 n.2, 54 n.17
Jacques, Raymond St. 63
Jankyn 182–3
Jenkins, Jacqueline 166–7, 171
Joan Beaufort, the Countess of Westmoreland 114–17
John of Arderne 29 n.29, 34, 41 n.58, 72, 72 n.54, 78, 156 n.5, 182, 184
John of Bordeaux 126 n.15, 127 n.17, 157, 164
John of Burgundy 35 n.42, 126–33, 154, 157, 159, 163–4, 198
    imperial powder 130
    pestis puerorum (children's plague) 31
John of Gaddesden 9, 45, 146

John of Gaunt 19, 114–15, 123
John of Trevisa 57 n.26, 101 n.53
Jones, Peter Murray 72 n.54, 151
Josian of *Bevis of Hampton* 15, 159, 179–82, 196
Julian of Norwich 8, 44, 159–62, 165–8, 170–3, 175, 178, 186, 196
Justinian plague (First Plague) 89 n.26, 91. *See also* plague

Kalas, Laura 9, 158, 158 n.12, 168, 168 n.43, 173, 178
Keiser, George 12, 122, 123 n.10, 126 n.14, 126 n.16, 132 n.29, 134, 136
Kempe, Margery 8, 151, 159–61, 165, 167–70, 170 n.46, 173, 175, 186, 196
   spiritual medicine 9, 159
King Arthur 136–8, 142
Kleinman, Arthur 190, 190 n.3
Knighton, Henry 165
Krug, Rebecca 67, 75

Labbie, Erin 197
Langland, William (Will) 4, 14, 31 n.35, 49–51, 50 n.5, 53–5, 59–60, 63, 68, 72, 78–81, 84–5, 160, 182–3, 187, 195
   on cardiocentric body 63–7
   on health in unhealthy world 75–6
   kynde knowyng 60
language of illness 40
Langum, Virginia 52, 65
Le Bone Florence of Rome 15, 159, 179, 181–2, 196
lechery 52, 69
leprosy 5, 14, 29, 35, 52, 52 n.13, 65, 69–70, 110
liver 72, 78, 130, 132, 137, 164
love
   lovesickness/love-madness 13, 40, 56, 62, 67–8, 80, 91, 92 n.32, 93–4, 102, 159, 195
   and medicine 17–18, 47, 56, 60, 64–5, 67
   Saunders on 93
Lydgate, John 4, 14, 28 n.23, 82–6, 83 n.9, 87 n.24, 88–94, 90 n.27, 92 n.32, 93–6, 98–9, 116–17, 119–20, 141–2, 195

   death of 117
   and Hoccleve 99–105

Macaulay, G. C. 73 n.56
MacCracken, Henry Noble 87 n.23
macrocosm/macrocosmic universe 7, 9–10, 22, 67, 78, 127. *See also* microcosm/microcosmic bodies
Magnani, Roberta 46
Magnus, Albertus 57, 60
malady 33, 52 n.13, 53, 56, 68–70, 92–3, 100, 102–3, 105, 110, 112, 122, 124, 149
malaise 13, 67, 78, 102, 195
mania 100–2, 112
Matheolus of Perugia 18 n.4
mating rituals 17, 19
Maxfield, David K. 38 n.51
McAvoy, Liz 169
McCann, Daniel 159 n.15, 170, 173
McKinstry, Jamie 87 n.21, 197
McNamer, Sarah 170
McVaugh, Michael 30
medical consciousness 1, 9, 50, 84, 117, 120, 153, 161, 168, 198
   and psychophysiological body 56–61
medical discourse 2–4, 9, 14, 22, 53, 104, 117, 124–5, 143, 154, 156, 159, 161, 195
medical emergency 5, 37, 40, 42
Medical Humanities 2, 5–9, 16, 190 n.3, 197
medical imagination 4, 9, 15
medical knowledge 4, 9, 13–14, 26, 61, 77, 91, 99, 123, 125, 134, 157, 159, 177, 180, 186, 196
medical language 29 n.26, 41, 50, 53–4, 119
medical/medicinal compound 9, 53 n.15, 65, 90 n.27, 130, 133–4, 156, 162, 170
medical practice 5–8, 25, 29, 34, 46, 53, 53 n.14, 71, 83, 127, 129, 146 n.60, 157–9, 161, 187, 194, 198
medical terminology 3, 12, 22, 29, 50, 53
medical treatment 3–4, 10, 13, 21, 40–1, 54, 60, 72, 74 n.56, 89, 112, 139, 156, 158, 161, 166, 197

medical writing 1, 3–4, 9, 13–14, 16, 18, 29, 34 n.40, 52, 115–17, 122–4, 127–8, 131, 136, 159–61, 165, 167, 169, 186–7, 189, 193, 196
medications 32, 55, 63, 65, 71–2, 76, 87, 99, 113, 125, 129–31, 133–5, 142, 144, 146, 156 n.5, 180, 186, 196
medicinal gardens 44–5
medicinal plants (plant-based ingredients) 44–5, 65, 125, 134, 180, 185
medieval medicine 27 n.22, 100
melancholy (black bile) 56, 66, 85, 87–8, 87 n.24, 93, 101–5, 105 n.57, 106–7, 112, 117
mental disorders 100
microcosm/microcosmic bodies 9–13, 22, 67, 78, 127. *See also* macrocosm/macrocosmic universe
    four Ages of Man 11
    four humors 11, 14, 22 n.12, 24, 76–7
    four temperaments 9, 11
    Microcosmic Man in the center of macrocosmic universe 10–11
    twelve winds 11
Middle English Dictionary (MED) 24 n.13, 28 n.23, 53, 53 n.14, 89, 90 n.27, 102 n.55, 162
misogyny 106, 108, 113, 182–3
moderation 25, 53, 72, 77, 87–8
modern medical theory 1–2
mood-altering effect 122, 156
Morrissey, Jake Walsh 88 n.25
Mount Grace 123 n.10, 170 n.46
myrr (nose infection) 162, 162 n.22

narrative medicine 2, 4, 12, 16, 16 n.34, 21, 23, 51, 60, 68, 70, 78, 82, 101, 106, 117, 122, 143, 149, 159, 190, 198
    features of (by Charon) 6
    and Medical Humanities 5–9
    narrating medicine for women 186–7
    principles of 194
    in Thornton household recipes 153–4
narrative poetry 1, 4, 17, 21, 89, 120, 122, 136, 139–40, 154, 156, 174, 189
New Jerusalem 108, 171, 173
New Testament 61

Nine Worthies 137
nonnaturals 11, 72, 120, 184

Ogden, Margaret 123–4, 125 n.13, 146
ointment 12 n.29, 156 n.5, 180
Olsan, Lea 146, 150–1
Olson, Glending 86, 174
original sin 141, 167–8. *See also* sin
Orlemanski, Julie 3, 18, 34 n.40, 39, 124
Oxford Bodleian Library MS Selden Supra 53 99

Page, Christopher 62
Palmer, James 68
pandemic 2, 7–8, 12, 16, 61, 82, 82 n.4, 91, 117, 198. *See also* Covid-19 pandemic, plague
Park, Katharine 146 n.60, 148, 157, 158 n.9
parturition 150–1, 153
passion 16, 168–73, 175, 196. *See also* compassion
Passus V 54, 65, 79
Passus VI 75
Passus XX 54
Paston II, John 163–4, 163 n.27
Paston, Margaret 159–65, 168, 178, 178 n.79, 186, 196
    grete myrr 162, 165
pathogen 4, 191–2, 191 n.7
Pearsall, Derek 79
Peck, Russell 51, 58
    emotive cognition 60
penitential system 50, 52, 60
personification 37, 55, 95–6
pestilence 1–2, 20, 28–32, 29 n.28, 34, 36–9, 50, 53 n.14, 54 n.18, 60, 79, 90–1, 96, 99, 103, 112 n.71, 119, 123, 126, 128–31, 138, 154, 157, 161, 164–5, 175, 191 n.5, 195
    diet and doctrine for 85–9
    great pestilence 165, 189
    and household healing 161–5
    lurking pestilence 105, 112, 139
    outbreak records 165–70, 192
    and penitence 53–5
    sovereyn pestilence 30
    to wounds 133–5
Pestis Secunda (Second Plague) 192

Petrarch, Francesco 3, 16
pharmaceuticals 25, 53 n.15, 65–6,
    65 n.43, 129, 161–2, 165, 179
phlebotomy 130, 144, 164, 185, 187
phrenitis 100–1, 112, 112 n.70
physic 24 n.13, 41 n.58, 53 n.14, 63, 112
    physical symptoms 2, 66, 69, 93, 103, 140
    physician and priest 61–3, 80
physiology 41, 122
Pickering Parish Church 145 n.57
plague 2, 4, 8, 12, 14, 21, 24, 28 n.25, 39,
    49–50, 49 n.1, 54, 65, 82, 83 n.5,
    84, 86, 89, 91, 103, 105, 107,
    126 n.14, 127–30, 138, 163, 165,
    168, 174–5, 189–92, 196, 198. *See
    also* Black Death; great mortality
    bubonic/buboes 1 n.1, 2, 5, 36, 36 n.43,
        61, 80, 112 n.71, 131–2, 189,
        191, 191 n.7
    in England (*see* England)
    First Plague (*see* Justinian plague)
    language of plague 192
    mortality 191 n.5, 192 (*see also* death
        (death poetry))
    outbreak records 165–70, 192
    plague tractates 1, 81, 163 n.27, 168
    pneumonic 1 n.1, 191 n.7
    preventative remedies for 54
    Second Plague (*see* Pestis Secunda)
    septicemic 1 n.1, 191 n.7
    strains of 1 n.1
    studies of 2 n.3, 3
    Third Plague 192
    treatises 4, 49 n.2, 82 n.2, 126,
        126 n.14, 130, 132, 154, 163–5
plague narratives 16, 20, 192–3
    vs. illness narratives 193–5
Plague of Athens 192–3
Plague of Justinian 192–3
plante of pees (plant of peace) 65
Poellinger, Mary Michele 136–7
poorys/pores 92 n.32
pragmatic approach 4, 8–9, 12, 25, 86–7,
    89, 120, 122–3, 131–3, 157, 196
prayers 12, 14, 45, 121, 125, 128, 133,
    142–3, 146–7, 149, 153, 156.
    See also charms, medical
premodern medicine/medical studies 1, 3,
    6, 8, 60, 103, 197–8

Pseudo-*Secretum Secretorum* 75, 77, 88–9,
    125, 138
psychophysiological body/organism 11,
    50, 53, 75, 80, 102, 125
    and medical consciousness 56–61
psychosomatic illness 100, 122
putrida (fever) 92

Rawcliffe, Carol 24, 26 n.18, 37 n.48,
    41 n.58, 45, 84 n.10, 99, 182 n.86
reading, therapeutic. *See* therapeutic
    reading
recuperation 6, 80, 103, 140, 146, 184
regimen sanitatis 1
Regimen sanitatis Salernitantum 120, 125,
    157, 171–2
regimens, medicinal 1–2, 24 n.13, 25,
    42–4, 53, 71–2, 75, 87 n.22, 116,
    125, 130, 147, 164, 178
religion 61, 69, 144
    healing language of 143
    religious community 73–4, 73 n.56,
        146
    religious culture 115, 148, 178, 187
    religious violence 136
resurrection 150
Rhazes 129 n.20
ritual performances 149, 153–4
Rogers, Will 184–5
Rolle, Richard 8, 134–5, 173
romances 3, 15, 19, 45, 56, 109, 131,
    135–6, 138–41, 141 n.48, 143,
    159
    virtuous women of 179–81
Rosenfeld, Jessica 69
Rose of Mary (rosemary) 12, 156, 160, 179
Rozenski, Steven 108

Sacks, Oliver 5 n.11
salus (health and salvation) 4
salvation 4, 29, 113, 134, 195
salve 53 n.15, 136–7, 140, 145
sanctification 74, 143–4
    sanctified verbal signs 148
Satan 63
Saunders, Corinne 93, 100–1, 180,
    180 n.81, 197
scarification 127, 130
Scogan, Henry 28 n.25, 29 n.28

self 67, 80, 154
    self-care 1, 5, 12, 42, 60, 120, 198
    self-doctoring advice 157
Seven Deadly Sins 52, 54, 65, 69, 195
    and confession 55–6
sickness 26 n.21, 62, 68, 94, 104, 110, 111 n.69, 119–20, 136, 153
sin 52, 55–6, 61, 66, 69, 74, 108, 141, 165, 167, 191. *See also* original sin
Siraisi, Nancy 11
skepticism 14, 20, 26, 60, 63, 161–2, 165
Smith, Dav 122 n.9
Smith, Kirk L. 26 n.19
Smyth, Karen 95
Snell, William 87 n.23
social body 50, 60, 189
sodeine violence 96
Solemnis Medicus 28 n.24
sovereyn pestilence 30
spicers (apothecaries) 164
spiritual healing 65, 177
spiritual medicine 9, 158. *See also* holy medicine
St. Anthony's Fire 134 n.34
St. Apollonia 148–9
Stavsky, Jonathan 181 n.83
Steel, David 193
stones (medicinal properties of) 156, 180, 184
storytelling 1, 6, 8, 13, 22, 34, 46, 51–2, 68, 111, 122, 136, 140, 195
    diagnosing storyteller's illness 78–80
    dialogic exchanges in 81
    storytellers 5, 7, 20, 22, 46–7, 78, 117, 194, 198
Strakhov, Elizaveta 94, 100 n.49
studia humanitatis 16
subjective narrations 5, 16, 189, 192
sugar stick medication 65–6
Suso, Henry 99–100, 100 n.49, 106–7, 116
Swynford, Katherine 114–15
Sylvester 69–70

tail-rhyme romances 135–6, 138, 147, 156
talk therapy 14, 51
temperaments 9, 11, 87, 100, 120
Ten Commandments 31
therapeutic medication 63, 113, 156. *See also* medications

therapeutic preparation. *See* theriac/treacle
therapeutic reading 4, 6–7, 9, 12–16, 26 n.18, 51, 51 n.7, 138–44, 153, 159, 159 n.15, 187, 196
    and *Vertu* of women's healing 178–9
    for women 173–4
theriac/treacle 53 n.15, 129, 162
Thornton, Robert 120–5, 123 n.10, 126–34, 136–7, 139–40, 143, 145, 147, 163–4, 196
    and Burgundy 126–33
    childbirth 149–53
    fever 147–8
    healing power of blood 144–7
    household medicinal recipes 153–4, 196
    London Thornton manuscript 85, 86 n.17, 120, 145 n.56
    reading for dis-ease 138–44
    Thornton Lincoln Cathedral MS 91 4, 14–15, 121, 123–4, 126 n.16, 132, 138–9, 143, 156, 163
    toothache 148–9
    wound treatments 133–8
Torrigiani, Pietro 57, 171 n.52
transgression 29, 36, 52, 55, 69, 141–2, 168
trauma 105 n.57, 117, 136, 138, 149, 151, 153, 193–4, 196–7
    emotional 92
    traumatic disease events 1–2, 7, 19
Trembinski, Donna 7
tresor 75
triacle (miraculous remedy) 32, 53 n.15, 65
Trinitarian 150
truth 34 n.40, 35, 38, 52, 65, 67
Turner, Marion 3, 39, 41, 46–7
typological analogy 150

urine
    color of 25–8, 26–7 n.21
    medieval medicine 27 n.22
uroscopy 10, 26 n.21, 92, 93 n.34
uterus 173, 178, 183

venomous matter/poison 65, 120, 131–2
verbal healing/speech act 146–7, 151–2

violence 112–13, 116, 136–7, 139, 141, 196
   hand-to-hand combat 136–7, 142
   religious 136
   sodeine 96
   against women 140
Virgil 152–3
Virgin Mary 15, 46, 71, 71 n.52, 74, 143, 149–51, 160, 170, 177–8
Virtue given of God 12, 12 n.29, 156, 156 n.5, 179
Voigts, Linda Ehrsam 41, 160, 163 n.27

Wack, Mary 56
wall painting 94, 145
Walsingham, Thomas 28 n.25, 36, 165
Watson, Nicholas 166–7, 171
Watt, Diane 178
Webb, Heather 56–7, 171 n.52, 172
Whitaker, Elaine 163 n.27
Winstead, Karen 108
women 2, 8, 11, 15, 40–2, 44, 74 n.56, 100, 106, 109, 113–15, 140, 153, 156–8, 169–70, 183–4
   literary 159
   medical recipes by 160
   narrating medicine for 186–7
   narratives of fictional women 159
   therapeutic reading for 173–4, 178–9
   transgressive 142
   virtuous women 15, 115, 143, 179–81
   woman's milk 150, 151 n.76, 153, 172
      (*see also* breast milk)
   women healers 41, 46, 116, 158–60, 158 n.10, 178, 180 n.81, 196–7
   and communal medicine 160–1
   vilification of 182–6, 196
wounds/wound treatments 133–8
wylde infirmitee 102. *See also* infirmity/infirmite

Yee, Pamela M. 70
Yersinia pestis 1 n.1, 191, 191 n.7
Yoshikawa, Nasoë Kukita 61, 174

Zweers, Thari 74 n.56

www.ingramcontent.com/pod-product-compliance
Lightning Source LLC
Chambersburg PA
CBHW062216300426
44115CB00012BA/2081